Changing Seasonality

Changing Seasonality

How Communities are Revising their Seasons

Edited by
Scott Bremer and Arjan Wardekker

DE GRUYTER

ISBN 978-3-11-221608-8
e-ISBN (PDF) 978-3-11-124559-1
e-ISBN (EPUB) 978-3-11-124591-1
DOI https://doi.org/10.1515/9783111245591

Library of Congress Control Number: 2023942056

Bibliographic information published by the Deutsche Nationalbibliothek
The Deutsche Nationalbibliothek lists this publication in the Deutsche Nationalbibliografie; detailed bibliographic data are available on the internet at http://dnb.dnb.de.

© 2025 the author(s), editing © 2025 Scott Bremer and Arjan Wardekker, published by Walter de Gruyter GmbH, Berlin/Boston
This volume is text- and page-identical with the hardback published in 2024.
This book is published open access at www.degruyter.com.

Cover image: Eamon O'Kane (2008). Falling Water Seasons Remix (painted whilst listening to In Utero by Nirvana). Oil on canvas 223 x 274 cm.
Typesetting: Integra Software Services Pvt. Ltd.
Printing and binding: CPI books GmbH, Leck

www.degruyter.com

"All because our young planet randomly collided with a rather large asteroid, resulting in a 23.5° tilt between the earth's rotational axis and its orbital plane around the sun" (Manuel Hempel).

Artist: Magnhild Øen Nordahl
Title: Parallel Sogndal
Year: 2016
Description: A sculpture in a public space installed with the pillar parallel to the Earth's rotation axis and the platform parallel to the Earth's equatorial plane.

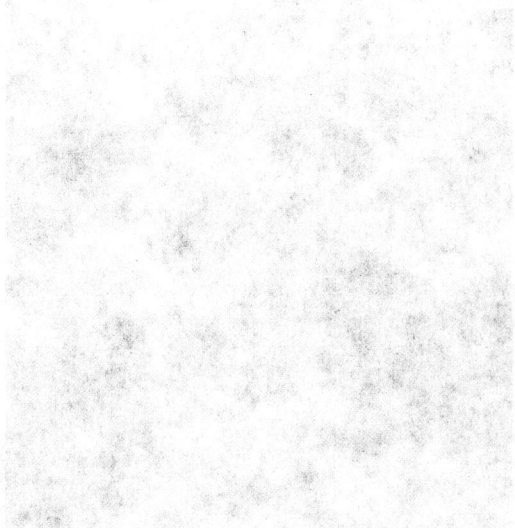

Preface

At its core, this is a book about how people adapt and build resilience to global environmental changes, like climate change. But in its own small way, we hope this book helps move conversations from how experts best deploy techno-scientific 'solutions' to these challenges, to how all of us – individually and collectively – culturally think, feel, and act relative to the environment, and particularly relative to seasons.

We the editors – Scott and Arjan – have worked for quite some years as social scientists studying (and supporting) adaptation and resilience to climatic and environmental change. And we have both spent time on both sides of the so-called science-policy interface, where science informs collective decision-making, working in local and central government. We have seen 'science in action' (to reference Bruno Latour); the ways scientific knowledge is established by scientists, and also how this knowledge finds its way into political and social spheres, settings where society is debating the best ways to respond to change. But this has come with some frustration at a growing reliance on science and technology over other ways of knowing. Science is an indispensable resource for well-supported decisions on climate adaptation, but it is rarely sufficient on its own; we almost never have 'perfect information', major uncertainties usually persist. Indeed, as Dan Sarewitz showed us almost 20 years ago, this uncertainty can see scientific evidence fuel disagreement and confusion on how to adapt, rather than narrowing down the list of best possible options.

What is more, science advice can come with a naïve assumption that decisions are mainly based on the best available science. Yet we have both witnessed, time and again, that other (often less explicit) influences often carry the day in public decision-making. Influences like values and emotions, political posturing, or cultural and common-sensical assumptions about the world; what we could call 'culture in action' to reference Ann Swidler. These are not irrational ways of making decisions; they are other legitimate ways of reasoning, as John Dryzek might say. They often are rooted in what societies and cultures value, and they are types of reason that we can all relate to because we employ them daily. Of course, this comes with its own uncertainties; people rarely agree unanimously on values, whether globally or locally, and judgements will change over time as well. But despite us all recognising the influence of culture and norms on decisions, the conversations on climate adaptation still mainly circle topics of science and policies, and as a result, we all continue to be frustrated by the lack of purchase that climate science is having in political, social and individuals' daily decisions. The recent Intergovernmental Panel for Climate Change 6th Assessment Report continues to recognise a relatively narrow spectrum of knowledges, mainly social and natural sciences, and local and indigenous knowledge.

So, we the editors have increasingly turned our attention to those overlooked knowledges wrapped up in our cultures, and in particular cultural frameworks for telling time and coordinating timely action. There is an important, often quite tacit, knowledge of the right time to take a certain action; there is 'good timing'. Many of us cannot express timings in words, it is a sense we have, and seasonal cultures and calendars are a perfect example of this. There is a season – a time – for everything.

As our backstories in the introduction show, we came to see the significant influence of seasonal cultures on people's daily decisions, in our research and private lives. It is easy to think of seasonal cultures as belonging to indigenous communities living close to the land in exotic locales (and indeed most research on seasonal cultures puts the focus there), but we saw how 'moderns' also live seasonally in a certain sense. Seasonality is present in the rhythms of plants and animals, on which subsistence and agricultural communities depend, but it is also embedded in social, economic and technological rhythms and trends. And, whether in small traditional societies or in highly modern cities, we saw evidence of long-held seasonal frameworks faltering and failing. This led to the CALENDARS research project, which sought to study but also engage with and potentially revise seasonal cultures with groups of people around the world, from gardeners to artists or climate scientists. We were a small group of social scientists who teamed up with these groups to uncover (for us but often also for the groups who took their seasonal habits for granted) the seasonal rhythms and patterns people observe in timing their actions. We could call this local or traditional knowledge, craft or institutional knowledge. Perhaps temporal knowledge?

As we worked with these groups, we became increasingly uncomfortable about our typical ways of analysing and reporting on these knowledges. Often, it is we scientists reporting on these extra-scientific ways of knowing, and extrapolating from them, in a scientific format: articles and books with ordered headings like 'method' or 'analysis' and laden with theory and technical language. This is important work, it is a field of scientific research after all, but we couldn't shake a feeling that this was somehow inconsistent with our commitments to other ways of knowing. We decided that this project leant itself to a different type of book. One which collected perspectives on seasonal change directly from the people we worked with – the gardeners and the artists for example – and let them show their experience in their own authentic voice. A book that would collect insights from many ways of knowing seasonal change, without requiring contributors to conform their account to particular scientific norms. And as the project progressed, our network of collaborators – scientific and extra-scientific – grew and we started to collect accounts from all over the world, in all manner of registers. This book is the result. It is probably customary to reflect on the hard work of assembling an edited volume, and while there was certainly some effort, it was not difficult finding people enthusiastic to write about seasonal change. This is a topic dear to many people's hearts it seems.

This book could not have been assembled – at least not by us – four years ago. When the CALENDARS project began in 2019, this topic was unknown territory for our small research team. Indeed, our particular focus – on how seasonal cultures are contested and change as templates for action – is lightly researched in the literature at large, so we had little to go on. We are very grateful to the extended project team, whose different lines of investigation together helped us advance understanding on this topic (in no particular order): Paul Schneider; Kerstie van Zandvoort; Bruce Glavovic; Sissel Småland Aasheim; Elisabeth Schøyen Jensen; Mathias Venning; Simon Meisch; Mark Thomas Young; Thomas Potthast; Eva Lövbrand; Sarah Strauss; Marta Bruno Soares; Kamilla Stølen; Stefan Sobolowski; and Håvard Haarstad. It is important too to underline how our understanding of this topic evolved though our fieldwork with the different societal groups that we partnered with in case study communities, whether they be teachers or gardeners, artists or coffee roasters, so we want to acknowledge their patience in sharing their seasonal lives with us. All of these discussions expanded further at a workshop that we held outside Bergen in May 2022, where we felt at last that we were on the right track, and we want to acknowledge the contributions of all our invited guests who joined us there and helped plan this book into a reality. Many of them are chapter authors. We want to acknowledge the folk at De Gruyter publishers who helped us through this process and saw value in a book that departed from some academic norms. And finally, none of this work would have been possible without funding from the European Research Council (ERC) under the European Union's Horizon 2020 research and innovation program (Grant agreement 804150).

Scott Bremer
Arjan Wardekker

Contents

Part VI **Planning & engineering**

List of images

Scott Bremer and Arjan Wardekker

1 When seasons no longer hold

Planetary scientists suspect that, when young, our planet met with an enormous celestial body in a random collision that tilted the earth's rotational axis relative to its orbital plane around the sun. This tilt has since determined which parts of our globe are most exposed to solar radiation at different points in its solar circuit, as a key physical pattern dictating the annual cycles of life on this planet. At a fundamental, material level we humans have evolved as seasonal animals, interacting with other seasonal species in a seasonally-cycling loop (1). "Seasons . . . will always be there as long as the earth is tilting" (2).

But in this book we are less interested in ideas of seasons as eternal laws of nature, and more focused on how seasons affect peoples' patterns of thinking, feeling and acting, *as part of our cultures*. As human communities physically evolved in a seasonal environment, so have their cultures likewise evolved to reflect this seasonality (1, 3, 4). Seasons culturally affect how we relate to our environment and to each other, and as these relations change – through shifts in resources, in governments, worldviews, technologies and skills, economic trade, and so on – so too do our seasonal frameworks. Our cultures affect the annual patterns we notice as meaningful for us, the values and emotions we attach to periods of the year and argue about, and the activities and festivities that we practice and coordinate at the 'right time' each year. Those frameworks provide a repertoire for how to tell the time of the year and live seasonally (5, 6).

This is an important point of departure for this book, for readers to reconsider seasons as cultural, because it implies that how we live seasonally is not only determined by 'the tilt'. It is also up to us – as individuals and communities – to (consciously and unconsciously) choose how we relate to seasons. Much of what we associate with seasons – the signs that cue seasons, the festivals, treasured seasonal activities, our diets and so on – have been settled on and made significant by human communities. They are the seasons we choose to see.

How then do we choose to respond when, in turbulent times, our seasonal cultures no longer hold? How do we adapt as the patterns we are accustomed to smudge together, and we lose our sense of seasonality?

Studies worldwide show us that communities today are critically re-examining their seasonal cultures and calendars to better adapt to fast-changing seasonal realities in the places they live (7, 8). Communities find themselves in a unique moment of accelerated and intersecting processes of changes – from climate change to globalisation – which are destabilizing seasonal frameworks as templates for timely action. Put simply, peoples' activities are poorly coordinated in time, and they feel they can no longer rely on cultural cues for knowing the right time to act. There are increasing accounts of populations whose seasonal activities no longer synch to the rhythms they track, endangering peoples' livelihoods and compounding hazards (9, 10). We see for instance: farming practices disconnected from a changing climate; fishing rhythms upset by altered ocean habitats; festivals losing meaning in an increasingly diverse society; or iconic seasonal tools made obsolete with advances in science and technology.

Now is an important moment to reflect on what seasonality means for us. How communities revise their seasonal cultures to reattune to the rhythms that matter to them is an important *adaptation challenge*. It is about how people alter their way of life to not just survive but thrive in heavily modified environments and rapidly changing societies, with a view to long-term sustainability. In this sense, this book links up to a small but growing number of scholars worldwide who are studying culture as a key capacity that avails communities to adapt to global environmental change (9); to cope and re-adjust to disruptions in the seasonal conditions that community life has been patterned to.

The way communities reorient their cultures to shifting conditions may affect whether these cultures serve as resources for living by seasonal rhythms, for adapting, or guide people down maladaptive pathways. On one hand, left alone, humans and other species in an environment will always incrementally co-evolve to "[re-]align with each other through timing to make living in common possible" (11, page 103). But the new seasonal patterns that emerge may be grossly unsustainable and unfair. It has become common practice, for example, for wealthy Norwegians to travel south in July – usually by plane – to find the summer conditions they expect in tropical locations. But the emissions from this unsustainable habit are steadily warming Mediterranean locations until summer's heat will become unbearable. Or consider examples where powerful groups like colonising nations – if left to it – have imposed calendars on the powerless. So, on the other hand, it might be necessary to rethink our seasonal cultures and have these discussions 'out loud', consciously and deliberately, extending a voice to groups normally marginalised, including the other species we share this planet with. Since seasons have different meanings in different social worlds – the different circles people move in and the activities they engage in – these are discussions that should be (and are) sparked in all of these social worlds, from the parliamentary chamber to the fishing club, or kindergarten.

With this book, we want to fuel the reflections and discussions about seasonal cultures that are ongoing within different social worlds around the world. We want to bring up seasons as a topic of out-loud conversation and argument, with a collection of chapters that show those messy moments when taken-for-granted seasonal cultures are contested and reinterpreted and changed. While other books look back at seasonal traditions anchored in the past (12), we want to focus on what happens when those traditions are turned upside down and communities of people (and plants and animals) experience and effect and experiment with new seasonal patterns of life (13). This is not to dismiss the important cultural heritage we have inherited, which continue to offer us important way-markers. But rather to celebrate the resourcefulness and creativity of communities who are constantly challenging what seasons mean for us, or what we pay attention to; whether through architecture, witch covens, a weather-proof road, virtual reality, computer games, communal lifestyles, workshops for realigning with swans, or spectacularly alien species of Japanese wireweed. We want to create a handbook for re-crafting seasonal habits.

To this end, the book is not only targeted at an academic audience but aims to be thought-provoking and meaningful for people from all walks of life. We have collected diverse cultural accounts of an eclectic group of authors witnessing changes in seasonality in different parts of the world and showing what these changes mean for them. It compiles concrete snapshots of people altering how they engage with seasonality in order to show both (i) how heterogeneous seasonal cultures are across and within communities, and (ii) the many and often intertwined processes transforming cultures. As you will see, seasonal change rarely boils down to a shift in climate alone; it almost always links up to other change processes such as deforestation, or migration. Chapters capture authors' own authentic voices, in their own style and for a broad audience, as they try to get a grip on a seasonality that is less and less easily grasped. In this way, we hope that the book can equally serve as a source of inspiration for scientists and artists, indigenous communities and engineers, planners and beekeepers, rugby players and ecologists, gamers and boaters, or indeed all of us who live our daily lives by seasonal rhythms.

When seasonality failed to hold for us

Up until quite recently, seasons seem a 'common-sensical' topic for us, the editors. If questioned, we might have answered that they are distinct divisions of the year, and in the Global North, that there are four: spring, summer, autumn, and winter. We might have associated each seasonal category with a host of taken-for-granted images, activities, and expectations, each deeply rooted in our cultures.

However, the last few years we each, separately, experienced messy moments when seasonal assumptions failed to hold for us. We came to question what constitutes a 'distinct' period of the year and see it as far more contested – across places, cultures, and contexts – and changeable over time. These moments gave us pause to deeply question seasonality, in both our professional and personal lives, and motivated us as social scientists to study seasonal cultures and assemble a rich picture of change told from diverse perspectives.

What will become of the summer rains?

I (Scott) was in northeast Bangladesh, in the settlement of Sunamganj Sadar, when I first started thinking about the importance of seasons for patterning community life. I was with a group of Norwegian researchers working with Bangladeshi partners to study the climate of that area, where the monsoon rains effectively start in summer, a few weeks earlier than they *should* according to the meteorological models. It was the summer month of Boishakh (mid-April to mid-May on the Gregorian calendar), and we were put up in a local politician's house. I had eaten something that didn't agree with my European constitution – a typical story – and I remember hugging the toilet bowl at around 5 o'clock in the morning and listening to the deluge of summer rains beating on the metal roof, coinciding with the morning call to prayer from the nearby minaret. And at that moment, faint from malnutrition, I felt like I was being inducted to that place, introduced to the local environmental and social rhythms that set a tempo to people's everyday lives there.

It occurred to me how familiar the summer rains must be for the people of that place, like an old relative visiting at the same time each year. Travelling around that area and talking to people, I saw how the rains culturally conditioned the modes of living and seeking a living; they provided a cue for routine action. Farmers harvested their 'boro' rice crop and set it to dry, households began to shore up their houses with flood defences, and as the flood waters rose and covered that area like an inland sea, settlements sat perched on islands (Figure 1.1). Farmers and labourers became fishers, and boatmen started plying their trade, taking livestock to market or kids to school. And while the floods could also bring suffering, illness, loneliness, and a loss of income, many saw this as part of a natural seasonal order. Indeed, when international donors funded works to dig out riverbeds and build high embankments or dikes to prevent flooding, locals were appalled. The lakes, normally filled by the summer floods and resupplied with fish fry, became stagnant. And the flood waters that crossed the embankments could not drain back into the river, leaving the land waterlogged. Locals took matters into their own hands to 'free the summer floods', through clandestine night-time actions carving holes in the embankments.

Figure 1.1: The fields around Sunamganj Sadar in northeast Bangladesh. Communities here live with unique rainfall patterns, affected by the Indian hill country that wraps around these lowlands. (Photo by: Scott Bremer).

So, I was concerned when I started to hear another common story, that seasonal patterns were increasingly unrecognisable to people there. The Bangladeshi calendar is organised by six seasons, each two months long, and marked out by some quite distinct reference points or signs. But people said that a changing climate meant they now struggled to distinguish between seasons, and could only make out three: summer, winter, and the monsoon. They saw a shifting pattern of summer rains – less rain falling at different times – with consequences for lake levels, fish stocks, the migrating birds, and their livelihoods. What's more, they missed the rains as a cultural cue that they timed their activities to, leaving them guessing at when to act. I asked if scientific forecasts could provide these cues, but they complained that the forecasts were not reliable in their area. People felt stuck in limbo – in an interregnum – between losing their cultural signs of when to act, but not having the scientific information to replace them. More than that, they missed the rains they had become so accustomed to; they missed their old relative.

"There are four seasons"

I (Scott) took these troubled thoughts with me from Bangladesh when I travelled on to visit my homeland of New Zealand, and they forced me to review the image of seasons that I grew up with. This was a disorienting process for me. I came to see how deeply the four seasons were embedded in my view of the world, to the point where I'd long taken them for granted as a law of nature. Seasons were the kind of elementary facts that appeared in our kindergarten curriculum and going through my old things I saw all my childhood books peppered with references to very recognisable symbols of seasons – sandcastles in summer, and snow sledges in winter. Maybe that's why I never questioned those seasonal categories before, even when they didn't hold for my seasonal experiences in New Zealand. I always assumed that somewhere in the world there were places where people lived with the authentic four seasons I had only read about or seen on the TV. That we New Zealanders lived with some errant seasons that didn't fit to the proper pattern, but that the world was a messy place and not everywhere could adhere to the ideal after all.

As I started talking to friends and family, I saw from the mystified looks I got that I wasn't alone in these seasonal assumptions. What could possibly be gained from studying something so common-sensical? At one point my friend Quinn quipped that he had the answers to my questions in his young daughter's school-book and thrust the page under my nose. The page was headed: "There are four seasons", and underneath were the season's names and symbols. 'Summer' was a shining sun; so far so good, New Zealand experiences hot summers. 'Autumn' though was an orange leaf, and here the framework started to crack. Almost all native New Zealand plants are evergreen, and while we have some imported European trees, you can go through vast tracts of New Zealand without ever seeing an autumn leaf. 'Winter' was a snowflake, yet for those of us living on the North Island, snow is something spotted on the mountain tops, and even these dustings are dwindling with ever warmer winters. Only on the mountain sides of the lower South Island can people expect to find themselves in the snow. Finally, 'spring' was a giant colourful flower, yet, again, most native plants have very modest blooms, typically small smatterings of white flowers.

This was an arresting moment, when I saw the school's common-sensical representation of New Zealand's seasons for what it was, a northern hemisphere transplant (see Figure 1.2). The thoughts of my own school days came rushing back, but now I felt tricked. This innocent claim that "there are four seasons" hid the particular seasonal patterns of New Zealand, with its unique geography and seasonal rhythms, as well as the competing cultural meanings associated to seasons. Before colonisation there may have been as many as 43 different calendars used by Māori

Figure 1.2: The shape of the year, as drawn by a child from Oslo. As researchers, we have asked groups to draw their year. This image is from a workshop with children in Oslo in 2020. The child thought she had drawn it "wrong" when she realised she had only drawn one month of snow, and she thought there should be two or three months. (Photo by: Elisabeth Schøyen Jensen).

tribes across New Zealand – espousing anywhere from two to six seasons – but with colonisation these were replaced with a standardised European calendar. And this European calendar continues to be stabilised in New Zealand through processes of globalisation; from the steady flow of European migrants, to the films we see, or the holidays we celebrate. That's how we have come to live by seasonal symbols that have never been authentic to New Zealand. It demands that we employ some elaborate manoeuvres, like spray-painting fake snow on the windows for Christmas holidays in December, to trick ourselves into acting seasonally.

Rhythms of life in a tourist town

At least in Europe, the classic four seasons seem to hold up. My (Arjan's) hometown in the Netherlands, a countryside town of some 11,000 permanent residents, sees the typical spring, summer, autumn and winter. Voorthuizen is located near the city of Amersfoort, in the centre of the country, on the border of the meadowlands of the Gelder Valley and the woods and heathland of the Veluwe region. It experiences the typical European agricultural and woodland rhythms. Autumn is harvest time and the forests turn red, yellow, and brown and the weather can be rainy and gloomy. Winter is quiet and at least somewhat cold, and although I've never got the hang of it many Dutch love ice skating during this season. Occasionally, there's snow or ice, but this is getting rarer compared to when I grew up. The local ice rink – a field equipped with a pump to flood it during winter (in the hope that the field freezes over) and a small shack that used to sell hot chocolate – finally gave up and closed this year after several years of being unable to open due to a lack of sustained frost: "The winters aren't really wintery anymore" (14). Spring is a time of meadows filled with flowers and young animals. The weather starts improving and the colours in the fields and woods brighten. Summer means warm weather and the time to wear shorts, swim in one of the local lakes and fens, and eat ice cream or fresh strawberries.

However, these typical agricultural and woodland rhythms are trumped by another: that of the tourist season. The region is perfect for outdoor activities, such as cycling, walking, horse riding, and so on. During the warmer months, the population triples or quadruples with tourists staying at the many camp sites and bungalow or caravan parks that surround the town. Unsurprisingly, such an influx of people has a huge impact on life in the town. I've often felt that the town really has two seasons: the tourist season and the 'off-season', and that the year is shaped like a wave (Figure 1.3). The off-season feels eerily calm and quiet. The streets, shops and cycling paths are deserted, and these months can be gloomy due to cloudy and rainy weather. But it also offers some solitude, as well as time for family during the Christmas holidays. For me as a local, the occasional sunny week in winter offers great opportunities for cycling trips on the uncrowded country roads and paths.

The tourist season ramps up slowly when the weather improves. Early visitors appear during sunny weekends, often people who have a fixed holiday home in one of the parks. The short holidays in April and May, such as Easter, King's Day and Pentecost, tend to have the first big peaks of tourism, with noticeably more people in the streets and on the cycling paths, and the local tourism agency and shopkeepers' organisation start organising the first events. Over the summer holiday period, July and August, the town turns into a hive of activity: Main Street gets crowded, local shops and restaurants do great business, and some farmers sell fresh fruit and crafts in small stalls alongside the country roads. There's a busy program of events, such as a biweekly fair, several festivals, flea markets, a marathon, hot air ballooning, and a flower parade. And while the intensity drops slightly after the official holidays end, tourist season goes on until it ends, often rather abruptly, when the rainy weather makes it impossible to deny that summer is over and it is time to clean up, rest, and wait for next year.

Figure 1.3: The shape of the year in a tourist town: from the solitude of the off-season to a hive of activity in the tourist season. (Photos by: Arjan Wardekker).

The CALENDARS project

As scholars studying how communities adapt to climate change, we saw malfunctions in seasonal cultures as an important but largely overlooked topic for research. So many of peoples' daily decisions are influenced by cultural categories like seasons – we draw on them as tacit repertoires for reckoning time – yet they remain largely unquestioned. Focus is instead put on improving the quality and skill of seasonal forecasts though, while important work, it has long been recognised that scientific information is not the only resource people draw on when making decisions on how to adapt. In many cases, culture trumps science. We wanted to study groups of people engaged in different activities or social worlds, as skilled practitioners of seasonal cultures; people who draw on seasonal frameworks for coping with the year-to-year variability in seasons, and how they tinker with and recraft these frameworks with an eye to more long term seasonal change.

This led to the CALENDARS (*Co-production of Seasonal Representations for Adaptive Institutions*) research project being initiated for a period of five-years from 2019, funded by the European Research Council, and conducted by a six-person team of interdisciplinary social scientists, mainly spread over Norway and New Zealand. CALENDARS case studies were global and diverse, including beekeepers, botanical gardeners, coffee roasters, artists, climate scientists, and schoolteachers and students in Bergen, Norway; grape growers in New England, USA; meteorologists in Ethiopia; amateur writers, conservationists, farmers, hunters, schoolteachers and students and local government on the Coromandel Peninsula in New Zealand. With each group we sought to collaboratively: (i) uncover the seasonal cultures that moves their activities; (ii) analyse how their cultures may be changing; and (iii) rethink how to revise the seasonal patterns of what they do.

Over this project, we have met so many folks with interesting stories to tell about how seasons are changing for them. We convened a group of these people – most of whom are authors of chapters in this book – next to Hardangerfjord in Norway in May 2022 (Figure 1.4). Spring's pattern was making itself felt there, and as we shared our stories over coffee, we looked out on the receding snow caps, the blossoming cherry trees, the lawn speckled with wildflowers, and heard the occasional call from high schoolers dressing up in overalls and partying in anticipation of the end of the school year. We distilled some key themes, discussed stories we missed, and agreed to pursue the idea of this book.

Figure 1.4: The dock at the Solstrand Hotel on Hardanger Fjord in Norway, where we met in May 2022 to share stories of seasonal change, and finalise a plan for this book. (Photo by: Arjan Wardekker).

Seasons and calendars as cultural frameworks

This book assembles a dizzying set of accounts of changing seasonal cultures. The reader is sent whirling from a gin distillery in the New Zealand bush, to the Chilean mountains, to the German lowlands. They peer into a Dublin shopping mall, witness a swan attack in Denmark, and tend to beehives in Provence. They bathe in the currents of the Indian Ocean, wade through Japanese wireweed in Norway, or dip a toe through a fishing hole cut in the Greenland ice. They imagine themselves as a toppling tree, or as a bridge engineer. They observe seasons in the mundaneness of their living room, before leaving this world and playing out seasons in the virtual realm, and on far-off planets. Making sense and drawing lessons from across these varied chapters is a journey of its own.

To help orient the reader through the stories between these covers, we here put forward a constellation of guiding concepts for thinking about seasons as cultural frameworks. The intention is not to provide the reader with a ready-made theory of what seasons are. The diverse accounts in this book shows that no such Rosetta stone exists. Rather we want to plant a few ideas in the back of readers minds, which might function as bridges between chapters, tools useful for thinking with, or hooks for hanging up insights. At least, it provides some insight into our own thinking about the book and how we have made sense of it all.

Seasons are flexible categories

Societies the world over adhere to frameworks of seasons, often with assumptions that seasonal categories are well-established and commonly held (15). And to some extent that's true. Season's names are commonly recognisable in societies, and they conjure up shared images and reference points that many agree on, for instance that summer is warm, or the dates of important holidays. But dig a little deeper and we discover that individuals and groups vary in the definitions and meanings they attach to seasons; ranging from quite precise descriptions of seasonal markers to more qualitative perceptions of seasons as patterns that someone "knows when they see them." People even differ on how they visualise the shape of the year, ranging from a circle, or spiral, to something resembling an amoeba, or the lines painted by sunlight on their balcony at different points of the year (16). In today's diverse, modern societies, there is rarely one accepted definition of seasons. People interpret and act on seasons differently.

If seasons are interpreted flexibly, it is because they are complex and fuzzy categories that defy precise definition. We experience seasons as changeable and ephemeral and see this reflected back to us in our cultures (17, 18). Seasons vary from year to year – no two summers are exactly alike – and merge into one another in transitioning from one season to the next. As Fischer and Macauley (17, page 66) note, seasons are poorly described as exact blocks of time like a clock hour or a calendar month, and better seen as movement between phases in the on-going cyclic flow of annual rhythms; *"Spring arises out of winter and becomes summer [. . .] There is not a moment in time at which we can say: winter has stopped, and spring has just begun."* In some ways we can think about this like dividing a flowing river into sections that make sense to us; the section with rock pools, the meandering section, the section where fish spawn and so on. Accordingly, where people decide to divide the flow into seasons depends on what periodic patterns are meaningful for them and what they pay attention to, whether that be rainfall, crop rotations or the school year for instance. Finally, to this complexity we can consider that seasonal patterns undergo long-term change over periods from a few years to millennia. The El Niño Southern Oscillation (ENSO) phenomena is an example, with global climate systems fluxing between El Niño warm and La Niña cold extremes and affecting seasonality over several years. But we can also see seasons change on a very slow arc over hundreds or thousands of years, with societies' technologies and land use, climatic change, the evolution and spread of species, or oscillations in and out of ice ages (19).

Finalising this book in the fjord city of Bergen in Norway, we the editors can distinguish quite divergent ideas here about seasonality. Most people we talk to think in four seasons, common to the temperate latitudes and European cultures, but disagree on where to draw the boundaries. Some define seasons relative to the tilt of the planet, marked out by the solstices and equinoxes. Others link seasons to the cycles of the sun and moon and define them by the months of the lunar-solar Gregorian calendar, associating spring with March, April, and May for example. Others define seasons by some weather threshold, the way autumn's onset is measured as a certain number of days in a row with temperatures below a particular value. And others still define the four seasons phenologically, according to the life cycles of plants and animals, such as when trees bud or birds migrate. But there is opposition to the four-season model too. Some people divide the year into two 6-month seasons according to sunshine hours, with a light and dark season. Others wryly refer to Bergen's wet climate in describing a single month of spring in May, and 11 months of wet autumn weather. Conversations about seasons also opened for very detailed discussion on the seasons of particular activities, such as tourist season, chainsaw season, or broken-hip season. In these conversations we see the year divided up in specialised ways, by patterns that are only visible to people experienced in these activities.

If we see seasons as flexible categories, it follows that there are many ways of studying them, whether through the rhythms of solar insolation, cyclical changes in temperature and rainfall, phenology of ecosystems, or as cultural frameworks (1). This is an important point for reading this book. While we recognise that seasonality is ultimately an earthly pattern in the natural world – being mindful of 'the tilt' – we do not think that this means seasons are first and foremost scientific categories, which can only really be apprehended through scientific measurements of nature, in things like rainfall or temperature. For us, the notion of dividing the flow of the year into parts and naming them is inherently cultural. That seasons are cultural categories and science is one cultural – yes, cultural – way of interpreting seasonality.

Seasons as cultural categories

Anthropologists have long studied population's seasonal frameworks as one of the earliest and "most basic scaffold[s] of peoples' sense of time" (4, page 94). Seasons are fundamental to how societies have made sense of the natural cycles around them in reckoning the timing of their activities; telling the time of the year for ensuring activities – whether fishing, planting crops or sharing stories – were done 'on time' (20) (Figure 1.5). Indeed, this could be a matter of life and death, as for instance planting crops in the wrong season or too late in the season could mean losing the harvest. Seasons then capture other forms of time than are meted out in our clocks. Insofar as time is defined as a rate of change then we see many types of time, or 'temporalities', pulsing through our landscapes and communities and our bodies (3, 21). The hydrology of a river – its flooding and drying over the year – is a cyclic rate of change that can be thought of as a temporal rhythm (22). So can tree rings, menstrual cycles, the regular appearance of storms, or the ticking of an air conditioning unit. Seasonality is about the temporal rhythms we choose to track and live by.

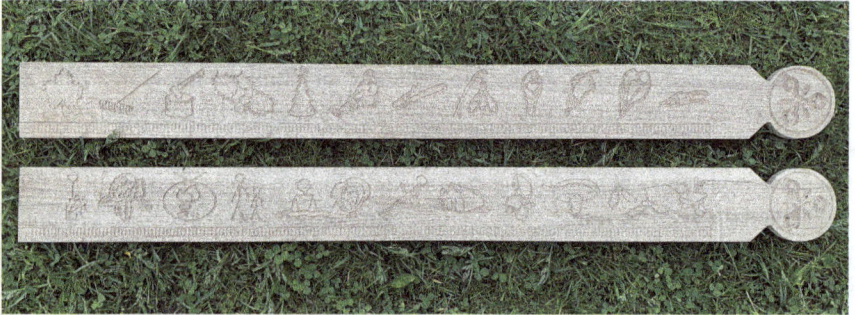

Figure 1.5: A reinterpretation of a traditional Norwegian 'primstav' or calendar, with symbols that mark the rhythms of the year, as contemporary reference points for gardening work and botanical research at the Bergen Arboretum, in Norway. These symbols trigger certain practices, and help coordinate the different activities in the gardens. (Photo by: Scott Bremer).

Seasonal frameworks guide communities through yearly rhythms, providing them with templates or schemas for attuning their activities with natural conditions, and with other activities in the community (6). This means developing repertoires of seasonal signs and markers to trigger certain practices, and a set of temporal reference points to coordinate between different practitioners (20). Or, as condensed in scriptures like the Christian Bible: "*To everything there is a season, and a time to every purpose under the heaven*". For example (23), beekeepers in western Norway track the hazel buds as signalling the start of the beekeeping season, as the moment when bees begin venturing out to collect nectar and the beekeeper needs to attend to the hive. Likewise, there are key reference points, as when hives must be transported to the fruit orchards *en masse* for pollination. This demonstrates what Bourdieu and other anthropologists note (6, 20), that it is through their activities and relations between activities that people perceive, experience and create seasonal categories. Activities are at once timed to and constitutive of seasons, meaning that peoples' activities become part of the seasonal pattern that they themselves associate with a time of the year. The beekeepers' activities are as much part of the beekeeping season as the flying bees or flowering valleys.

Seeing seasons as particular to activities helps make sense of why there are so many interpretations of seasons in our increasingly heterogeneous and specialised modern societies. While the rhythms of the hazel tree are of great importance to the beekeeper, they are likely invisible to the hotelier who is tuned to tourist season, or the engineer who is monitoring the seasons in the wear on key infrastructure. It also explains why it is important to have some shared names for seasons – such as 'summer' or 'monsoon' – that everyone in a community can relate to in some way, in order to coordinate the diverse activities going on in a population (15, 24).

If seasonal categories are functional for organising activities, they are also important for symbolising, valuing and give meaning to the chaotic world around us. They are written into the stories we tell about ourselves in the world. In this way, seasons are cultural themes that underlie our music and art, poems and histories, philosophies and proverbs and festivities (12, 25). The budding hazel may have practical significance for a beekeeper, but it is also part of an awakening nature that European cultures have traditionally associated with spring, fertility and new life, optimism, light and air, the colours green and yellow, Easter and a host of other Christian holidays for example (17). In this vein, seasons are often employed as metaphors representative of the different stages in a person's life (or the life of an organisation or civilisation or project . . .), from birth and vibrance over spring and summer, into the decay and death of autumn and winter (17). These are symbolical and emotional connotations of seasons that people culturally relate to. Seasons are central to human experience; our human relationships to each other, and to nature.

Seasonal cultures and calendars are claimed as part of the intangible heritage – the social and festive practices, representations, expressions, knowledge and know-how – that communities create, use and transmit from generation to generation. Recent interpretations of the Lascaux cave paintings suggest that tens of thousands of years ago, ice age hunter-gathers were already painting symbols for tracking the seasonal behavior of animals (26). Today, calendars and cultures continue to order social life around the world, and we see efforts to record and protect these. There are initiatives to codify the calendars that indigenous Australians use for timing activities in synch with the weave of rhythms that they track – the weather, soil, plants and animals – in deciding when to conduct controlled burn-offs for example (8). Sometimes this protection is formalized through efforts to register calendars on UNESCO's World Heritage List. The Traditional Chinese Seasonal Calendar was registered in 2016, and Project Mausam is an ongoing initiative to inscribe the monsoon patterns, cultural routes, and maritime landscapes of the Indian Ocean on the list (27).

But protecting seasonal cultures comes with difficult questions. First, the decision of whose calendar to protect is highly political and contentious. Why, in a country as geographically and culturally diverse as China, is only one calendar recognised on the Heritage List? Surely communities experience and live by different seasonal patterns on the tropical southern coast compared to the mountainous interiors, on the steppes, or the flood plains of the major rivers? Second, preservation of traditional calendars can overlook how they evolve and are *"constantly recreated by communities and groups in response to their environment"* (see UNESCO 2003, Article 2.1). Back to Indigenous Australian calendars, recent efforts to codify these include an appreciation for the modified environments these communities live in now, and the technologies they have at hand (28).

For navigating the cultural accounts in this book, a reader might find guidance in a definition, which we have been working from in recent years, of seasons as: *"individuals' and groups' perceived patterns in yearly rhythms that they segment into periods meaningful for them, and effect practices that maintain or change these patterns"*.

Seasons as perceived patterns

> *Summer still raging while a thin*
> *Column of smoke stirs from the land*
> *Proving that Autumn gropes for us.*
> (Song at the beginning of Autumn, in, A Way of Looking; Elisabeth Jennings 1955)

We can think about seasons as patterns that individuals and groups look for in the impossible tapestry of tangled rhythms that flow through the year. As we noted for the beekeepers, these rhythms are as much the 'natural' rhythms we see in the environment as they are the social or cultural rhythms we effect in our environments. The patterns that people discern depends on the rhythms that matter for them, and how they perceive a coherence between these rhythms, or a 'wholeness'. What the Norwegian beekeeper names 'spring' is not only the budding hazel but the whole complex weave of rhythms coming together over a period; when temperatures and light increases, bee's leave the hive, beekeepers open the hive and feed the bees sugar, the fruit growers organise how many hives they need for pollination, biosecurity laws on when hives can be moved take effect, and so on. Rhythms are largely interrelated – e.g. warming temperatures affect when bees leaving the hive – but some rhythms may simply coincide or happen at the same time without being related to the others. Beekeepers might for instance associate tax returns with the pattern of spring, but this rhythm has no apparent relation to bees or sunshine. When rhythms rework themselves into a different pattern, a new phase, then the beekeeper may bracket this as a new season and call it 'summer': when the snow has melted to reveal wildflowers, the first honey is harvested, the colony grows strong and swarms, children are home for the holidays and help out, and beekeepers start rearing queen-bees (3).

One way of visualising seasons could be as the patterns formed in a kaleidoscope. In this way, seasonal patterns are observed by someone peering into the tube, and as the tube is rotated – the way the year cycles – the pattern holds for a moment before the beads (or rhythms) move into a new configuration and the person perceives a changed pattern. Importantly, each person using the kaleidoscope will interpret the pattern differently, noticing some elements more than others, and looking at how the elements fit together. Indeed, the kaleidoscope is a fitting parallel to seasonality because it has often been used to symbolise change on one hand and harmony on the other.

Elisabeth Jennings, in her poem 'Song at the beginning of Autumn', captures this way of looking at (and smelling and feeling) seasonal patterns, and sensing departures from these patterns. Though she writes about summer "raging", and in an earlier stanza describes the summer colours on the landscape and trees heavy with growth, she notices a single column of smoke and remarks on this as a feature reminiscent of autumn. For her, the bonfire signaled that the summer pattern was coming apart and an autumn pattern starting to form into place. The poem also shows how seasonal cultures – in names like 'summer' and 'autumn' and symbols like bonfires – frame what we pay attention to. While Jennings noticed the bonfire, other rhythms may have gone unsensed.

Of course, the above is only one way of thinking about seasons as culturally perceived patterns, and many others are possible. But it is a useful concept we have been working with and we think it can help readers make sense of the chapters in this book which approach seasonal patterns in unique ways.

Seasons as practices and technologies

> *But I am carried back against*
> *My will into a childhood where*
> *Autumn is bonfires, marbles, smoke;*
> *I lean against my window fenced*
> *From evocations in the air.*
> *When I said autumn, autumn broke.*
> (Song at the beginning of Autumn, in A Way of Looking; Elisabeth Jennings 1955)

It may be intuitive that seasons are the patterns we notice, and that what we notice is culturally mediated or influenced. But many would still assume that, while seasonal categories might be cultural, the patterns we make sense of are inscribed "out there in nature" and we respond. That seasonal rhythms – e.g. linked to the Earth's circling the sun or global weather patterns – are independent of humans, and would repeat for millions of years whether we were here to notice them or not. It is less intuitive to think that human communities affect the seasonal patterns we find significant, through the activities we do and the ways we interact with an environment. We already discussed how beekeepers' activities are an inseparable part of spring's pattern; that the behaviour of honeybees and their material effect on ecosystems is influenced by the beekeeper's practices to the extent that we can say that beekeepers affect seasonality – phenological rhythms – in an environment.

In the modified environments people live in today, natural and cultural landscapes merge into one another and become one; humans and their environments co-evolve with one another. Gan and Tsing (11), in writing about the seasons of a satoyama forest in Japan, note how generations of repeated procedures for tending the forest – in conjunction with natural interspecies co-evolution between trees and mushrooms for instance – have effected a particularly patterned seasonality. The bonfire in Jennings' poem implies that by altering the timing of our practices, we can alter the seasonal patterns that we live by. For Jennings, the activity of lighting a bonfire evokes feelings of a new season, even as the current season still "rages". With seasons so closely associated with activities, this implies that in deciding on the timings of actions – like lighting bonfires – we can affect what seasonal pattern or period people feel like they are part of (even as many 'natural' seasonal rhythms remain unchanged). Or as Jennings writes, when she "said autumn, autumn broke."

Societies regularly affect seasonal patterns through their built environments and infrastructure, as highlighted in the case of the Bangladesh stop banks, which altered annual flooding regimes. To take another case, studies worldwide (e.g. in India (29), or Burkina Faso (30)) demonstrate how the construction of an all-weather road can do more to transform the seasonal pattern of life in a remote community than any changes in the climate or ecosystem. As roads are established, communities change their seasonal practices; connecting to markets and urban rhythms, travelling to the city for seasonal work, changing movement patterns and the goods they use over the year (31). Air-conditioned offices and indoor shopping malls might also change the seasonal perceptions and behaviour of the people who spend much of their time in these structures (32, 33). Moreover, the maintenance of infrastructures in turn introduces a raft of new seasonal rhythms, through resealing roads at different time of the year for example (34).

Meteorological and climate science is affecting how communities apprehend seasonal patterns and exercise control over those patterns. Our communities – especially indigenous communities – have long drawn on complex seasonal patterns that helped them read the time of the year in the weather, plants, animals, the land- or sea-scape (7). But in modern times many of us have swapped such observations for weather forecasts on the television, radio or smart phone apps (35). This usually means tracking just two or three rhythms – temperature, precipitation and wind – in forming an impoverished picture of seasonality. Indeed, some seasonal patterns like graphs of average rainfall per month, were invisible to us before developing methods for measuring rainfall and statistical infrastructures for calculating such averages and recording these data. A more recent development has been the production of seasonal forecasts, which are currently limited to assessing whether the next month or two will be warmer or cooler, wetter or drier, than the average. These forecasts are used by different groups, from hydro-electric companies predicting reservoir water levels to farmers planning cropping, in planning seasonal activities in advance (36).

Altogether, technological and scientific developments are changing communities' relations to seasons. On one hand, forecasts are reducing uncertainties around seasonal conditions – on the likelihood of a summer heatwave, or dry spring for instance – and providing people with a sense of seasonal control. Rather than acting according to seasonal traditions, people can *optimise* the timing of their activities for best results. On the other hand, reducing seasonal patterns to a few scientific measurements are estranging us from those seasonal symbols we draw inspiration, identity and meaning from. Thomas (37) captures this so eloquently in his poem 'Spring Equinox'. He provokes the reader by asking them to abandon the stories and imagery they grew up with: *"Do not say, referring to the sun / 'Its journey northward has begun'"*. He quips: *"The age demands the facts, therefore be brief – / Others will sense the simile – and say: / 'We are turning towards the sun's indifferent ray'."*

Seasonal frameworks change with time and people

It follows then, if we see seasons as cultural categories linked to communities' perceptions and activities, that seasonal frameworks evolve with changes in a community's environment, and in how people in the community relate to that environment and each other. To start with an obvious example, the calendars recorded by Ice Age communities around 17 000 years ago in the Lascaux cave. The seasons tracked by these populations must have been significantly different to our seasonal frameworks today given they were living in the tail end of an ice age, in an environment with no resemblance to the landscapes of today, cohabiting with species that are mostly extinct or have evolved, securing their livelihood through hunting and gathering, and with different cultural symbols and beliefs through which they made sense of the world. But what about just 500 years ago, in early modern Norway?

As the chapters on the primstav folk calendar show (38, 39), seasons held quite different meanings and practical significance for Norwegian communities just a few hundred years ago. The framework itself was different. The primstav was aligned with a lunar-solar calendar, but at the time it was the Julian calendar. Moreover, the most widespread sword or plank shape captured the year in just two seasons of winter and summer; one on each side of the plank. Within this framework, the symbolic markers of these seasons were associated with Christian saints and holy days, which were appropriated and reinterpreted into agricultural cues and proverbs tailored to the conditions of particular valleys and fjords and the technologies of the time (for more detail read 39). Consider how differently the year is patterned seasonally in today's Norway; founded on a Gregorian calendar and notions of four seasons that are roughly standardised across the whole country, where modern urbanised communities are increasingly detached from agricultural rhythms, and where the diversification of religions and growing atheism empties Christian holy days of meaning for many.

In the past few years, we (Scott and colleagues) have run workshops asking groups of Bergen residents to re-create primstavs for today. All groups have opted to return to the two-season calendar of a bygone era, but populated those seasons with updated markers or reference points for today. While some remain constant like Christmas or Saint John the Baptist Day, most have changed to reflect the school calendar, other holy days like the Muslim festival of Eid, global days of significance such as United Nations Day or Women's Day, technical reminders to change the car's winter tires, reminders to plan for the release of new computer games, or for local cultural events such as film or music festivals. Importantly, these primstav drawing workshops are not straight-forward. While groups of people do arrive at many shared reference points – Christmas is a common one – other annual markers are hotly contested, especially when groups are limited to how many symbols they can include. This demonstrates another major change from Norwegian society 500 years ago; today, society is more heterogeneous, and people contest different seasonal patterns.

And here we want to come back to the imperative for this book; why this volume is important now. Seasonal cultures have always, and will always, evolve and adapt with our communities. People and their cultures can be remarkably resilient (40). Yet, many argue that the processes changing seasonal cultures have been, until recently, rather gradual. In many cases this enabled communities to incrementally – even mundanely – adjust their ways of seeing and doing in the world; changes that only appear dramatic when compared over hundreds of years. What marks our epoch today is the 'great acceleration' in societal and environmental changes, in a global and interconnected way, that characterises what some term the Anthropocene (41). It is perhaps for this reason that communities attest to not just deviations from the seasonal frameworks, but a sense that they collapse altogether.

Highlighting change processes – climate change and all the others

Going through the chapters in this volume, a reader should keep an eye out for the diverse and intertwined processes coming together and affecting communities' and individuals' seasonal frameworks. These may range from significant global change Processes with a capital P, such as climate change or globalisation, down to extremely personal adjustments in how an author themselves experiences the seasons in their daily life. Sometimes these processes are quite apparent, highlighted and discussed by the author, while other processes are shown in more subtle ways and only discernible by reading between the lines. And more often than not, these change processes are entangled; they come together and interact in effecting seasonal change. Scott Bremer's (42) chapter for example shows how processes of globalisation, commercialisation and the increasing spectacle of sport have together transformed rugby from a seasonal pass-time into a year-round source of entertainment and revenue, with attendant shifts in the rules and playing style. Miriam Jensen's chapter (43) highlights clashes between the seasonal calendars of different river users, including non-human users like swans, where these clashes are concurrently affected by climatic change, a growing infrastructure of paths, shifts in land use, the timing of public holidays, and changing management regimes of the river. So, while the book is divided into six broad themes of change, this was not an easy division to make.

In this sense, this book is not all about climate change. Global climate change is obviously one of the major underlying change processes affecting seasonality, in weather patterns, phenology, sea temperatures, and so on. It undergirds many of the changes in the environment that we experience, and which feature in these chapters. It also significantly affects societies' relations to the environment, through a host of policies and taxes, technologies and research projects, news stories and so on. Our awareness that it's changing re-shapes our relationship to the climate and seasons, and what we notice. A warm February day in Norway is now not only greeted with a smile, but also a sense of foreboding. Indeed, over half of the chapters in this volume link to climatic change in some way. But climate change interacts in complex ways with other processes in undermining seasonal cultures – it rarely boils down simply to a change in average temperatures, or the frequency of storms. Rosario Carmona and Jessica Rupayan (44) show how climate change impacts on the transhumance cycles of the Pehuenche people are exacerbated by a legacy of environmental degradation, resource privatisation, monocropping, government subsidies, and ultimately, urbanisation. To reduce this to a climate problem is a simplification that ignores the weave of rhythms, meanings, practices and more that constitute seasonal cultures. As such, there is no specific section of the book on climate change. Rather, climate change is woven into many of the chapters, intermingled with other changes such as ecological, social, (geo)political, and technological developments. We encounter changing seasonality not in a piecemeal way, but in the interaction of many rhythms and changes in the world around us.

Adapting seasonal cultures

A final important theme to look for in these chapters relates to how individuals and groups are re-crafting their cultures to changing seasonal conditions and meanings. How they are *adapting* cultures as a resource for coordinating and attuning timely action in their communities. Cultural frameworks have always helped communities cope – through adjustments – to seasonal variability from year to year. But facing a wave of change processes, some are significantly re-drawing – re-imagining even – the patterns and reference points that serve as coordinates through the year. We will come back to adaptation in the conclusion, suffice for now to note the diverse ways authors in this book go about responding. One common plea, for example, is to reconnect with the rhythms that pulse through our environments, but which have become invisible to us. Another is to look to traditional and inherited wisdoms, and how they can be appropriated to today's predicaments. A third is to re-coordinate the timings of activities with each other and the environment, to follow the frictions and re-establish a semblance of stability. And others still propose boldly experimenting with new seasonal ways of life, played out in virtual worlds, or in the plants that track a shifting climate and choose to "have a go". Read together, these chapters put forward a rich portfolio of ways in which we can (and do) respond.

Encounters with seasonality

In a chaotic and changeable world, the seasons – summer, winter, the monsoon and so on – can feel like stable and lasting cultural landmarks to orient ourselves. We've come to see seasons as dependable categories for dividing up the year and setting order to annual cycles. They are grounded in our histories, inscribed in ancient calendars dug up from bygone eras. We are brought up on seasonal symbols, like winter's snowflake, in our story books. Our everyday speech is filled with seasonal references and proverbs, as is our poetry and literature. We hold valued seasonal memories, perhaps of picking summer fruits or huddled around the fire in autumn. Indeed, seasons can seem like societies' building blocks; attached to religious festivals, shaping diets, signalling traditional practices and holidays for example. Seasonal frameworks are deeply cultural and specific to the places we live. They set a rhythm to our lives, often without us consciously thinking about it.

But on closer inspection, seasons are quite unstable and unreliable. They fluctuate of course – no two summers are the same – but their meanings also change over time. We see a cultural perspective on seasons provides purchase for analysing the nuanced ways in which seasons change for communities, and why that matters for their everyday lives.

We encounter seasonality, and changing seasonality, in many aspects of our lives: from our cultural backgrounds, to the places we inhabit, our daily lives, and the work we do. In this book, we've invited a wide range of authors to explore how they encountered changing seasonality in their academic, professional, or personal experiences. We collected these according to six themes:

(1) Evolving history and heritage: seasonality is deeply rooted in our cultures, and becomes apparent when we examine historical artifacts and practices, immigrant experiences, religion, and Indigenous perspectives.

(2) Relations to nature: seasons play a large role in the cycles of plants and animals, and the way we as humans relate to those. Yet, the natural world encounters many changes, as do the ways we interact with nature.

(3) Creativity and the arts: seasonality can inspire creative pursuits, and we explore how cultural expectations of seasons might be embedded, or questioned, in arts such as photography, paintings, games, and poetry.

(4) Rhythms of daily life: we face many changes and disruptions in our daily lives, from technological to social, environmental and personal, and wonder about the role of seasonal patterns in those.

(5) Professional practices: work engages with many seasonal rhythms in the world outside the office building, which may be our local surroundings or the global stage, and we explore the views of both practitioners and academics on that.

(6) Planning and engineering: the places we inhabit are designed to be in sync with seasonal rhythms, often in hidden ways, and we will explore the interactions of spatial planning, engineering, and infrastructure with changing seasonality.

Together, these chapters offer a diverse and deep but accessible repertoire of perspectives, based on concrete real-life experiences. We hope that they may trigger reflection and inspire communities and individuals to revisit the ways in which they encounter and engage with changing seasonality.

References

1. Kwiecien, O., T. Braun, C. F. Brunello, P. Faulkner, N. Hausmann, G. Helle, . . . & S. F. Breitenbach. "*What we talk about when we talk about seasonality—A transdisciplinary review*". *Earth-Science Reviews* (2021): 103843.
2. Muir, J. "Tilting the frame: How the seasonal characteristics of light informs image". In: Bremer, S. & A. Wardekker (eds.) Changing seasonality: How Communities are Revising their Seasons. De Gruyter: Berlin, 2023.
3. Adam, B. Timescapes of modernity: The environment and invisible hazards. London: Routledge. 2005.
4. Roncoli, C., T. Crane, & B. Orlove. "*Fielding Climate Change: The Role of Anthropology*". In S. Crate and M. Nuttall (eds.). Anthropology & Climate Change: From Encounters to Actions. Walnut Creek, Calif.: Left Coast Press: 87–115.
5. Munn, N. D. The cultural anthropology of time: A critical essay. *Annual review of anthropology*, (1992): 93–123.
6. Bourdieu, P. *Outline of a theory of practice*. Cambridge: Cambridge University Press, 1977.
7. Chisholm Hatfield, S., E. Marino, K. P. Whyte, K. D. Dello, & P. W. Mote. "*Indian time: time, seasonality, and culture in Traditional Ecological Knowledge of climate change*". *Ecological Processes*, 7, (2018): 1–11.

8. Leonard, S., M. Parsons, K. Olawsky, & F. Kofod. "*The role of culture and traditional knowledge in climate change adaptation: Insights from East Kimberley, Australia*". Global Environmental Change, 23 (2013): 623–632.
9. Adger, W. N., J. Barnett, K. Brown, N. Marshall & K. O'Brien. "*Cultural dimensions of climate change impacts and adaptation*". Nature Climate Change 3 (2013): 112–117.
10. McNeeley, S. M., & M. D. Shulski. "*Anatomy of a closing window: Vulnerability to changing seasonality in Interior Alaska*". Global Environmental Change, 21 (2011): 464–473.
11. Gan, E. A. and Tsing. "*How things hold: a diagram of coordination in a Satoyama forest*". Social Analysis, 62 (2018): 102–145.
12. Groom, N. *The seasons: A celebration of the English year*. Atlantic Books Ltd, 2013.
13. Bastian, M. "Taking a chance in unseasonable environments". In: Bremer, S. & A. Wardekker (eds.) Changing seasonality: How Communities are Revising their Seasons. De Gruyter: Berlin, 2023.
14. Pasker, R. "Getreur in Voorthuizen, want na 35 jaar komt er einde aan de ijsbaan: 'Merken al jaren dat het niet meer kan'." *De Gelderlander*, 10 March, 2023. (https://www.gelderlander.nl/barneveld/getreur-in-voorthuizen-want-na-35-jaar-komt-er-einde-aan-de-ijsbaan-merken-al-jaren-dat-het-niet-meer-kan~a76eaab5/).
15. Orlove, B. How people name seasons. In S. Strauss & B. Orlove (eds.). *Weather, climate, culture*. New York: Berg. 2003: 121–140.
16. Hofseth, A. "This is what the year actually looks like". *NRK Beta*, 01 January, 2018. (https://nrkbeta.no/2018/01/01/this-is-what-the-year-actually-looks-like/).
17. Fischer, L., & D. Macauley. *The Seasons: Philosophical, Literary, and Environmental Perspectives*. New York: SUNY Press. 2021.
18. Ingold, T. *Being Alive: essays on movement, knowledge and description*: Oxen: Routledge. 2011.
19. Chambers, L.E., R. D. Plotz, S. Lui, F. Aiono, T. Tofaeono, D. Hiriasia, L. Tahani, O. Fa'anunu, S. Finaulahi, & A. Willy "Seasonal calendars enhance climate communication in the Pacific". *Weather, Climate, and Society, 13* (2021): 159–172.
20. Munn, N. D. "*The cultural anthropology of time: A critical essay*". Annual review of anthropology (1992): 93–123.
21. Bastian, M. "Fatally confused: Telling the time in the midst of ecological crises". *Environmental Philosophy, 9* (2012): 23–48.
22. Krause, F. "Seasons as rhythms on the Kemi River in Finnish Lapland". *Ethnos, 78* (2013): 23–46.
23. Hempel, M. "*Losing seasons in the landscape; when the weather, bees, trees and people fall out of synchrony*". In: Bremer, S. & A. Wardekker (eds.) Changing seasonality: How Communities are Revising their Seasons. De Gruyter: Berlin, 2023.
24. Douglas, M. *How institutions think*. Syracuse: Syracuse University Press. 1986.
25. Harris, A. *Weatherland: Writers and artists under English skies*. Thames & Hudson. 2015.
26. Devlin, H. "Amateur archaeologist uncovers ice age 'writing' system". *The Guardian*, 5 January, 2023. (https://www.theguardian.com/science/2023/jan/05/amateur-archaeologist-uncovers-ice-age-writing-system).
27. Pearson, N. "*Claiming the winds: Monsoon in the Indian Ocean*". In: Bremer, S. & A. Wardekker (eds.) Changing seasonality: How Communities are Revising their Seasons. De Gruyter: Berlin, 2023.
28. McKemey, M., E. Ens, Y. M. Rangers, O. Costello, & N. Reid, N. "*Indigenous knowledge and seasonal calendar inform adaptive savanna burning in northern Australia*". Sustainability, 12 (220): 995.

29. Vedwan, N. "Culture, climate and the environment: Local knowledge and perception of climate change among apple growers in northwestern India". *Journal of Ecological Anthropology, 10* (2006): 4–18.

30. Nielsen, J. Ø., & A. Reenberg. *"Temporality and the problem with singling out climate as a current driver of change in a small West African village"*. *Journal of Arid Environments, 74* (2010): 464–474.

31. Krauss, W. *"Weather and infrastructure: The Flax Road"*. In: Bremer, S. & A. Wardekker (eds.) Changing seasonality: How Communities are Revising their Seasons. De Gruyter: Berlin, 2023.

32. O'Kane, E. "The nature of art: Changing seasonality in my artwork". In: Bremer, S. & A. Wardekker (eds.) Changing seasonality: How Communities are Revising their Seasons. De Gruyter: Berlin, 2023.

33. Hitchings, R. *"Seasonal climate change and the indoor city worker"*. *Transactions of the Institute of British Geographers, 35* (2010): 282–298.

34. Young, M. "Artifacts and seasonality: How we guide the built environment through time". In: Bremer, S. & A. Wardekker (eds.) Changing seasonality: How Communities are Revising their Seasons. De Gruyter: Berlin, 2023.

35. Hide-Bayne, D. "Apps and me: how apps are shaping my experience of the New Zealand environment and seasons". In: Bremer, S. & A. Wardekker (eds.) Changing seasonality: How Communities are Revising their Seasons. De Gruyter: Berlin, 2023.

36. Venning, M. "Forecasting seasons: Using science-based climate forecast information to dictate seasonal agricultural rhythms in East Africa". In: Bremer, S. & A. Wardekker (eds.) Changing seasonality: How Communities are Revising their Seasons. De Gruyter: Berlin, 2023.

37. Thomas, R. S. "Spring Equinox". In "The Stones of the Field". Druid Press.

38. Axtel. S. et al. *"Healing roots and unsettling legacies"*. In: Bremer, S. & A. Wardekker (eds.) Changing seasonality: How Communities are Revising their Seasons. De Gruyter: Berlin, 2023.

39. Schøyen Jensen, E. *"Thinking with the primstav today"*. In: Bremer, S. & A. Wardekker (eds.) Changing seasonality: How Communities are Revising their Seasons. De Gruyter: Berlin, 2023.

40. Strauss, S. "Are cultures endangered by climate change? Yes, but . . . .". *Wiley Interdisciplinary Reviews: Climate Change, 3* (2012): 371–377.

41. Edensor, T., L. Head, & U. Kothari. "Time, temporality and environmental change." *Geoforum* (2019).

42. Bremer, S. "Telling the year by the rugby season, and getting confused". This In: Bremer, S. & A. Wardekker (eds.) Changing seasonality: How Communities are Revising their Seasons. De Gruyter: Berlin, 2023.

43. Jensen, M. "Feral swans and frightening encounters". In: Bremer, S. & A. Wardekker (eds.) Changing seasonality: How Communities are Revising their Seasons. De Gruyter: Berlin, 2023.

44. Carmona, R. & J. Rupayan. "Chasing the seasons: Pehuenche experiences of rapid socioecological change in the Southern Andes". In: Bremer, S. & A. Wardekker (eds.) Changing seasonality: How Communities are Revising their Seasons. De Gruyter: Berlin, 2023.

Part I **Evolving history & heritage**

Sara Axtell, Carson Brown, Jena Brune, Kirsten Lovett,
Merissa Lovett, Maureen Springer, and Anna Vangsness
2 Healing roots and unsettling legacies

Unsettling: Understanding our relationship to place

The Mississippi and Minnesota Rivers come together in the area currently known as the Twin Cities of St. Paul and Minneapolis. This confluence, or '*Bdote*' in the Dakota language, is central to the creation story of the Dakota people, and Dakota have lived here since time immemorial (1).

The earthwork mounds built by the ancestors of the Seminole people shape the land that is now called southern Florida, and the Seminole continue to live in this place (2).

As descendants of European settlers, living in what is now Minnesota and Florida, our peoples' histories in North America began much later. Throughout the 1800s, Scandinavian settlers were arriving at the same time the U.S. government was systematically displacing and exterminating Indigenous peoples.

Broken treaties, the U.S.-Dakota War, Dakota internment at the Fort Snelling concentration camp, and the largest mass execution in the history of the United States preceded the Dakota Expulsion Act of 1863, and collectively resulted in massive land dispossession and the ethnic cleansing of Dakota people from Minnesota (3, 4).

Repeated American military campaigns, the forced exile of the Indian Removal Act of 1830, and concentration camps like the one at Egmont Key were perpetrated against the Seminole and Miccosukee peoples (5, 6). Similar atrocities occurred across the entire continent.

These histories live in our institutions and policies, and in our very bodies, thoughts, and actions. Reckoning with this history must centre on a process of land return. Many of us who are descendants of those European settlers are also asking ourselves what within our culture allowed these brutalities, and what we can do in our own generation to help repair these cultural ruptures.

European settlers both experienced historical trauma in Europe and inflicted trauma in North America (7). For descendants of settlers, reconnecting to our European roots requires us to face these histories, a task that often collapses into guilt, overwhelm, and immobilization. We need communal rituals and structures to sup-

Acknowledgements: We would like to express gratitude to Monica Siems McKay and Janice Barbee for providing feedback and perspectives on this essay.

port such an intense reckoning. We need tools that bridge past and present, victim and perpetrator, there and here, pain and joy, in order to heal and contribute to repair.

Finding healing roots: The primstav

Our group was formed in the spring of 2019, drawn together by our common search for such bridging tools. We were heavy with the weight of trying to understand and reckon with our own histories. Exhausted by the pace of our own lives and by the sense of disconnection we experienced from the world around us. Many of us had been learning from the examples shared by Indigenous and African American elders and teachers, as well as from elders in our own cultural communities, that reconnecting to earlier cultural practices can bring a different kind of balance to our lives. In the words of Robin Kimmerer, botanist, writer, and member of the Citizen Potawatomi Nation:

> In a colonist society the ceremonies that endure are not about land; they're about family and culture, values that are transportable from the old country. Ceremonies for the land no doubt existed there, but it seems they did not survive emigration in any substantial way. I think there is wisdom in regenerating them here, as a means to form bonds with this land (8, page 250).

In our search for ceremonies for the land in our own histories, we came across the primstav. The primstav, a calendar dating back potentially as far as 11th century Norway (9), contains a rich store of folk knowledge for understanding humans' relationship to the natural world. Figure 2.1 shows an example of a primstav in progress. When was the right time to plant winter rye? To shear sheep? When do the salmon start to run, and the bears come out of their dens? Working with the primstav brings phenology, folklore, and art together with a study of history and culture.

Figure 2.1: Drawing a primstav, the summer side: work in progress. (Photo by: Sara Axtell).

We have found that primstav study can serve as a guide to unlearn and resist the oppressive systems that are present in modern western culture. While capitalism views land as commodity, the primstav demonstrates that our ancestors experienced the land as physical and spiritual sustenance. The modern western scientific model sees only the material, but the primstav allows for animist possibilities of meaningful, intelligent interaction with landforms, plants, and animals within a larger web of kinship.

Similarly, the modern construct of whiteness requires us to forsake cultural and ancestral connections in favour of a racialized identity, a process which strips away people's humanity. We use "whiteness" here to refer to what Coleman and colleagues call "a socially constructed ideology emanating from legal, economic, and cultural practices (10, page 500)." It is a product of culture, not culture itself. Like capitalism, whiteness makes people and places interchangeable across disparate contexts, rather than seeing them as singular and situated. Part of this ideology is to position whiteness as neutral, the blank default space, outside of and superior to all "other" identities. To occupy this elevated and presumably objective space, whiteness must erase the diversity and richness that European cultures generated before they were "white." This dehumanization of self and "other" is the prerequisite for continuing atrocities towards Native peoples and the land. For us, working with the primstav has been part of restoring a more rooted identity, and regaining some of our humanity lost to whiteness, helping to create the kinship conditions in which our current scale of violence is inconceivable.

We have been exploring this together, as a collective during this past three years. Interacting with the plants and animals and landforms with whom we are living and making meaning together about these experiences. Working with the primstav has helped us to slow, to pause, to notice. It has helped us to understand and be connected to rhythms and cycles in the natural world. It has also allowed us to be more connected with our ancestors and create space within ourselves and our communities to reckon with the legacies that we carry. What follows are some themes from our personal and collective learning.

Working with the primstav has allowed us to slow our pace, notice what is going on around us, and develop a deeper sense of place

Community around the primstav has been an invitation to relationship and to responsibility. It reminds me to slow down and spend time with the kin outside. Sketch their details, learn their cycles, and reciprocate the gifts offered. It encourages me to question and to research. What words for these times and tasks are used in Norway? How do they relate to Dakota descriptors? It reminds me to attend to both the literal (time to bring out the mittens) and the metaphoric (time to mend the fences – what relationships need boundaries or repair?) In Figures 2.2 and 2.3, you see pages of primstav journals, where we record primstav days and observations about what is happening on the land. These opportunities to engage serve as a disruption to the habits of scarcity and detachment while supporting our ongoing, communal practices of learning, unlearning, and healing. (JB)

One of the most powerful aspects of the primstav study for me, has been the practice of paying attention to what is happening on the land around me through-out the year. I have had the joy of becoming acquainted with many of the native plants in Minnesota. Learning their names, along with when they bloom and fruit, and their relationships to other kin, has brought me into a deeper relationship with this place. This, in turn, brings up important questions about my relationship to this land as a descendant of settlers. I'm grateful that our primstav study group provides a community and structure in which to work with these questions. (MS)

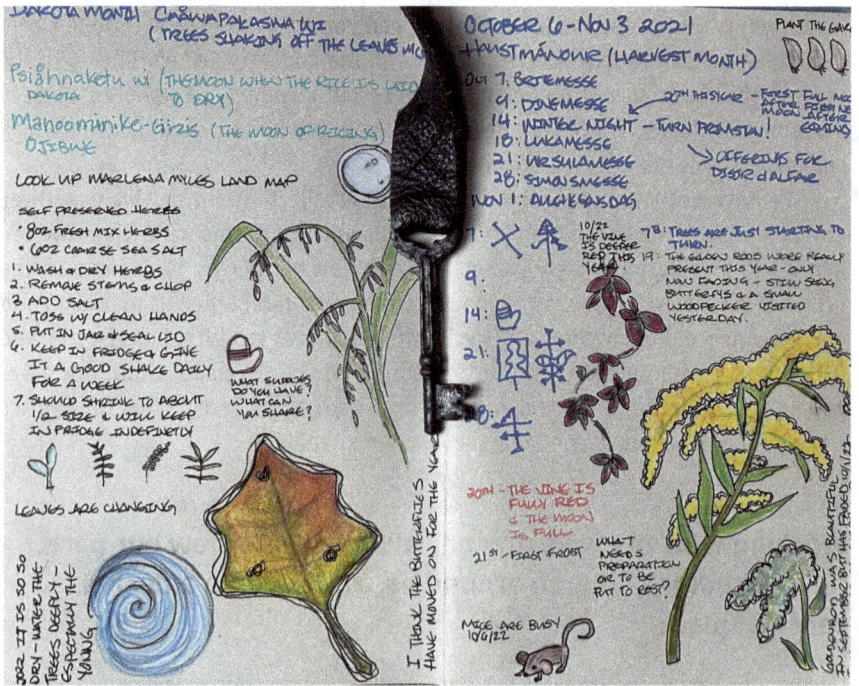

Figure 2.2: Primstav Journal. (Photo by: Jena Brune).

The primstav creates space for ritual. It helps us make sense of and be fully a part of the rhythms that surround us

I have an offering practice that is a way to connect with the land I live on while being an immigrant here. The primstav has added something traceable to my own ancestors to my existing land practice, and this has allowed an integration to happen that continues to be a profound experience. I feel a connection to my ancestors as well as a connection to the land. It doesn't mean there aren't any problems on the land, but it does help me to connect here and be guided by the ancestors and what they might have done in this situation. (KL)

The primstav has helped me to understand the rhythm of the seasons: which trees hold onto their leaves the longest in the fall? When do the elderberry, the pear and the honeysuckle begin to flower in the spring? The seasonal rituals embedded in primstav teachings help me to be a part of these rhythms. Offering porridge to the land on 'Sommermål' and seed to the birds on 'Christmas'. Weeding the gardens on 'Syftesok'. Ways to express gratitude and care. (SA)

Figure 2.3: Primstav Journal. (Photo by: Maureen Springer).

The primstav leads us to reconsider and repair values and practices within western culture that cause harm or ill health

There are primstav dates in July related to the hay harvest and cooperative work, which got me thinking about cooperative work in my life. At first thought, I'm often doing a lot of work on my own (gardening, cleaning and cooking for example.) But with more reflection, I was able to identify cooperative work in my life such as helping a friend move, helping others with yard work, and participating in neighborhood trash clean ups. This reflection brings to mind the principle of gift for a gift (reciprocity): how community bonds become stronger when we support each other. It has left me thinking about small ways to resist individualism by inviting cooperative work into my life, and how I can live in reciprocity with the seasons and with plant and animal beings who inhabit this land. (AV)

The primstav helps us to grapple with the legacies of this history, and how we can contribute to repairing the harms we have created

After living in northern California for 35 years, I was eager to learn about the land, seasons, and original inhabitants of my new home in Minnesota. I read books, went for walks, talked to neighbors, visited museums and farms, but I didn't have a scaffold on which to hang my learning, so it didn't gel. Group study of the primstav, with an "unsettling" lens, gave me an organizing structure to observe the cycles of this new place and ponder my personal role within it as a white settler on Dakota land. (CB)

Summer on the primstav calendar helped me to understand the dualities inherent in where I am living: my ancestors lived in the temperate zone while I now live in Florida. The primstav helped me reconcile the rainy/dry season climate of the subtropics with the traditional knowledge and seasons of my Scandinavian ancestors. The primstav and study of root culture also allowed me to find a meeting ground for the different histories of this land and the communities of Native/non-native people, animals, and plants. (ML)

In these past three years, the rhythms of the primstav have led us into a deepening relationship with the land and with our ancestors. It has helped to restore our connection to the seasons, both the seasons in the land where we are living and those in our ancestral places. It has opened up space to reckon with our own history and begin to learn a different way of relating to the world around us, more unsettled and more connected.

The authors

Sara Axtell is the great-great-grandchild of Norwegian settlers, and lives with her family on Dakota treaty land (1805, 1837, and 1851 treaties). She teaches at the University of Minnesota and with Healing Roots. She feels profound gratitude to elders at Healing Roots and the Cultural Wellness Center as well as to elders and teachers in the Indigenous communities in Minneapolis.

Carson Brown is a psychiatrist and writer, as well as a parent, partner, daughter, sister, friend, neighbor, and basketball coach, interested in collectively envisioning and embodying the radical shifts needed to rebirth a sustainable and just society, and hopefully having fun in the process.

Jena Brune uses relationship, creativity, and accountability as a framework to guide her work partnering with youth, adults, and families as a Minnesota based youth worker, transformational coach, and restorative facilitator. She holds deep gratitude for Healing Roots in helping her to recognize the resilience and tools of her Norwegian and Finnish heritage while building a community which can support and navigate the work of acknowledgment, repair, and connection.

Kirsten Lovett is a Shamanic Coach/Mentor at Now Moment Journey specializing in helping people identify their unique shamanic gifts through developing relationships with spirits of Nature.

Merissa Lovett has lived in Florida on Seminole/Miccosukee land for thirty years. She is passionate about sharing, dreaming and other animistic practices to empower people who are called to remember the old ways. These practices help practitioners enter the Otherworld to solve problems, recover ancestral knowledge, and heal.

Maureen Springer is a descendant of German and Irish settler ancestors, an aunt/daughter/sister, artist, art therapist, and apprentice with Healing Roots. She lives with her partner in St. Paul, Minnesota, three blocks away from the Mississippi River on Dakota treaty land.

Anna Vangsness grew up feeling connected to her Norwegian roots through family stories and cultural foods at Christmas time. She has lived on Dakota land for most of her life, currently residing with her family in south Minneapolis. She is a mental health therapist at Community University Health Care Center and studies as an apprentice with Healing Roots.

References

1. Minnesota Humanities Center. "Bdote Memory Map." As accessed on October 9, 2022. (https://bdotememorymap.org/memory-map/#).
2. Seminole Tribe of Florida. "The Ancestors." History: Where we came from. As accessed on October 9, 2022. (https://www.semtribe.com/stof/history/the-seminole-ancestors).
3. Minnesota Historical Society. "The U.S.-Dakota War of 1862. Historic Fort Snelling". As accessed on October 10, 2022. (https://www.mnhs.org/fortsnelling/learn/us-dakota-war).
4. Minnesota Indian Affairs Council, the Minnesota Humanities Center, and the Smithsonian Institution's National Museum of the American Indian. "Relations: Dakota and Ojibwe Treaties. Why Treaties Matter." As accessed on October 10, 2022. (http://treatiesmatter.org/treaties).

5. Seminole Tribe of Florida. "The Long War. History: Where we came from." As accessed on October 9, 2022. (https://www.semtribe.com/stof/history/the-long-war).

6. Miccosukee Tribe Indians of Florida. "History." As accessed on October 9, 2022. (https://www.miccosukee.com/history?fbclid=IwAR1gf9g0TqcmZKx41KuNpZWG4o9OA3JELWpcSjYI1Y MPNIShOUhT6OaTOKM).

7. Menakem, R. *My grandmother's hands: Racialized trauma and the pathway to mending our hearts and bodies*. Las Vegas: Central Recovery Press, 2017.

8. Kimmerer, R. W. *Braiding Sweetgrass: Indigenous Wisdom, Scientific Knowledge, and the Teachings of Plants*. Minneapolis: Milkweed Editions, 2013.

9. Stokker, K. *Marking Time: The primstav murals of Sigmund Aarseth*. Decorah, IA: Vesterheim Norwegian-American Museum, 2003.

10. Coleman, B. R., C. R. Collins, and C. M. Bonam. "Interrogating Whiteness in Community Research and Action." *American Journal of Community Psychology* 67 (2021): 486–504.

Elisabeth Schøyen Jensen
3 Thinking with the primstav today

This chapter is about the traditional Norwegian calendar, the primstav. Historical, local, or just different, examples of time keeping practices, calendars and objects like the primstav (that you will get to know better very shortly), can be things that are good to think with. They can be used for reflection on time and time practices; how we "do" time, including what seasons mean to us today.[1] The primstav displays not only abstract time, but also concrete time. It is not an empty calendar grid, but filled out and meaningful for a specific time, place and society.

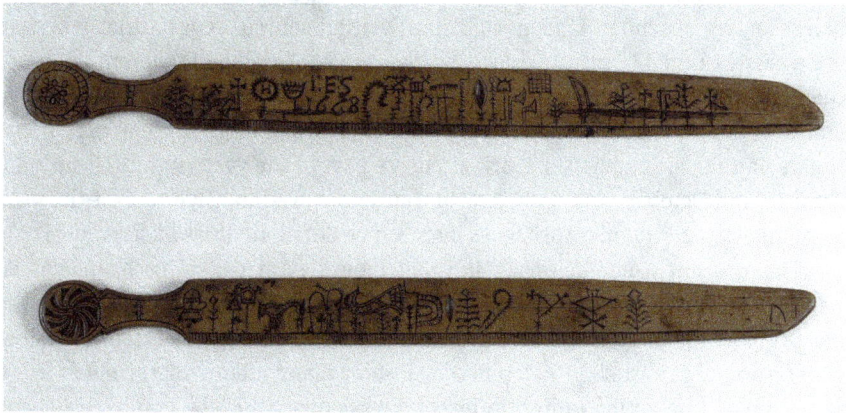

Figure 3.1: The traditional Norwegian two-sided perpetual calendar, the primstav. Top: summer side, that starts April 14th, marked by a tree with leaves. Bottom: winter side, starting October 14th, marked by a mitten. (Photo by: Anne-Lise Reinsfelt, Norsk Folkemuseum; licence: Creative Commons BY-SA; https://digitaltmuseum.no/011023128311/primstav).

Maybe you use Microsoft Outlook or Google calendar to keep track of time in everyday life? Or a free paper calendar provided by your local grocery store, workplace, or union? Or maybe a printed version of your children's school calendar on the fridge door provides the main basis for planning? Or a Moleskin planner perhaps? The calendar function of your smart phone? Or something else? In reading, think about how the primstav is both similar and different from the time

---

1 See for instance Birth 2013 (1) or Bastian 2012 and 2017 (2, 3) for scholarly discussions of how different time keeping practises and objects connect us to different phenomena, people, events, and so on.

keeping tools many of us use today. How did the primstav coordinate its users, and what do our time keeping tools coordinate us with?

The primstav

Calendars made of wood in different shapes and formats (4), on which weekdays, Sundays and Saint Days are marked with notches and symbols, were in use in many parts of Europe before paper almanacs and calendars became more widespread (4, page 9; 5, page 61). Notches and symbols made these time keeping tools accessible also to the illiterate.

The primstav is the Norwegian version of this perpetual calendar design. The oldest known specimen is from 1457, but written sources suggest that it was in use already in the 13th century, possibly also earlier. Based on the Julian 12-month calendar, the primstav divides the year into two six-month sides, a summer side and a winter side. This division of the year into two, a bright and, in traditional Norwegian farming societies, work-intensive part of the year running from mid-April to mid-October, and a dark, cold, but less work-intensive part of the year from mid-October to mid-April, goes back to pre-Christian times in Norway (5).

The primstav would be carved in wood, typically ash, oak or birch, and can be found in many different shapes; round, oblong, more or less rectangular, but the most common is this sword-like shape as in Figure 3.1 (see Figure 3.2 for an example of a round primstav). A notch marks each day, and often a bigger notch every seventh day. In addition to this, different days connected to the Catholic calendar of saints are marked with carved images and symbols. It was set in Norwegian state law in 1247 to be observant of the holy days, and the main purpose of the primstav was to keep track of religious events or celebrations. The primstav itself did not originate from the clergy though, it had its place at home and in everyday life and was carved by local wood carvers with quite a lot of variation. An examination of approximately 90 primstavs from eight different museums and collections in southern Norway found on average 62 days marked with symbols with a lot of variation in which days are marked and the symbols used to mark them, depending on region of origin (7).

The primstav was a practical time keeping tool that, in everyday use, took on many more mundane purposes in addition to the religious. Local rules of thumb, proverbs and sayings were connected to the different days marked to give advice on farming activities, practical seasonal preparations, weather predictions and other everyday preparations. The symbols marking the different Saint days or feasts would mainly be connected to the specific Saint in question and would

Figure 3.2: Round primstav (winter side), dated 1501. (Photo by: Adnan Icagic, Kulturhistorisk Museum, Oslo University; licence: Creative Commons BY-SA; https://digitaltmuseum.no/0210211796802/primstav).

often relate to the cause of death and martyrdom of said Saint. In use and with time, these symbols would often be reinterpreted into something more relevant to everyday life. For instance, Alver (1981) notes that few probably remembered that the knife that often marked August 24th referred to poor Saint Bartholomew being skinned alive and then decapitated. Rather, the knife was read as marking a day that was known as a good time to slaughter the calves (5, page 157). 'Barsok' or Saint Bartholomew's day was also known as the first autumn day, and the weather on that day gave predictions for the coming autumn. The fish hook often marking St. Andrew's Day (patron saint of fishermen), November 30th, was read as this being a good time to go fishing for the Christmas celebrations. With time, some symbols seem to have developed independently of their saintly origin altogether. Some primstavs will, for instance, have St. Thomas sitting on a beer barrel or just a beer barrel marking St. Thomas' day, December 21st, as this day was known as the day for brewing beer for the Christmas celebrations. You should also have all the wood you need for Christmas in the woodshed by this day. If not, it was said in some parts of the country that 'Tommes' might come and do mischief (5, page 103). Here the mischievous 'Tommes' seems to refer to some sort of spirit or pixie (a 'nisse' in Norwegian) rather than to the holy Saint Thomas.

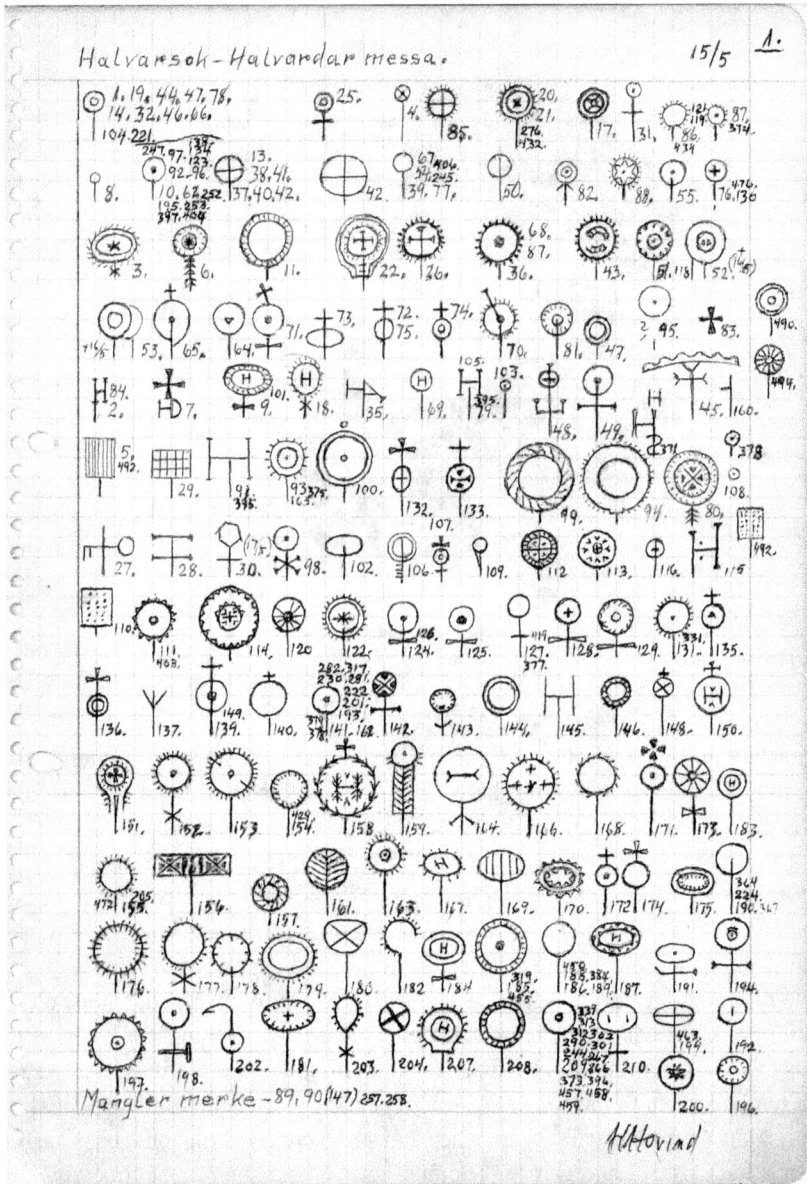

Figure 3.3: Primstav markings for May 15th, St. Hallvard's day. In the late 1980s, Kaare Hovind travelled around different museums in Norway and noted down, among other things, the symbols used on different primstavs. This image is from his notes (https://arkivportalen.no/entity/no-NTNU_arkiv000000046229; this image © NTNU University Library, used with permission).

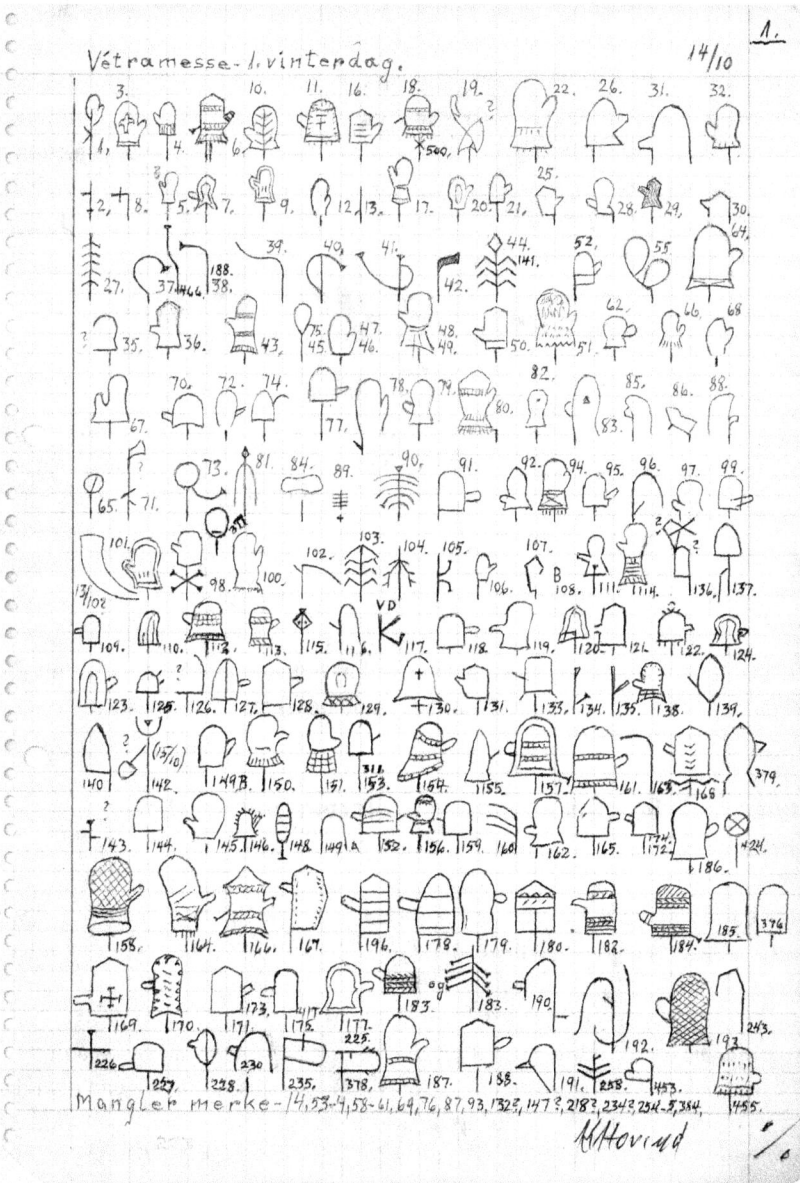

Figure 3.4: Primstav marking for October 14th, St. Calixtus' day or winters day. (This image © NTNU University Library, used with permission).

These traditions and sayings have little to do with the doubtful apostle Thomas. The rake found on July 10th, the Day of Saint Canute or 'Knutsok', as far as we know has little to do with the devout Danish king Canute either, but the day was known as time for haymaking. Just a few days before this, on Saint Sunniva's Day, July 8th, you will often find a scythe. Again, there is no particular connection to the tale of Saint Sunniva, but this is haymaking season and so we find both scythe and rake. Two more examples follow:

May 15th, St. Hallvard's day

The symbol for St. Hallvard's (see Figure 3.3) day is normally a millstone as Hallvard, according to the tale, was killed when trying to save a persecuted woman. His body was then dumped in the Drammen River with a millstone around his neck. Miraculously he floated so his body could be found and buried in consecrated ground. St. Hallvard's day was also known as the time for sowing grain, which the millstone can be a reminder of, though this reminder was observed differently in different Norwegian climates and geographies. In the southern part of the country this was known as the peak day for sowing, while further north it was known as the earliest possible day for sowing grains, "but only if there was no ice on the lakes" (5, page 139). Also, now farm animals could be let out to the outfields.

October 14th, St. Calixtus' day or winters day: First day of winter

The symbol for St. Calixtus' day (see Figure 3.4), or winters day, is supposedly a pontifical of Pope Calixtus I, a papal glove or a hat, but historians find few traces of Saint Calixtus having been well known or important in Norway. It is assumed that this day was marked first and foremost as the first day of winter as in pre-Christian times, and that the symbol for this day was read (and made) as a mitten, symbolising the cold season coming (5, pages 75 & 92). This is the day you turn the primstav from its summer side to its winter side. Sometimes the day would be marked with a tree without leaves. The weather this day gave predictions for the winter coming. One saying goes that "all that feeds man" should be indoors by now, and it was a bad omen if snow would fall on an open barn door from now on. Also, from this day, the horses should wear bells, as the days grow darker and you might not see them coming.

The primstav gradually went out of use for various reasons and was a relic in most places already by the end of the 17th century (5). By this time, both the Protestant Reformation and the Gregorian calendar reform had reached Norway. Also, paper almanacs gradually became more widespread. All these things, together with other more general societal changes and developments, made the primstav obsolete as a practical time-keeping tool. However, you find it as a treasured traditional item even today, valued for its beautiful handicraft and as a symbol of a bygone traditional farming society.

The primstav displays concrete, local time-telling practises from a historical period when Norwegian society as a whole was deeply attuned to Catholicism and to the seasons, where all activities had to be coordinated with the changing seasons. What do our time-telling practices, calendars and yearly events tell us about our society today?

The author

Elisabeth Schøyen Jensen is a PhD candidate in the CALENDARS project at the Centre for the Study of the Sciences and the Humanities, University of Bergen, Norway. Her background is in Sociology and Science and Technology Studies and she has previously worked at CICERO – Centre for International Climate Research.

References

1.   Birth, K. "Calendars: Representational homogeneity and heterogeneous time". *Time & Society* 22 (2013): 216–236.
2.   Bastian, M. "Fatally Confused: Telling the Time in the Midst of Ecological Crises". *Environmental Philosophy* 9 (2012): 23–48.
3.   Bastian, M. "Liberating clocks: developing a critical horology to rethink the potential of clock time". *New Formations* 92 (2017): 41–55.
4.   Harris, A. *Time and Place – Pocket book on the art of Calendars*. Little Toller Books, 2019.
5.   Alver, B. *Dag og merke – Folkeleg tidsregning og merkedagstradisjon*. Universitetsforlaget, 1981.
6.   Zerubavel, E. *Hidden Rhythms: Schedules and Calendars in Social life*. University of California Press, 1981.
7.   Kismul, H. *Primstaven*. Bergen Faktorforening, 1979.

Helen Cornish

4 Enchanting cyclical time: Living through the Wheel of the Year

The four Greater Sabbats of the witches' year are Candlemas, May Eve, Lammas and Hallow-e'en. The four Lesser Sabbats are the equinoxes and the solstices. These are the natural divisions of the year, and all of them were celebrated by our pagan Celtic ancestors in Druidic times (1, page 47).

Contemporary witches embrace the divinity of nature and the seasons in their ritual calendar, the Wheel of the Year. In this chapter I show how these celebrations help approach the world in more magical and less rational ways. On the surface the calendar marks the regular passing of time in an orderly and chronological manner, but the use of ritual and myth can create more experiential ways of measuring the turning year, which emphasises cyclical rather than linear time. First, I explain how witchcraft today is a modern, rather than ancient, practice with several 'paths' or traditions. I sketch some of the influences and histories that have shaped the festival calendar, and offer some examples of seasonal celebrations expressed through myth, ritual, and folklore. Modern practitioners celebrate witchcraft as a global practice, but different climates and seasonal flows make it tricky to establish shared festivities. Creative approaches provide opportunities for eco-spirituality and environmental action as well as transformation through the seasonal cycle.

Contemporary witchcraft is a thoroughly modern magical-religious practice – creative and inventive – while simultaneously fashioned as revitalising traditional, even ancient, customs. It is one of many thriving European Pagan Nature Religions established in the twentieth century, which share a view of the earth as inherently spirited and as a source of divinity. They honour the turning seasons and the growing cycles of life and death, always to return. Modern witchcraft traditions are inspired by entangled intellectual and creative European movements from the eighteenth century, intertwined with ritual magic and spiritualism, drawing on Earth Mysteries and New Age concepts. Today's practitioners cover a range of 'paths'. Some are Wiccans who follow initiatory covens set up by Gerald Gardner in 1950s England. Others work in more informal ways, inspired by occult influences such as Ancient Egyptian magic, or feminist traditions that reclaim female power. And some witches work in a solitary fashion and see themselves as inheritors of wise women and cunning men skilled in folk magic, imagined as prac-

Acknowledgements: With thanks to the Museum of Witchcraft and Magic and Vivienne Shanley for the Wheel of the Year photograph.

Figure 4.1: The Wheel of the Year at The Museum of Witchcraft and Magic (© Viviane Shanley). In contemporary witchcraft the witch's year is divided into eight major festivals. These festivals mark the passage of the sun through the year and relate directly to the agricultural cycle. The wheel also represents the continuity of life, death, and renewal. (Used with permission).

tical ancestors who walked with one foot in the spirit world. These diverse traditions hold in common an acknowledgement of seasonality that celebrates the ebbs and flows of an animated natural world in the wheel of the year.

The Wheel of the Year is a coherent and balanced sequence of eight festivals over the duration of one calendar year. The four solar events (solstices and equinoxes) are interspersed with the cross-quarter days as distinct festival celebrations, encapsulating the essential concepts and vital mysteries of the Old Religion, as depicted in the painted wheel that turns in the Museum of Witchcraft and Magic (Figure 4.1 and Table 4.1). Rural and folkloric customs take their place in the seasonal cycle. Each event corresponds to the European growing seasons but is also intertwined with myth cycles, emphasising birth, death, and rebirth. Deeper resonances are found through the lunar and astrological cycles.

Diverse pantheons or paths offer mythic inspiration, but Wiccans favour the eternal battle between the kings of oak and holly to the echoes of the Wild Hunt. At midsummer, and the height of the sun, the holly king rises and challenges the reigning oak king whose death symbolises the weakening sun and the dying greenery. In turn, at midwinter, the aged holly king is slain by the youthful oak king who welcomes the returning light and warmth. The lifecycle of the god and

Table 4.1: Wheel of the Year markers.

Date	Festival	Event
31 October	Samhain/All Hallows Eve	Fire festival/cross quarter day
21 December	Yule/Midwinter	Solstice
1 February	Imbolc/Candlemas	Fire festival/cross quarter day
21 March	Ostara/spring	Equinox
1 May	Beltane/May Day	Fire festival/cross quarter day
21 June	Midsummer	Solstice
1 August	Lughnasadh/Lammas	Fire festival/cross quarter day
21 September	Mabon/Michaelmas	Equinox

goddess, sensuous and fertile, is venerated, and echoes the agricultural calendar: following the cycle of light and dark through honouring St Brigit at Candlemas or Imbolc; planting seeds at the vernal equinox; embracing the rising sap and the fertility of all at Beltane; admiring the growing crops at midsummer; rejoicing in the corn harvest at Lammas; and the apple crop at Mabon; preserving the fruits of human endeavours to survive the long, cold, dark winter, and acknowledging the proximity of the ancestors and the world of spirit at Samhain; and yule celebrations at midwinter, when the longest night anticipates the return of the sun from the underworld. In between, the equinoxes hold moments of balance, before the light tips into darkness and back again.

The ritual cycle encapsulated in the Wheel of the Year is considered by witches and other magical-religious practitioners to have old and deep roots in nature's annual rhythms, favouring ancient pagan senses of time founded in spiritual reverence for an animated natural world. Many believe the ancient Celts welcomed the New Year in at the end of October, at Samhain (All Hallows Eve), a time of potency, where the veils between the worlds are said to be thin. They describe the great fire festivals of Celtic Ireland and point to standing stones and burial chambers that face the midsummer sunrise or the midwinter sunset. They observe that in the days before the modern clock, daily events were dictated by seasonality; time to turn the cattle out to grass, to plant the seeds, or harvest the crops.

Historians have disputed the coherence of these origin stories and suggest the contemporary map is a modern and rationalised selection of disparate farming, grazing, and hunting markers; the cycle of Catholic feast days; as well as numerous pageants, fires, and fairs founded in historical Britain and Ireland. The initial solar calendar sketched by eighteenth century Druids aimed to revitalise a lost spirituality, while twentieth century Wiccans and Druids filled the spaces between with the cross-quarter days. By the mid-1960s the Wheel of the Year was a recognisable eight-fold cycle, each festival identified by a variety of names depending on which origins are being evoked, Celtic, Anglo-Saxon, or English (2).

It is important to recognise the ritual Wheel of the Year as a modern construction. Nevertheless, at the same time, the Wheel is a more experiential, emotional, and sensory way of apprehending the cycles of the year. It is a means to situate practitioners in time and space, and to foster attention to the natural world around them, rather than quibble over the extent to which it is, or is not, historically authentic. It introduces different registers of time, enchanted and mythic, which respond to the flow of the seasons and the imagination rather than to the regulated order of clock time. The eternal battle between light and dark, life and death, is conceived of as a spiralling cycle, rather than a linear chronology of no return. To the contrary, the Wheel of the Year holds at its heart the celebration of return, rebirth, and renewal.

Irregularities in seasonality and the emphasis on European seasons pose questions for witches and druids following the orderly calendar in different places worldwide. For example, should Beltane be celebrated on the first of May regardless, to raise the power of collective magical action, or piecemeal as and when the blossoms arrive, as an acknowledgment of the plant's efforts. Or, given the global reach of modern witchcraft traditions, when and how to celebrate Beltane in Australia where the hawthorn is an invasive pest, and the month of May does not herald the arrival of summer. Practitioners across the world turn to their surroundings and adapt as appropriate to the climate, embracing pluralistic practices. In the southern hemisphere the elemental directions are inverted as they honour the land beneath their feet and pay attention to the life cycles of local flora and fauna, taking inspiration from both Indigenous Australian and European mythological traditions. The sense of perpetual return remains anchored in the cosmos, the solstices and equinoxes, as open arms to welcome the cyclical patterns of light and dark.

Challenges are compounded by the climate emergency, ushering in disruption, out of step with anticipated seasonality. While modern witches are found across the political spectrum some actively engage in environmental politics, following an eco-spirituality that embraces inspirited senses of the earth and ethical imperatives to care for the land. Many are inspired by the universal goddess as a symbol of an enduring, interconnected, sacred cosmos, and by *Spiral Dance*, Starhawk's guide to eco-feminist and earth-based activist spirituality that outlined rituals produced by the East Coast Reclaiming Collective in the 1970s (3). Starhawk's ecological activism continues to provide a beacon for twenty-first century ecologically minded witches. They recall witches in the 1980s marching alongside Greenham Common protesters in the United Kingdom, carrying out rituals to ward off global threats. Sarah Lyon uses the fluctuations through the Wheel of the Year as motivation for raising magical energy and transforming consciousness: as revolutionary action (4). As Alice Tarbuck writes, the work of witchcraft "is often deeply connected to, and seeks to serve, steward and understand our earth, to advocate for its protection" (5, page 140). Witches of Instagram and WitchTok (TikTok channel) provide platforms for community and initiate opportunities for collective action. Seasonal festivals over the solar, mythical, folkloric, and agricultural cycles offer space for rituals that foster connections to the environment, to renew strength and purpose.

The Wheel of the Year can be seen as a magical phenomenon. At first glance, it measures time according to the conventional chronological calendar, an orderly sequence of annual festivals. On closer inspection, seasonal tales disrupt rationalist order through battles for control over light and darkness, of ventures into the underworld, or chasing across the night sky in the wild hunt (6). Cyclical solar markers, annual agricultural events and folkloric customs combine with mythological tales and suggest that time and space are not so well ordered after all. For magical practitioners in the twenty-first century, these seasonal celebrations offer an experiential framework for personal and collective transformative possibilities; creative, sensory, and enchanted.

The author

Dr Helen Cornish is an anthropologist (Goldsmiths, London), who has carried out ethnographic research on how histories are navigated by practitioners of modern witchcraft. She is interested in how experiential and sensory forms of knowledge of and about the past are entangled with empirical sources and formal histories. One of her key research sites has been the Museum of Witchcraft and Magic in Boscastle, Cornwall, UK.

References

1. Valiente, D. *Witchcraft for Tomorrow*. London: Robert Hale Ltd, 1978.
2. Hutton, R. *The Stations of the Sun: a history of the ritual year in Britain*. Oxford: Oxford University Press, 1996.
3. Starhawk. *The Spiral Dance: A Rebirth of the Ancient Religion of the Great Goddess*. New York: Harper Collins, 1979.
4. Lyons, S. *Revolutionary Witchcraft: A Guide to Magical Activism*, Tantor, 2020.
5. Tarbuck, A. "Witchcraft in the Anthropocene". In Tarbuck A. & C. Askew (eds.). *The Modern Craft: Powerful voices on witchcraft ethics*. Watkins Media Limited, 2022.
6. Greenwood, S. *The Nature of Magic: an anthropology of consciousness*. Oxford: Berg, 2005.

Marjolein Pijnappels

5 Exploring dynamic eco-calendars for a modern world

A land in suspended seasonality

The Netherlands today seems suspended in seasonality. We hardly get a hint of the time of day or year when we work from our artificially cooled or heated, and electrically lighted offices. Or only briefly when we transverse the outdoors to our climate-controlled cars, which drive us to our climate-controlled homes. We eat strawberries and other summer fruits year-round thanks to technology and global supply chains. We are no longer at the mercy of sunlight, storms, and downpour, because we have harnessed and stored its powers for ourselves. What's not to love? Well, although our climate-controlled indoor spaces seem suspended in time, our bodies are not. Our endogenous circadian clocks are locked to the solar day and our biology also follows the seasons (1). Circannual rhythms are connected to mood, suicides, reproduction, birth weight, timing of human births, sleep and mental illnesses (2).

When we cut ourselves loose from natural cycles, we traded connection for comfort. Our disconnect from the natural cycles and seasonal woes has enabled us to grow and consume far beyond the carrying capacity of our planet's ecosystem. The 'Western' way of life has a major impact on the planet: raw materials are being depleted, our waste is accumulating, and our climate system disrupted. Armed with all our knowledge and technology we have proved unable to find sustainable solutions for poverty, hunger, and inequality in the world.

To restore the connection with our biological cycles and ecosystems, and explore how we can recalibrate this connection in a post-modern world, join me on a trip to the island of *Pongso no Tao*, before travelling back in time to the pre-Christian, Dutch delta.

Acknowledgements: I am very much indebted to the insights gained from my ongoing conversations and correspondence with Sutej Hugu, regional coordinator for East-Asia in the Indigenous and Community-conserved Areas (ICCA) Consortium and native to *Pongso no Tao*. His wisdom was invaluable in writing this chapter. Any unforeseen errors with respect to interpreting Tao mythology are all mine.

The mythic eco-calendar of *Pongso no Tao*

Often, when looking to transform our society, we first move away from the cause of the mess. We look towards practices in other, seemingly more spiritual places of the globe, hence the popularity of Tai Chi, yoga, meditation, and indigenous herbalism in 'Western' countries. It is the dream of returning to an innocent state and assuage the guilt of overconsumption. I too am not immune to the lure of a faraway place, where presumably peace-loving people live in balance with nature.

The Austronesian *Tao* people, who live on the small volcanic island *Pongso no Tao* (Orchid Island), off the coast of Taiwan, have been a source of inspiration and wisdom, searching for another way of timekeeping and relating to ecologies. Tao secure their livelihoods alternating between fishing for migratory flying fish, coral reef fishing and agriculture. They organize their year with an eco-calendar calibrated by biological rhythms (3).

Their adaptable calendar, *ahehep no tao*, divides the year roughly into three seasons. There is only one, the *rayon* season, where it is permitted to catch the flying fish the community depends on (4). Tao add leap months every couple of years, extending the *rayon* season, not by mathematical calculation, but by observation of the flying fish population. The decision is a communal one as well, taken by Tao elders, and meant to balance human needs to the needs of the flying fish. It is practical as well as mythological, part of the inter-species compact between Tao ancestors and the ancestor of flying fish.

Teachings from our own indigenous eco-traditions

Trying to overlay the Tao calendar on our modern world, built on consumerism and disconnected from our ecology, is a fool's errand. Sutej Hugu, regional coordinator for East-Asia in the Indigenous and Community-conserved Areas (ICCA) Consortium and native to *Pongso no Tao*, told me so himself. "If you would print our calendar", he explained kindly, "it would have our thirty names of the phasing moons, the days, and the intercalation (*inserting the leap month, Eds*). But to us the calendar is more than this phenomenon. We are all embedded in an inter-species habitat. You feel the weight of the relationship. Some are more near and some more far. That is the first principle of the calendar." The Tao calendar is not an object existing in isolation or outside of the world, rather it connects Tao to the spiritual world and their natural environment (5).

To connect to our local ecologies in the 'West', we must turn to our own ancestry and establish connections to our own habitat, and we must experience that connection physically, through our bodies. These three overlapping domains, ancestry, ecology and physiological experience, are the ingredients for a modern eco-calendar.

Instead of putting our hopes on faraway, idealized practices, we must uncover or develop our own, localized, ecological practices. Tracing back Dutch indigenous ecological knowledge systems might be an impossible task. Centuries of Roman hegemony and Christianization have assimilated or erased the indigenous Germanic-Celtic hunter-gatherer-farmer communities and their oral traditions, arguably the last who may have upheld an ecological knowledge system (6). What we do know comes from Norse and Icelandic mythologies, the undoubtedly biased accounts of Roman rulers, or disguised as Christian rituals. Northern European ancestral tree-cult, symbolized by holy trees (where churches later came to be built) stands in sharp contrast with the mass deforestation of the Netherlands that was completed in 1871, when the last tree of the last primeval, eight-thousand-year-old forest was felled in Beekbergerwoud. Had we felt the weight of the relationship with living trees as our ancestors did, we might have grasped the importance of ancient forests and trees for biodiversity and soil health before scientifically uncovering the central role of ancient trees in the mycorrhiza, as hubs that connect and support other trees in a forest (7).

Although the people living in the Netherlands are now part of the same ecosystem, our ancestry is diverse because of centuries of migration. Today we have ancestral roots stretching to all parts of the planet, and as our forebears travelled here, they brought their traditions and seasonal festivals with them. What can we learn by tracing the roots of all our cultural heritages? What can we integrate from the broad range of festivals and ecological traditions?

It is a given that our world is an unfathomably different world than that of our ancestors. But again: our biology is the same. While our bodies are attuned to the solar day, they are now disrupted by a work culture of long hours, shift work, extended commutes, and the 24-hour availability of almost everything (1). We are expected to stay productive members of society all through the year, even when daylight is sparse and our bodies thirst for rest. The Germanic ancestors didn't have four seasons, they named two: a light and a dark half. The dark half was for preparing for winter and hunkering down. The light half was for being productive. Could our calendars make room for daylight-tied productivity? Alert us to seasonal adaptability of working hours? Slowing down in the darker half of the year, eating foods that sustain our bodies like beets, pumpkin, and winter carrot, instead of summer fruits whose winter growth cost us precious energy. Working longer hours requires less electricity in summer, when daylight is abundant, than in winter. Living by our physiological cycles might possibly attune us to our ecological environment and curb greenhouse gas emissions. Surely, it will give us the sensitivity and guide to adapt to new and uncertain ecological conditions.

Figure 5.1: A (re)imagining of an eco-calendar for a modern world, divided in winter and summer half, and the twelve lunar months, hours of daylight added as fluor green flares. (Photo by: Marjolein Pijnappels).

How to reconnect with our ecology in a modern world

The big challenge for the peoples of the modern world is how to reconnect with our ecosystem and biological cycles, while living in a market economy, severed from the surrounding habitat. We are connected to the world around us, but not in a bodily way. We gather news from across the world about climate change disruptions, war, and ecological collapse through our computers, but it's a digital, cerebral connection, not one that is observed, experienced, and felt first-hand.

We can still observe the trees and the moon through our climate-controlled homes' windows, but their presence does not weave into our daily lives. A conscious practice of observing the natural world and observing the state of our own bodies might re-establish that connection. Spending time outdoors to experience and sense the seasons and calibrate our inner physiology with the outside environment. Noticing the patterns and rhythms and applying them in our own lives, such as eating regional foods grown in the season, making conscious decisions to take rest when days are short, and planting indigenous species in our gardens. In Figure 5.1, I have started to experiment with what such an eco-calendar might look like for me.

The Tao eco-calendar faces its own challenges. Tao way of life, mythology and ecosystem knowledge system have all been significantly interrupted by martial law, forced displacement, introduction of marketable exotic species, dumping of nuclear waste, and replacing ancient Tao names with Chinese names to boost tourism, confusing the Tao history and connection with their ancestral lands. Since the eighties Tao fishing and harvesting according to the interspecies pact and calendar has all but disappeared. Elders like Sutej Hugu work hard not just to preserve it for posterity, but to bring it back to life. Because of climate change the Tao calendar is disrupted and needs to be adapted. "The effect of climate change goes beyond our knowledge," reflects Hugu. "But we always know the way, and we will innovate to keep the living tradition. We continue to follow the teachings of the flying fish."

Maybe it is terribly naive to think modern societies have the capability to live on natural cycles again, but it is equally naive to believe we can go on living as though we are separate from our ecosystem, that resources are infinite and that technology will solve all our problems. By uncovering our own roots, wherever we are from, and feeling the weight of our relationships to the species and habitat that surround us, we become aware of our own biological cycles and how they are always responding to the world around us. Let that guide us to a new framework, a flexible eco-calendar that honours this biology and helps us adapt to a transforming world.

The author

Marjolein Pijnappels, MSc, is a transdisciplinary researcher and designer. She has a degree in marine ecology and worked as climate change communicator for the first two Dutch climate change research programs before founding and running an information design studio for twelve years. She draws inspiration from techno-, bio- and mytho-logy to connect people, challenge them and start dialogues. She also creates science-based (future) stories and hopeful alternative worlds.

References

1. Foster, R.G. & T. Roenneberg. "Human Responses to the Geophysical Daily, Annual and Lunar Cycles." *Current Biology* 18 (2008): 784–794.
2. Swaab D.F. et al. "Biological rhythms in the human life cycle and their relationship to functional changes in the suprachiasmatic nucleus." *Prog Brain Res*. 111 (1996): 349–68.
3. Hugu, S. "Tao Worldview". In A. Kothari and A Salleh (eds.) *Pluriverse: A Post-Development Dictionary*, Tulika Books, 2019.
4. Lin, C-N. & B-W. Tsai. "Implementation of Indigenous Knowledge on Local Spatial Management: A Case Study in Orchid Island (Lanyu), Taiwan." *Sustainability* 13 (2021).
5. Hugu, S. "Community-Managed Fisheries: Stories from the Tao." *Oxford Real Farming Conference 7–13 January 2021*, video lecture.
6. Wassmann, P. "The Hidden Pathways of Germanic Mythology: On the Neglected, Demonized, Repulsed and Repressed Archetypical Representations of Original Germanic Culture." Chiron Publications, 2019.
7. Simard, S. W. et al. "Partial Retention of Legacy Trees Protect Mycorrhizal Inoculum Potential, Biodiversity, and Soil Resources While Promoting Natural Regeneration of Interior Douglas-Fir." *Frontiers in Forests and Global Change*, 3 (2021).

Natali Pearson

6 Claiming the winds: Monsoon in the Indian Ocean

With its boundlessness, depth and fickle liquidity, the sea lends itself to a different way of thinking about the seasons. There is no doubt, of course, that there are seasons at sea. Sailors, fishers and coastal communities know the rhythms that play out across the surface, in the skies above, and through the water column below. Such rhythms reflect the changing seasons and implicate different communities from those on land.

But seasonality at sea is not just about when the coral spawns or the whales migrate; nor is it only about the position of the stars or the ebb and flow of the tide. Increasingly, political claims are being made on the ocean's seasons that require us to reconsider what the ocean is capable of, and what we are asking of it. These claims—to pasts, and to futures—have seen the seasons of the sea reframed as *"natural and cultural heritage"* and used as political tools to advance particular narratives. As it relates to the sea, therefore, the notion of changing seasonality is not only about adaptation to increasingly irregular climatic rhythms, but also about the growing attention that nation states and international institutions are giving to these seasons and the strategic opportunities they present.

The ocean is conceptually slippery. It evades definition and resists the frameworks we impose on it. We may have tried to master it with technology—ships, charts, lighthouses—yet we are constantly humbled by it. Nautical charts might delineate maritime boundaries and zones, but there are no walls or fences at sea. Nationalism and imperialism have defined and driven many of our encounters with the ocean, yet the high seas, which make up almost two-thirds of the world's ocean, remain beyond the jurisdiction of any one state (1).

Despite—or because of—this perceived elusiveness, the ocean has always been subject to claims and contestations. Not only has the myth of the sea as empty space (2) elided the existence of indigenous knowledge systems, it has also overlooked the ocean's abundance of resources, even as it has created the very conditions that have enabled these resources—deep ocean minerals; oil and gas; fish, kelp and other forms of oceanic sustenance—to be extracted and exploited (3).

Acknowledgements: I wish to thank the organisers of the April 2022 'Heritage as Claim Making' workshop in Norway, in particular Edyta Roszko from CMI-Chr. Michelsen Institute and Knut Rio from the University of Bergen. It was at this workshop that I first encountered Scott Bremer's work on seasonality. I would also like to thank Cheng Nien Yuan and Wayan Jarrah Sastrawan for comments on early drafts of this chapter.

But minerals, energy and food are not the only things that can be pulled from the sea. In recent decades, maritime archaeologists and historians have drawn attention to the significant cultural resources to be found in our oceans and rivers. Across the Indian Ocean, for example, shipwrecks, sunken ceramics and other forms of material culture testify to long histories of mobility and exchange (4, 5). With the introduction of the 2001 United Nations Educational, Scientific and Cultural Organization (UNESCO) Convention on the Protection of the Underwater Cultural Heritage, these sites and objects have been transformed, their historical and archaeological significance reconfigured as heritage. This process of creating heritage has in turn created political opportunities—including, in the Indian Ocean, for the seasons of the sea to be folded into broader strategic initiatives under the banner of heritage.

Fringed by land and defined by sea, the Indian Ocean encompasses a vast sweep of our blue planet. For centuries, and despite the distances involved, this ocean has connected the east African coast, the Arabian Peninsula and lands of the Middle East, the Indian sub-continent and the archipelagos of Southeast Asia (6). To facilitate these connections, seafarers relied on seasonally reversing winds that affected the ocean's surface currents. Known as the *monsoon*, the word's etymology reflects the significance of these winds to many different communities. Monsoon is derived from the Portuguese '*monção*', which in turn comes from the Arabic '*mawsim*', meaning season (7, 8). In the northern Indian Ocean, warm humid winds blowing from the southwest prevail from June to November—the summer monsoon. From December onwards, this weather pattern reverses itself, with cold, dry winds blowing from the northeast—the winter monsoon. The rhythmic predictability of the monsoon meant seafarers planned their outward and return voyages with both care and precision. Harness the wind and minimise time spent at sea; but delay departure, even by a few weeks, and risk missing the monsoon altogether.

For millennia, these seasonal winds defined trade and travel in the Indian Ocean, sustaining long-distance commercial networks and creating a rich legacy of cultural, material, and intellectual exchange that endures to this day. Increasingly, however, there are concerns that the monsoon is losing its power and predictability—that the seasons are shorter or too intense, or that they arrive too soon, or too late (4). These changes affect global shipping networks and supply chains. More urgently, they have severe consequences for coastal communities, who experience drought, flood, and other disasters because of irregular monsoonal rainfall.

As an idea, however, the monsoon holds remarkable strategic power—perhaps more so than ever. In 2014, India sought to harness this power with the launch of Project Mausam, the use of *mausam* connoting the monsoon and the navigation corridors enabled by these winds.[1] Project Mausam's objective was as ambitious as its scope: to inscribe, as a transnational mixed (natural and cultural) route, the monsoon patterns, cultural routes and maritime landscapes of the Indian Ocean on the UNESCO World Heritage list (9). Some 39 littoral states, from east Africa to Southeast Asia, were identified as probable partners.

To date, however, not a single other littoral country has come on board. Critics have suggested that rather than focusing single-mindedly on World Heritage status—which requires a site to be of outstanding universal value and meet at least one of ten selection criteria—India should instead have channelled its energies into developing deeper and more significant partnerships in its efforts to revive Indian Ocean culture (10).

In its attempt to revive romanticised theories of historic connectivity, mobility and exchange, India's initiative has been compared with China (11, 12). China launched its own transnational initiative called the Belt and Road in 2013, a year prior to Project Mausam's conception. The comparative success of these two initiatives—both transnational in scope, stretching across overlapping periods and geographies, and with similar themes of cooperation and shared heritage—by two of the world's most strategically important countries, remains contested.

What is clear, however, is that India's interest in inscribing monsoon routes as heritage offers valuable insights into what seasonality means at sea. At a surface level, seasonality is expressed in the cadence of change—the changing winds, the arrival of the rains, the swirling currents. Dive deeper, however, and we see the work that the monsoon, as a form of transnational maritime heritage, is being asked to do. Initially presented as a cultural initiative, Project Mausam is more clearly understood as a geocultural project that uses maritime connectivity to advance contemporary political claims of India. While scholars continue to debate the precise nature of these claims (9, 11), one thing is certain: the monsoon, and the project that takes its name, is undergoing great change. Just as climatic patterns are shifting, so too is the regional architecture across and beyond the Indian Ocean. Whether these changes are part of an existing rhythm, or the beginning of a new one, remains to be seen.

---

1 Initially launched as the Mausam Initiative.

The author

Dr. Natali Pearson researches and teaches at the Sydney Southeast Asia Centre, the University of Sydney, where she is affiliated with the School of Humanities. Her research focuses on the protection, management, and interpretation of underwater cultural heritage in Indonesia. Her first book, *Belitung: The Afterlives of a Shipwreck*, is published by University of Hawai'i Press (2023).

References

1. McVeigh, K. *'One of the Most Important Talks No One Has Heard Of': Why the high seas treaty matters*. The Guardian, 2023.
2. Hofmeyr, I. *Oceans as Empty Spaces? Redrafting our knowledge by dropping the colonial lens*. The Conversation, 2018.
3. Reid, S. 'Imagining Justice with the Abyssal Ocean', in *Laws of the Sea*. Routledge, 2023: p. 70–93.
4. Hofmeyr, I. & C. Lavery *Exploring the Indian Ocean as a Rich Archive of History – Above and Below the Water Line*. The Conversation, 2020.
5. Pearson, N., *Belitung: The Afterlives of a Shipwreck*. Honolulu: University of Hawai'i Press, 2023.
6. Tagliacozzo, E. *In Asian Waters: Oceanic Worlds from Yemen to Yokohama*. Princeton University Press, 2022.
7. Tripati, S. & L. Raut, "*Monsoon Wind and Maritime Trade: A case study of historical evidence from Orissa, India.*" Current Science (2006): 864–871.
8. Indira Gandhi National Centre for the Arts *Concept Note: Mausam / Mawsim – Maritime Routes and Cultural Landscapes*. 2014.
9. Ray, H.P. "Project Mausam'. India's Transnational Initiative: Revisiting UNESCO's World Heritage Convention', in B. Schnepel & T. Sen (eds.) *Travelling Pasts: The politics of cultural heritage in the Indian Ocean world*, Brill, 2019.
10. Bhalla, M. *India Should Revive the Mausam Initiative – But Not as it Stands Now*. The Wire, 2020.
11. Singh, R. & T. Winter. "From Hinduism to Hindutva: Civilizational Internationalism and UNESCO". *International Affairs 99* (2023): 515–530.
12. Sharma, R. *Project Mausam hits a Chinese wall*. The New Indian Express, 2017.

Tanguy Sandré, Arjan Wardekker, and Jeanne Gherardi

7 While waiting for the sea ice: Stories of changes from Ittoqqortoormiit (Kalaallit Nunaat)

For me, the sea ice actually brings thoughts of warmth and light. Not the frozen nothingness as it is often portrayed. There is one tool especially that helped Inuit survive, the qulleq, the oil lamp, which the women tended. Ikummataa is what feeds the light in the qulleq – fuel from the fat of seals, walrus, whales, and other animals; those animals that come from the sea ice. And in traditional times that light meant warmth and it provided a light by which families shared their stories, their knowledge, and much laughter (1).

Changing sea ice

For many small communities in the Arctic, climate change-driven variations in the sea-ice thickness and extent are a central experience of recent environmental transformations. In Ittoqqortoormiit (Box 1), Kalaallit Nunaat (Greenland), sea ice is a 'character' that featured in many stories we were told. Discrepancies and mismatches between sea ice conditions and those expected based on local knowledge and recent memories were often described. Together with the community, we[1] have been exploring how these modifications have impacted on local people, through their stories of changes. How do sea ice changes reframe the way this *kalaaleq* (sing. 'Greenlandic') community experiences seasonality, resilience, and environmental and climate change?

---

[1] Tanguy Sandré and Jeanne Gherardi have both conducted repetitive fieldworks within the community from three weeks to two months in autumn 2021, summer 2022 and autumn 2022. Together with Arjan Wardekker, we have explored how resilience and challenges to the community's resilience are expressed in our ethnographic materials and experiences.

Acknowledgements: The authors wish to acknowledge the participation and invaluable insights and meaning offered by the inhabitants of Ittoqqortoormiit. Gratitude is especially expressed to Mette Pike Barseljasen for her key facilitator role, Erling Madsen for the opportunity of taking part on polar bears' patrols and Olena Madsen for her translation in the Tunumiisut we used.

The authors were funded through Belmont Forum project SeMPER-Arctic (Norwegian Research Council Grant Agreement 312938 and French National Research Agency).

Box 1: Ittoqqortoormiit (Tunu, Kalaallit Nunaat).
Ittoqqortoormiit is the northernmost community on the east coast of Kalaallit Nunaat (Greenland), located at the mouth of Kangertittivaq. The town was founded in 1924–1925 by Ejnar Mikkelsen mainly to reaffirm the Danish sovereignty and block further Norwegian claims on the east coast. The community has long relied on subsistence hunting as its principal source of livelihood. In recent years, Ittoqqortoormeermii, the inhabitants of Ittoqqortoormiit, have been facing multidimensional transformations driven by: 1) increased institutional marginalisation: since the *Self-Government Act* (2009), Ittoqqortoormiit municipality was incorporated into a much larger unit of local government, named Kommuneqarfik Sermersooq, ruled from the capital Nuuk, at least two day's travel away via Iceland, 2) decreasing population and services: 354 inhabitants in 2022 compared to 530 in 2005, and an absence of doctors, 3) ecological restrictions: more restrictive quotas for hunting, 4) changing climate and sea-ice conditions.

"Naluarnga!" ("I don't know" in Tunumiisut/East Greenlandic). This is an uncommonly short *kalaalleq* word, performed as a refrain during the autumn 2021. The days were getting shorter at the mouth of Ugeer ('Winter' in Tunumiisut), and we were randomly asking locals: "When will the ice wrap itself again around the 350-inhabitant town?" I quickly understood that this question was heavily derived from a western worldview, one which aims to foresee and control. At the same time, convergent stories were told: "It was earlier before, we are now waiting a long while for the ice to be stable and thick enough to be safely covered by the tracks of sled dogs and snowmobiles." In June 2022, the question could have been inverted: "When will the ice melt again around the 350-inhabitant town?" But we researchers have learnt. We already know that the question does not fit the context. We therefore pay further attention to new convergent stories: "This is very unusual that there is still ice now"; "we haven't seen that for 20 years"; "it must be hard for the hunters all this ice."

What do those recurrent and convergent stories tell us about the connectedness of a small community with the sea ice? How does it document changing sea ice conditions driven by a warmer climate? How does it help us to understand a cultural experience of seasonality and to grasp the "space between seasons"?

In recent years, in the Arctic as a whole, sea ice conditions have been particularly impacted by climate change. "Since the late 1970s, Arctic Sea ice area and thickness have decreased in both summer and winter, with sea ice becoming younger, thinner and more dynamic (very high confidence) (2, page 76)". This statement from the Intergovernmental Panel on Climate Change (IPCC) seems to suggest linearity or a relative simplicity in describing observed changes. Discussions with community members in Ittoqqortoormiit were challenging this description and interrogating its local saliency. The framing of sea-ice evolution in these discussions was centred on anomalies and difficulties in apprehending the dynamic of experienced changes, rather than as a process of continual decline.

In Kalaallit Nunaat, especially for the community dwelling on the east (e.g. Ittoqqortoormiit) and the north-west coast (e.g. Qaanaaq), the conditions of ice are crucially linked to the practice of subsistence hunting. In Ittoqqortoormiit, except residual seasonal tourism, hunting is the only source of income for the town. Dogsledding and snowmobiles are used to hunt prey (polar bears, walrus, narwhals, muskox, seals, etc.) on the ice. A reduction in the length of the sea-ice season is strongly connected with a decline in the dog population in recent years: the shortening of the sea-ice season directly reduces the period of rentability of a large pack of dogs that are becoming too expensive to feed. If dogsled-based hunting is threatened by rapid changes, fishing, which is the first source of income in the country but has always been limited in the community, is seen as a potential opportunity (Figure 7.1). With changes in sea-ice conditions, the use of motorboats is growing in the fjord. Technological changes are thus combined with human/non-human reconfigurations: a shift in the relations between human and dogs, but also between humans and other species, such as the polar bear.

How sea ice changes affect inter-species relationships

The door shudders. The streets whitened by the arrival of winter contrast with the colourful houses that nestle the 350 inhabitants of the town. The darkness is receding, the northern lights erasing green clouds carefully intertwined during the night. Other tints will soon emerge. The shiver of the door stops. The handle creeks. The schedule is too early for each noise not to have its own meaning. His imposing frame appears and suddenly freezes. For a moment, the sounds fade away. Shortly afterwards, he evaluates: 'It's not cold.' Our eyes meet and talk to each other. It's six in the morning and the polar bears patrol sets off (fieldnotes, Tanguy Sandré, 2021).

Among the stories we were told in Ittoqqortoormiit, many were focused on polar bears. It was especially true in the autumn 2021, when polar bears were around the town, much closer than usual, and it was therefore a favourable season for polar bear stories. In recent years, changes in sea ice extent and thickness have been associated with an increase of visiting polar bears. As one community member underlined: "20–25 years ago, the hunters had to drive a longer way to hunt polar bears. Now, they're coming inside the village." It is also inconceivable now for Ittoqqortoormeermii to venture outside the town without being armed. Being prepared for a random encounter appears to be a basic rule. A few years ago, a polar bear patrol was set up in Ittoqqortoormiit. The patrol consists of a single person who is charged with assuring the town is free of polar bears before the school opens. At six in the morning, the patroller drives around the town, slowing down on spots where polar bears have been noticed in the past, for instance down the Kuuk (River), at the garbage dump or nearby Qinngaaiva/Walrus Bay.

Changes in sea ice redesign relationships between inhabitants and polar bears, whose behaviour is affected by those sea ice conditions. Hence, it reframes the way polar bears are perceived among new generations (3), who now commonly perceive polar bears as a threat: "All the community is scared of meeting polar bears. They don't want their kids to be outside after the weather gets dark because they're afraid there might be a polar bear. It's quite normal that we get visits from polar bears inside the town"; "it is very different now, when I was a kid, we used to go skiing on the ice and mountains everywhere, and now we cannot venture out there without a gun because there can be polar bears everywhere." Both hunting practices and local leisure activities are impacted by this permanent threat.

Interstices and local experiences of seasonality

Another set of stories focused on how the sea ice determines local views on seasons and seasonality. Among most human groups, living conditions are strongly associated with seasonal calendars, which provide a common structure for community life. Under complex changes, notably co-driven by climate and environmental crises, cultural calendars have to be rearticulated to keep making sense of local experiences. The changing sea ice, and its practical local consequences, affect hunting activities. Hunting periods are framed at the intersection of biological and migration cycles, sea ice conditions, hunting and community practices, values, and knowledge, as well as institutional and environmental regulations. Seeing seasonality in this multifaceted way, as an intersection of rhythms, allows for a nuanced and local (and respectful) understanding of changing dwelling conditions. It goes beyond a 'western', science-based framing of seasonality, to see seasons as local frameworks and shed light on ways of navigating with the flow of seasons, rather than acting according to rigid calendars. Even if "seasonality is the most basic scaffolding of people's sense of time, structuring fluctuations in resource availability and deployment of adaptive responses (4)", a "neglected aspect of climate change adaptation is the role played by communities' cultural relationship to seasons (5)".

A dominant representation of seasons follows a four-season division of the year. In Tunumiisut, at first glance, the four-season categorisation appears relevant. Hence, winter (Ugeer) and summer (Mannginner) are extremely present in the narratives collected, with notable but less frequent occurrences of spring (Manngileqqaarner) and fall (Ugiatsar). Nevertheless, our observations and storylines from our interviews suggest that the life of the community is driven by a duality marked by the presence or absence of sea ice.[2] The season – and the stories of these periods – determine what activities take place in the community. The interstices between those two sea ice seasons are characterised by lassitude, high unpredictability due to high year-to-year inconsistency, as well as more frequent winter-like storm events and hurricanes in autumn. Not much can be done in these 'in between' periods, and as our local conversation partners kept reminding us – 'naluarnga', I don't know – it's a fool's errand to predict when the transition will happen. This attitude characterised how the community handled seasonal variability and change: they wholeheartedly accepted the inherent uncertainty, and the inability to reduce it, and trusted in the community's resilience to weather the transition period. In-site observation suggests that this is more than an attitude, rather a way of being in the world. This provides an interesting contrast with Western perspectives and our work in climate science which is characterised by much more of a focus on predic-

Figure 7.1: A woman fishing on thin ice. Taken by Tanguy Sandré, June 2022, Ittoqqortoormiit. (Photo by: Tanguy Sandré).

---

2 We cannot rule out that the timing of the repetitive fieldwork might influence our perspective on this duality.

tions and projections, and where irreducible uncertainties are associated with frustration. We might be able to learn much on Arctic resilience from how communities navigate these seasonal interstices. The local experience of seasonality also provides clues on how to deploy downscaling of science-based understandings to make climate science more locally meaningful to these communities.

The authors

Tanguy Sandré (he/him) is an interdisciplinary PhD Research Fellow at the CEARC and LSCE Research Centres, University of Paris Saclay, and visitor researcher at the SVT, University of Bergen. He is involved in two European projects on resilience in the Arctic (SeMPER-Arctic, 2020–2024) and existential risks within non-Western communities (PREFER, 2022–2027). His research interests notably include: the plurality of knowledge, critical ethnography, epistemology, issues of adaptation and resilience.

Jeanne Gherardi is an assistant professor at the University of Versailles St Quentin and member of the LSCE research centre. She has a background in paleoceanography and paleoclimatology. She is currently conducting narrative-based transdisciplinary research on the Arctic region. She is coordinating the 'SeMPER-Arctic' interdisciplinary project aiming to study the concept of resilience of Arctic communities through the collection and analysis of local stories.

Arjan Wardekker is a Senior Researcher at the Centre for the Study of the Sciences and the Humanities (SVT), University of Bergen. His work focuses on urban & community resilience and climate change adaptation. He is particularly interested in the role of perceptions, narratives and framing, and the interaction between science, policy and society, in building resilient communities.

References

1.   Gearheard, S. F., L. K. Holm, H. Huntington, J. M. Leavitt, & A. R. Mahoney (eds.) *The Meaning of Ice: People and Sea Ice in Three Arctic Communities*. Hanover, NH: International Polar Institute Press, 2013.
2.   IPCC. "Technical Summary". In *Climate change 2021: The physical science basis*. Oxford: Oxford University Press, 2021.
3.   Lund, N. H. S. 'Changing times for people and polar bears.' In *The Inuit World*. New York: Routledge, 2021.
4.   Roncoli, C., T A. Crane, & B. Orlove. "Fielding Climate Change in Cultural Anthropology". In S. A. Crate & M Nuttal (eds.) *Anthropology and Climate Change: From Encounters to Actions*. New York: Routledge, 2009.
5.   Bremer, S., B. Glavovic, H. Haarstad, E. S. Jensen, T. Potthast, P. Schneider, M. Bruno Soares, et al. "Changing seasonality: recalibrating institutions' seasonal calendars". *Ambio*, (submitted).

Rosario Carmona and Jessica Rupayan

8 Chasing the seasons: Pehuenche experiences of rapid socioecological change in the Southern Andes

Seasonal cycles in Pehuenche territory

Climate change has a direct impact on the seasons. These changes can produce a significant impact on Indigenous communities living in close interdependence with the territory. Furthermore, these impacts are often entangled and reinforced by other socio-ecological processes altering the way communities organise themselves. The commune of Lonquimay, located in the southern Andes in Chile, illustrates this situation. It has been socially, politically, and economically marginalised, and today it is the second poorest commune in La Araucanía, Chile's poorest region. At the same time, Lonquimay is very susceptible to environmental changes and especially vulnerable to drought. In writing about the changing seasons in Lonquimay, I spoke with Jessica Rupayan about her experiences. The quotes in this chapter are hers.

More than half of Lonquimay's population are Pehuenche people living in rural areas. The Pehuenche are a sub-group of the Mapuche People, who have co-habited with the millenary pehuen tree (*Araucaria araucana*), whose common English name is the Monkey Puzzle tree. These trees provided them shelter and food, especially during colonisation times. Its seed, the *piñon*, has a high nutritional value, and its resin has medicinal properties. Thanks to this, and other factors that are difficult to perceive for those who have not lived with these ecosystems and their spirits, the pehuen is considered a sacred tree. Pehuenche means 'people of the pehuen' in the Mapuche language.

Pehuenche life is inscribed in diverse activities that rhythmically shape seasonality. The Pehuenche's economy and culture are based on a two-level transhumance[1] cycle: *pukemtuwe* (cold season) and *walügtuwe* (warm season). These levels refer to both space and time. The *pukemtuwe* corresponds to the coldest season. It is also the lower altitude zone where the Pehuenche live and spend most of the year —each community has its *pukemtuwe*, which is subdivided into family plots. During the *pukemtuwe* season, work is focused on caring for the house, animals, and crops. The *walügtuwe* coincides with the warmer season and

---

1 Transhumance is a type of pastoralism based on the seasonal movement of livestock.

is also the mountain area, which is inaccessible in cold months due to snow, but when temperatures rise it opens for grazing and the gathering of non-timber forest products such as *piñones* and mushrooms. Although these seasons are associated with specific characteristics, their limits are not fixed as they depend on the weather, the territory and altitude conditions. Each community and family climb to the *walügtuwe* at the time they consider most appropriate.

The alternation between *pukemtuwe* and *walügtuwe* inscribes the Pehuenche economy in the rhythms of nature. In this way, this cycle implies a temporal organisation, but also a social practice and a mode of spatial production. It maintains the Pehuenche's connection with the territories that have ancestrally articulated their identity. More than a productive season, the *walügtuwe* is a space and a time of connection that nourishes the soul, allowing the body and mind to rest in the rhythm of life. At the *walügtuwe*, the Pehuenche recover their strength and energy for the cold months ahead.

> The *walügtuwe* provides us with food, spirituality and connection with the family and animals. You find a place to rest. When we get there, you notice different energy, which is transmitted from the pehuen, the quillay (Quillaja saponaria), the ñirre (Notofagus antartica) and many other trees . . . and from the birds, the condor (Vultur gryphus). Everything is enriched with that energy that we need for the year, life, and health –physical, mental and spiritual.

In the old days, the whole family went to the *walügtuwe* to spend the warm months there tending the animals, collecting *piñones* and sharing stories about the ancestors. The ancestor's energy is transmitted through the territory, enabling the Pehuenche to pass on their knowledge intergenerationally. "We always went with our grandparents; they told us stories." The elders share relevant ecological information with the children, such as how to take care of the pehuen and collecting the *piñon*. But above all, they transmit vital information about how to be *che* (people), that is, what to take and what to give in reciprocity. Being communal, the *walügtuwe* house tiny wooden constructions where families store tools and protect themselves during the night. Children fall asleep listening to owls and wake up with the animals' first steps.

> My grandmother said, 'listen, here comes this animal.' With that sound, you learn to listen to the silence, the noise, who is who, the feet. If the animal goes up or down, how long ago it passed, or if a puma is stalking it.

It was a joy feeling the morning's energy and welcoming it with a prayer. To share a mate tea, chat without schedules and clocks, and let the conversations about dreams flow. Then, going out to look at the animals, identifying one's own and those of others, trusting the neighbours will do the same. Coming back and eating *piñones*.

Eating *piñones* is a distinctive symbol of the Pehuenche identity. In other words, to be Pehuenche is to eat *piñones*. Moreover, the local economy is based on selling this seed to visitors. Today, women also commercialise by-products such as flour and culinary preparations. Some even refer to the *piñon* as 'Pehuenche gold.'

Seasons of change

In contemporary society, Pehuenche transhumance cycles have come to be entangled with the productive and economic dynamics imposed by state policy, which have encouraged the exploitation of forests and livestock throughout the twentieth century. Deforestation and overgrazing have created many pressures for Pehuenche economies, which are now highly dependent on state aid and development programmes that encourage competition.

In this context, the Pehuenche perceive many climatic impacts, including rising temperatures and reduced rainfall. Snow is softer and melts faster, decreasing water storage in the mountains and drying the springs. The drought deepens the water scarcity scenario produced by a legal regime that privatises water and leaves it in the hands of entrepreneurs who do not live in the territory. Those who do not have water rights cannot take it from the rivers that flow past the doors of their house.

Drought reduces grasslands. To cope with this situation, Pehuenche families have shifted from crops for human consumption, such as wheat and quinoa, to crops for animal feed, such as alfalfa and oats. These crops are promoted by state policy, which also encourages the use of pesticides that can decrease soil productivity, and reinforce the impacts of environmental degradation and climate change. Feed deficits impact the health of livestock, already affected by environmental changes.

The transitions between the seasons have tended to homogenise. The warmer and cooler periods of the year seem to be blurring, and the transhumance cycles of *pukemtuwe* and *walügtuwe* blend.

> Before, the seasons were clear. They were characterised by the fall of the leaves in autumn, and the trees blossomed in spring. In September, you could see the buds, and in November, everything was in bloom. Today, they flower in August. Formerly, in April, we had the first rains, but now it is still warm, the rains fall in May, and everything has moved. Piñones used to fall in the first half of February; you could even eat some at the end of January. Nothing is the same. And I do not know when it changed so drastically.

Because of this, the signs indicating the time to go up to the *walügtuwe* have been delayed, creating weeks of uncertainty where the only option is to buy more fodder. But it is not only the time that is slipping away but also the places. The *walüg-tuwe* have moved higher and with them, their energy and grasslands. Families and their animals must now walk to more distant and inaccessible areas, such as ravines, or even lease private land. In the mountains, the *piñones* are evasive, dropping off weeks later than usual, just when children are due to go to school in March. But how could Pehuenches come down to drop their children off if their school supplies can only be bought thanks to *piñones* sales?

Climate change also affects the native flora and fauna. The medicinal herbs have diminished, and native trees are weaker. The most affected species is the pe-huen. The quantity and quality of the *piñones* are not the same; their taste and tex-ture has changed. To not lose them, Pehuenche must sell or process them quickly. In many houses, finding them on the plate is no longer possible. "We used to toast *piñones* until November. But not anymore. They do not even make it to June."

The changes in the pehuen impact livelihoods, but above all, Pehuenche's knowledge and identification systems. For example, the Pehuenche used to pre-dict the weather with the seeding, but this is no longer possible; the relationship between seeding and cold season intensity does not correspond anymore. Dis-trustful, the youth no longer trust traditional knowledge.

Although the spiritual connection is maintained, the *walügtuwe* are less vis-ited than before. In addition, the more changeable temperatures have made the nights in the mountains colder, sometimes making it more challenging to stay up there. For many, the *walügtuwe* is now a space outside the productive rhythms. Becoming just a memory.

> When I return to the territory, it is like going back to previous lives, not only remembering childhood or past years but also going back to another time. A space in which one has already lived and is not living now . . . it is like entering the unconscious.

It is not change that affects Pehuenche culture. It is the disruption of the rhythms and cycles that enable the construction of their territory. Being dynamic, these rhythms have given the Pehuenche a sense of belonging and stability to face multiple challenges and adapt to extreme conditions. Today the seasons are slipping away, and this disturbance brings perplexity and sadness; the days have lost structure. The void opens the space for other activities, regulated by the calendar of state policy and the homogenisation of agricultural and livestock practices. Life becomes predict-able, making reading nature's signs irrelevant. In addition to immense economic pressures, the lack of connection to the land makes it easier to move to the cities. In urban spaces, rituals are replaced by duties. Alarm clocks supplant birdsong, and the morning mate is shared with the email. The pehuen calls them, but not everyone recognises their language anymore. Something is missing, but how to know what?

Nature has rhythms. They are neither homogeneous nor fixed, but change and adjust to each other in search of a balance that allows the reproduction of life. Thanks to our unique capabilities, humans have learned to become independent of many of these rhythms. Paradoxically, this makes our lives more monotonous.

Aligning ourselves to the rhythms of nature may seem restrictive. Nevertheless, allowing ourselves to flow with an order beyond our control can be a step towards achieving contentment, something so elusive these days. The happiness that the Pehuenche find with the *walügtuwe* is not just due to the products, services, or contributions this season provides –although these are fundamental. The relevance of the *walügtuwe* lies in the fact that it inscribes Pehuenche's life in a major order. An order is not perceived as superior, untouchable, or immutable but in constant dialogue with their daily rhythms. In these spaces and times, now fugitive, the Pehuenche remember who they are: a strand of this web we call life.

Figure 8.1: Pehuen, 2023. (Artwork by: Rosario Carmona).

The authors

Rosario Carmona is a painter and anthropologist, with an MA and PhD in Anthropology. She has a diploma in Political Ecology (CLACSO) and in Indigenous Rights (Fondo Indígena). Currently, she is a researcher at the University of Bonn, Germany, and the Research Center for Integrated Disaster Risk Management, Chile. Her work analyses the coherence between international agreements and national climate governance in terms of Indigenous Peoples' participation and recognition.

Jessica Rupayan belongs to the Mapuche-Peheuche People and was born in Lonquimay. She is a lawyer and advocate for Indigenous Peoples' rights, the defence of nature and climate justice. She is founder of the National Coordination of Indigenous Women in Chile and the Foundation Tayiñ Rakizuam. Currently her work aims to strengthen Indigenous Peoples, and especially Indigenous women's participation in climate policy in Chile.

Part II **Relations to nature**

Hope Flanagan and Linda Black Elk

9 Gifts of the plant world

Introduction

Hope Flanagan is a cultural educator and storyteller in the Minneapolis Native community who teaches and leads plant walks in Native communities across the state of Minnesota. Linda Black Elk is an ethnobotanist and food sovereignty activist on the lands of the Oceti Sakowin (what is now known as North Dakota). Both are holders of indigenous knowledge about the gifts of food, medicine and materials that plants share. What follows is a transcript of a conversation held in October 2022 about what they have been observing in the plant world.

Conversation

Hope:

I was just listening to a report about farmers in the United States having a high rate of suicidal ideation and suicide attempts. To me it wasn't any real surprise because I think farmers are acutely aware of what's going on environmentally. And I think the two of us are out there with the wild plants almost every day. We're seeing a lot of things going on that I think the lay person isn't seeing. So for many people it's easy to be in denial of some of the big changes that are happening. And one of the things I keep running into is the expression of environmental depression or environmental anxiety.

Linda:

I think it's so important to think about that. My husband and our youngest son and I were out yesterday. We were driving down the road and my husband stopped on the gravel road and there was a tree covered in choke cherries. Fresh, not dried. Some of them are even still red. And we just stared at it for a while. And of course, we were grateful to be able to harvest some more on one hand, but on the other hand, we kept talking about the fact that we normally harvest those at the end of June and July and August. For most Lakota people, the name of the time of year that is around July, late July and August is *Çaŋpasapa Wi*, which means "The Moon When the Choke Cherries Are Black." And we were collecting them on October 3rd. An ethnobiologist up in Michigan said today he was collecting raspberries. Raspberries that were flowering. And he said it was the second time this season that they've been flowering. I was thankful to be able to collect those choke cherries, but it did give me anxiety. It made me think I'm benefiting off of climate change, which is a whole other level of anxiety. And what am I gonna do? Make the best of it? You know, so crazy.

Hope:
That happened to me today as well. I had taken a group out about two or three weeks ago to pick New England aster roots. And there weren't any. And I said, well, it must be because it was such a dry year. I wasn't seeing the plant. And then the last few days, they've been producing flowers like crazy. So our pollinator meadow was really, really busy. And then I went picking nanny berries after that. This is really not normal plant behaviour. Our readers might not be aware that almost always the months of the calendar in the different Native languages correspond to what's going on seasonally. And I did bring this up with an elder up there in Canada, Ogiimagwanebiik, and she said when you see that the months don't match what is happening with the plants, the plants are right. The plants are right. They're not wrong. It's us. We're the ones that are wrong. People need to be paying attention.

Linda:
I think that's so profound – "the plants are right" – because, you know, they are. They're doing exactly what they're supposed to do. They're doing exactly what the temperature and precipitation are telling them to do. Tonight, we're supposed to actually get our first hard freeze. It's supposed to get down to 21 degrees Fahrenheit here in North Dakota. And so everyone is picking their gardens and all sorts of stuff. But I started to think, if the raspberries are flowering, what's going to happen to those raspberries tonight as it freezes? What's going to be their reaction to that? And then how will that affect their blooming time next year? Will they still go dormant successfully now, and then bloom successfully next spring? I don't know.

Hope:
That's an excellent question. We really don't know. I've been seeing lilacs blooming the last few days. And, you know, that can't be easy on the plant, producing blossoms twice a year. Where are they going to get energy to continue to keep this up? So I think we get some really false starts in this because we're seeing some plants that are saying, "I'm in stress. I'm going to try as hard as I possibly can to reproduce."

I was seeing that stress with some of the old oak trees and acorn production, they were just full, just solid with acorns. And these were some of those old oak trees. Oak trees around 'Bde Maka Ska'. I wouldn't be surprised if those weren't oaks that had been purposely raised by Dakota community there. Because the acorns are very sweet, easy to process, hardly any tannins. So they're delicious, but they were just everywhere.

Because of climate change, the wild rice is changing. To the north of our 'Dream of Wild Health' farm, it was flooded. To the south, it was drought. We were able to take the students out and show them how to harvest. But that whole point is moot if there isn't any rice because of climate change. So there was some celebration that you currently have some rice in the Minnesota River. And that was exciting, and I think we've got to look for some of those celebratory moments. Like, yeah, we've got some rice and we can do some of our old tribal practices from a long time ago. I think we have to look at what we can celebrate.

Linda:
So what foods are there that we can collect that maybe we haven't been framing as foods? I don't spend a lot of time in acorns. But a friend of mine from the Shakopee community is out at the Klamath Reservation right now doing acorn processing because that's a great food source. But if the rice isn't going to be there, then maybe we should be looking to the acorns. It's just a complete fruit basket upset as far as I can see: to not be able to predict what's going to be there and what's not going to be there. What you're saying about looking for what we can celebrate is so important, because it speaks to resiliency and adaptability.

I was talking to someone else today and they asked me what my thoughts are about the future. And even though I probably do have a bit of anxiety around it, I'm super hopeful because you and I both know from being outside all the time that humans and plants are very resilient and very adaptable. Most of the population has had it drilled in their head that we're separate from the landscape. And that the best areas are pristine areas that humans have been removed from like national parks. People tend to think of those as healthy areas. But the truth is areas that have had people removed from them tend to not be very healthy areas. And that's because traditionally, we are part of the landscape.

We can be doing things to move adaptability along and to kind of help plants along. Like one example that I think of is wapato. We're about to go out and get Sagittaria latifolia in a couple of days. And I was always taught to go ahead and dig up the big ones, but always replant the little ones. You're selectively harvesting and always leaving some. If we start to rekindle a lot of these relationships with plants that people don't think of as food anymore. You know, everyone's going for the rice instead of the acorns. Maybe if we rekindle those other relationships, like with the acorns, the rice will get a break. And the acorns, we can do some plantings and have a positive impact, so that the plants are better able to

handle the impacts of climate change. We've got to quit trying to remove ourselves from it. I think that's the really clear message. Maybe that's what a lot of
this is, a message to pay attention, to see. We are so interwoven with all of it. We
can't ever extract ourselves from it.

The authors

Hope Flanagan has been a cultural educator and teacher in the Minneapolis Native community since
the late 1970's. She has taught in an Ojibwe Immersion classroom for 10 years, and for the past 14
summers taught the youth about the wild plants and cultural ways at *Dream of Wild Health* (1). She
has been a storyteller of the legends in the Native community since they were passed to her by Ona
KingBird in 2008. She leads plant walks on the reservations in Minnesota and for the Native agencies
in the area, to share the gifts of food, medicines and utility carried by the plants. She brings plants to
community members who can no longer gather them, so she keeps an eye on what is going on with
the plants, animals, birds, and insects around the state.

Linda Black Elk is an ethnobotanist and food sovereignty activist who specializes in teaching about
culturally important plants and their uses as food, medicine, and materials. She spends much of her
time, gathering, food and medicine to feed and heal her family and community. Linda currently
works and resides on the lands of the Oceti Sakowin in what is now known as North Dakota.

Reference

1.   https://dreamofwildhealth.org/

Michelle Bastian

10 Taking a chance in unseasonable environments

It is late November here in Scotland and it has been unseasonably warm. I keep forgetting and dress as if it is a winter like any other. In my down jacket, waiting at the bus stop, I find I'm ridiculously overdressed. But it's not only me who is confused. As a major newspaper pointed out just the day before (1), after an unprecedented heatwave this summer and above average temperatures every month so far this year (2), the UK is now experiencing a 'second spring', with many plants sending out new shoots or even flowering. In my own garden, the irises I put in last winter had flowered as expected in May. But sometime around October they started coming up again and their pots are now full of green shoots, although no flowers as yet. For many this can create a deep sense of unease, with the seasons seemingly out of synch. While we know local weather can always be unpredictable, the seasons by contrast can seem reliable, even a bit dull, appearing in culture and literature as "the tired formula of a repeating seasonal cycle, a there-and-back walk up and down the hill" (3, page 451). But as literary scholar Sarah Dimick has suggested (4), this once reliable seasonal form is becoming disordered as climate breakdown challenges the taken-for-granted round, changing not just weather patterns, but the seasonal indicators that we glean from the behaviour of the plants and animals around us.

In the case of my irises, once I started looking into it, I realised I needed to be careful about reading them as a new disorder of the seasons. In fact, this behaviour can be completely normal, even encouraged. Having a second flowering in a year is called reblooming, repeat flowering, or 'remontancy' (i.e., coming up again). And it is not that uncommon amongst certain flowers. Indeed, breeders of irises have sought to cultivate this trait deliberately (5). Around here, I've seen the arrival of snowdrops startle and concern people as being "too early". But as one close observer told me, when she checks her records, this too can be perfectly within their usual behaviour. Working out whether a behaviour is untimely, or within the expected seasonal range, is part of the job of phenologists, those people who study yearly lifecycle timing within ecosystems. Since the late 1990s their work has become widely influential, as, despite the traps laid by irises and snowdrops, climate change is indeed shifting when plants and animals move through their life stages. According to the UK government's Spring Index, for example, spring has advanced more than 8 days on average since the early 20th century (6). And, as we will see, this change in seasonal timing is having wide ranging effects across ecosystems. That is, while we look to many plants and animals for our sense of seasonality, the cues they themselves look to – whether this be light, temperature, water levels or wildfires – are proving just as unsettling and confusing for them.

One of the most dramatic concerns that phenologists have had about changes in seasonal timing has been about the potential rise in 'trophic mismatches'. These can occur when a creature becomes dangerously out of synch with its food source. One example was reported in 2014, where breeding puffin pairs on the island of Røst in Norway had dropped from 1.5 million to between 350,000 and 400,000 over the past 35 years (7). A contributing factor appears to be a mismatch between the timing of puffin breeding, and the spawning times of the herring that they feed on. The suggestion is that this mismatch arises because puffins and herrings appear to be telling the time in different ways, according to different cues. As Lief Nøttestad suggested in the report, puffins are guided by the changing length of daylight, responding particularly as the days lengthen in the spring. Because our rotation around the sun is (fairly) constant, this means that the puffins are also fairly regular in their nesting each year. The spawning time of herring, however, is guided by the temperature of the ocean, and this can occur from February to April with earlier spawning when the seas are warmer. Nøttestad explains,

> When the herring spawns early in the spring, as we've observed in recent years, the larvae drift northwards before the puffin's nesting season has fully started. The result is a mismatch between the puffin and its food. (quoted in (7))

Thus, while the relatively steady temperatures of the Holocene have supported sufficient overlaps of puffins and herring, climate change may prove these timing strategies no longer workable.

It can be easy to assume that being in synch is a good thing. However, other examples of shifting seasonal cues show what happens when species that were previously out of synch start occurring together. Recent observations of two Australian parrots, Little Lorikeets and Eastern Rosellas – both beautifully coloured birds that build their nests in tree hollows – have reported new conflicts between them over nesting sites. Birdwatchers have apparently not seen them in competition before, but in 2021 James Fitzsimons reports seeing these parrots squabbling over a nest site in Melbourne during May (southern autumn). The Lorikeets were thought to be unusually nesting at this time due to cues given by unseasonal eucalypt flowering (8, page 108). While this is a one-off example, and more research is needed, we can see how mixed-up seasonal cues can cascade across an ecosystem. In this case, shifts in temperatures and/or rainfall may have led to early flowering by the eucalypts (9), which in turn changed the timing of the Little Lorikeet, leading to new conflicts with the Rosella. Seasonal timing is indeed a community affair!

Other processes interfering with seasonal timing include our ways of managing landscapes, which can interfere with the ways that other beings tell what part of the year they are in. This may not be so apparent in the Northern Hemisphere, particularly in temperate regions, where it is difficult for land managers to directly change dominant seasonal cues, such as the length of day or the ambient temperature. However, in the Southern Hemisphere, as well as in tropical regions, a greater variety of cues are used, with more plants responding to rainfall and/or wildfires for germination. Over evolutionary time, these cues have proved to be better markers of conducive environments for young plants. However, these markers are also more likely to be transformed by extensive land management schemes, such as those used frequently in Australia.

A first example is the alteration to river flows. In the Murray-Darling Basin, dams, weirs, and reservoirs are some of the tools used to maintain high water flows in summer for agricultural purposes (10). Research by Lyndsey Vivian and her colleagues (11) has shown that this practice is particularly problematic for native riverside grass species. These grasses experience the high water levels as 'unseasonal', having evolved with low levels in summer. In addition, unseasonal summer flooding increases methane emissions (a significant greenhouse gas) from wetlands when they are used as reservoirs. Researchers have urged land managers to be more aware of the consequences of disrupting wetland and forest landscapes along the Murray-Darling (12), partly because this also disrupts what we might call their 'timescapes'. So while the case of the herrings and the puffins showed us how mismatches can occur between individual species, here the conflicts in timing involve whole ecosystems. Land managers must find ways of negotiating between the forested wetland temporalities, which have evolved over millennia, and temporalities of downstream agricultural landscapes, which often rely on introduced species such as rice and cotton that tell time in quite different ways.

A second example are fire tolerant plants, or pyrophytes, which use wildfires as a key indicator for when to germinate. In Australia, a range of plants may sprout following the end-of-dry-season wildfires, leaving new seedlings to benefit from the cleared landscape, the ash fertiliser, and the coming wet season. However, climate change is causing more intense wildfires, as well as unseasonal fires in what has generally been the 'wet season'. New seedlings emerging at the start of a prolonged dry period are finding it tougher to hold on until the right conditions for their growth return (13). In terms of land management, seemingly unsolvable conflicts in timing arise once again. This is because the rise of controlled burning regimes, as part of reducing the levels of dry vegetation that fuel large fires, are becoming much riskier during the traditional end-of-dry-season period. Hotter and drier summers are reducing opportunities to initiate safe burns, particularly since autumn rains are also decreasing (13, 14). Thus, while ecologists are encouraging land managers to implement burns at times that are seasonally appropriate for native vegetation, climate change is putting the times of plants, wildfires and safe landscapes significantly out of joint.

Finally, one of the more surprising examples of how climate change is affecting seasonal cues are the mismatches occurring *within* individual species. Scientists are finding cases where the timing of male and female flowers might themselves be following different cues and so diverging from one another. Dioecious plants, for example, have male and female flowers on separate plants. To produce viable seed, not only must male and female plants be in the same area, but their flowering times must also overlap (14). Changes in these plants, due to climate heating, is seen as putting them at particular risk of what is called 'phenological isolation'. In 2020, cases in India were found where male Eastern cottonwood (*Populus deltoides*), a key industrial forestry variety, flowered unseasonally in the northern autumn, making them wildly out of synch with the female flowering trees that produced catkins in the spring. The suggestion is that male plants might respond differently to cues of higher temperature or dryer conditions isolating them in time from their female counterparts. Elsewhere, studies have suggested that timing of a plant's own flower and leaf development might be getting out of synch, or even that 'below-ground growing seasons' – or the timing of root growth – might not be lining up with the parts of the plant growing aboveground.

Far from being a dull *fait accompli* then, our knowledge and experience of the seasons derives, not just from the weather, but from the cues that we receive from the plants and animals around us. Their complex methods for working out when to initiate various life stages do not rely on fixed internal rules, but adapt and respond to their changing environments. This is why the usual seasonal variations that inevitably occur can be taken in most creatures' stride. The worry is that with climate change and large-scale landscape change, both caused by human activity, cues that once worked reliably enough now risk leading more-than-human communities wildly astray. However, there is also the view that timing things right has often arisen from taking a chance and seeing what happens. As horticulturist Alys Fowler commented, when reflecting on the UK's 'second spring,' "Many plants are opportunists – if the temperature is right and the day length OK . . . they will have a go. I guess there is some evolutionary advantage to that" (quoted in (1)). Perhaps my irises, then, with their willingness to have a second shot, could represent something very powerful. Not that everything is going wrong, but instead reminding us that seasonal time is part of a continual experiment, a time that can never really be taken for granted.

The author

Michelle Bastian is a Senior Lecturer in Environmental Humanities at the University of Edinburgh and an Associate Professor II in the Oslo School of Environmental Humanities. Her work looks at the role of time in human and non-human environments. Currently, she is exploring seasonal timing in plants and animals and how this is changing in a time of climate breakdown.

References

1. Gayle, D. "'Second Spring' as Uk Experiences Record above-Average Temperatures." *The Guardian*, 25 Nov 2022 2022. (https://www.theguardian.com/uk-news/2022/nov/25/second-spring-as-uk-experiences-record-above-average-temperatures).
2. https://www.metoffice.gov.uk/hadobs/hadcet/cet_info_mean.html
3. Given, M. "Attending to Place and Time: Seasonality in Early Modern Scotland and Cyprus." *European Journal of Archaeology* 23 (2020): 451–72.
4. Dimick, S. "Disordered Environmental Time: Phenology, Climate Change, and Seasonal Form in the Work of Henry David Thoreau and Aldo Leopold." *ISLE: Interdisciplinary Studies in Literature and Environment* 25 (2018): 700–21.
5. Fan, Z., Y. Gao, Y. Ren, C. Guan, R. Liu, & Q. Zhang. "To Bloom Once or More Times: The Reblooming Mechanisms of Iris Germanica Revealed by Transcriptome Profiling." *BMC Genomics* 21 (2020): 553.
6. https://jncc.gov.uk/our-work/ukbi-b4-spring-index/
7. Jakobsen, S. E. "Puffin Chicks Die of Hunger" (https://sciencenorway.no/barents-sea-birds-climate/puffin-chicks-die-of-hunger/1399632). (Accessed 16 January 2023).
8. Fitzsimons, J. A. "Little Lorikeet *"Glossopsitta Pusilla"* Nest Hollow Preparation and Inter-Specific Aggression in Melbourne, Victoria." *The Victorian Naturalist* 138 (2021): 107–09.
9. Beaumont, L. J., T. Hartenthaler, M. R. Keatley, & L. E. Chambers. "Shifting Time: Recent Changes to the Phenology of Australian Species." *Climate Research* 63 (2015): 203–14.
10. O'Gorman, E. *Flood Country: An Environmental History of the Murray-Darling Basin*. Collingwood, VIC: CSIRO Publishing, 2012.
11. Vivian, L. M., J. Greet, & C. S. Jones. "Responses of Grasses to Experimental Submergence in Summer: Implications for the Management of Unseasonal Flows in Regulated Rivers." *Aquatic Ecology* 54 (2020): 985–99.
12. Treby, S. & P. Carnell. "Impacts of Feral Grazers and Unseasonal Summer Flooding on Floodplain Carbon Dynamics: A Case Study." *Ecohydrology & Hydrobiology* Early View (2022). (https://doi.org/10.1016/j.ecohyd.2022.12.007).
13. Miller, R. G., J. B. Fontaine, D. J. Merritt, B. P. Miller, & N. J. Enright. "Experimental Seed Sowing Reveals Seedling Recruitment Vulnerability to Unseasonal Fire." *Ecological Applications* 31 (2021): e02411.
14. Hultine, K. R., K. C. Grady, T. E. Wood, S. M. Shuster, J. C. Stella, & T. G. Whitham. "Climate Change Perils for Dioecious Plant Species." *Nature Plants* 2 (2016): 16109

Berit Gehrke and Michael D. Pirie

11 Plants in a world of changing seasons

Plants can be used as calendars for tracking seasons, particularly in temperate climate regions. Each year we witness a sequence of new growth, flowering, fruiting, and senescence. With each cycle, plants track optimal conditions for growth, they flower in time to engage their likewise seasonally dependent pollinators, and they avoid perils such as frost or drought that come with changing temperatures through the year. An annual record of plants' seasonal growth is laid down in successive concentric rings that can be read from their woody stems. Although a single tree lives and dies in one place, populations of tree species span geographic ranges and timeframes that subject them to an ever-shifting seasonality. Extremes of changing climates can push them into new territories and to the brink of survival. In this chapter we explore the plant calendar and adaptations to changing seasons throughout time and space using larches and the Arboretum in Bergen to highlight the various topics touched upon.

Plants can change dramatically in appearance through the growing season. Flowers appear, advertising themselves with bursts of colour, leaf buds open and leaves expand, age, and fall. The visual impact of these changes is extraordinary because they tend to occur across individuals of a single species more or less simultaneously. Our understanding of the phenomenon even has its own name: 'phenology'. Most people living in temperate climates can relate to phenological changes and are able to name the seasons in which they occur: the appearance of flowering bulbs and the development of leaves on trees heralds spring. Meadows grow tall and forest canopies close in during the summer. In autumn, we are struck by the abundance of fruit and changing colours of the leaves. The absence of flowers and seeming lifelessness of trees without leaves denotes winter (Figure 11.1). The phenology of plants such as flowering of hazel and elderberries has been recorded in Europe for more than a hundred years (1). Even today we track the seasonality of plants producing allergy-causing pollen, such as grasses and certain trees, or plants of agricultural importance such as apples and grapes.

Plants track seasons both with externally observable phenological responses and with a visible but usually hidden record of past seasons in their woody annual growth rings. To understand these rings, it can help to understand that in a tree trunk between the bark and the wood lies a thin layer of actively dividing cells, the vascular cambium, where cell division and hence growth occurs (Figure 11.2B). The rate of tree growth and stem thickening follows the seasons, being active during summer and slow or dormant during winter. In spring the plant mobilises nutrients stored in the roots and stem to form an often-lighter zone of loose tissue

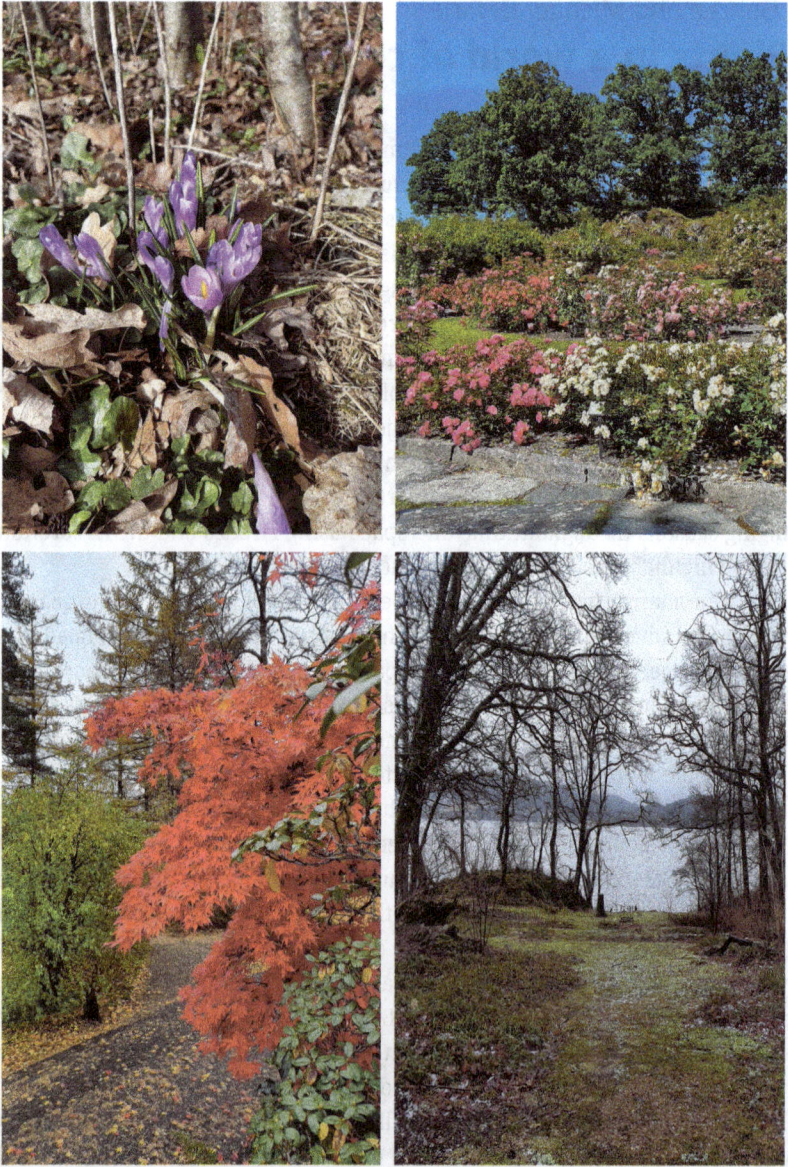

Figure 11.1: Temperate climate phenological seasons as reflected in the Arboretum of the University Gardens in Bergen. Spring: *Crocus vernus* 'Milde'. Many people visiting the Arboretum eagerly await the mass flowering of the Milde crocus as the first sign of spring. Summer: flowering roses in the rosarium against a backdrop of oaks in full leaf. Autumn: Japanese maple (*Acer palmatum*) with stunning red foliage. Winter: leafless trees in 'the Garden of Eden' with a view of the Fana fjord. (Photos by: Berit Gehrke).

with large cavities which allow the tree to transport water and minerals quickly from the roots to the crown. The cells in this early season wood are thin-walled and not very robust. Subsequently, more thick-walled cells are formed in a much denser tissue that mainly provides structural support. Thickness of annual rings also tracks climatic and other conditions. Tree rings can therefore be used to infer past climate events. There is a dense record of such data for many Northern Hemisphere temperate climate regions reaching back several hundred years. Particularly wide rings in larch, for example, are associated with years in which cool conditions in July–September were followed by high precipitation in May–July in the year after (2).

The onset of visible phenological events such as flowering or leaf emergence are linked to adaptations of plants to climate (mostly temperature and precipitation), availability of nutrients, pollinator abundance or light levels. Many plants also maintain an internal clock, which can be more complex. Plant seasonality takes many forms. One particularly striking phenomenon is seasonal leaflessness, as exhibited by deciduous (as opposed to evergreen) trees. Periodic leaflessness can allow plants to tolerate seasons that are unfavourable for growth, such as cold winters or dry summers, and to withstand catastrophic events such as freezing (3). Deciduous plants pre-empt such hard times with a controlled process of deliberate aging known as 'senescence'. The advantage of leaf senescence is that nutrients such as nitrogen can be reabsorbed, stored, and reused. Prominent changes in leaf colours result from the mostly green-reflecting photosynthetic pigments being broken down. Leaves turning yellow, red, and brown therefore reflect no less than a recycling mechanism of plants. Outside the northern temperate zones, other kinds of vegetations display other phenologies or seasonality, such as in seasonally dry ecosystems in which deciduousness is a response to periods of plentiful water supply alternating with drought (4).

Evolutionary adaptations to the environmental conditions are often inherited and therefore shared in groups of closely related species. However, very similar traits can also evolve repeatedly in distantly related organisms when a strategy is particularly successful. An interesting example is the evolution of deciduousness in larch (the genus *Larix* – Figure 11.2). Larch is the common name for a group of 10–13 closely related species of trees distributed only in cold-temperate regions of the Northern Hemisphere, with greatest diversity in northern North America and northern Asia. Species of larch can also be found in Europe as well as in mountainous areas in China and Japan (5). Larches are mostly pioneer species in mixed-coniferous forests. Their deciduousness sets them apart from most other conifers which retain their needle shaped leaves throughout the year, various of which we bring into our homes as Christmas trees to remind us of sea-

Figure 11.2: Japanese larches (*Larix kaempferi*) in the Arboretum of the University Gardens in Bergen. These trees have been planted around 1961. A) Two pendant male cones on the left and 2 upright fresh female cones on a branch with young shoots. Larches have male and female flowers on the same tree, often on the same main branches. Many of the needle like leaves are clustered in short shoots, a typical characteristic of all larches. B) The outer bark of a Japanese larch. C) An older and dried up open female cone. The seeds have already dropped. Female cones of larches persist on the trees. D) A tree trunk cross section showing the outer bark surrounding inner wood with a darker heart-wood and pale, living sap-wood. The thickness of the annual rings clearly varies, as is

sons of growth. *Larix* is considered an early successional tree: it moves in following disturbance and is typically replaced by spruce (*Picea*) and pines (*Pinus*) later on (6). Larches do not grow well in the shade, such as that cast by stands of their evergreen relatives. Intolerance of shade is offset by more efficient use of nitrogen and carbon, the building blocks of life, allowing larches to establish on poor soils. They are often one of the first trees to establish following fire and can become dominant at the tree line where, with increasing elevation, other species dwindle away (5).

Due to their pioneer character, responses of larches to seasonal changes – changes in climate such as in temperature and precipitation – can be expected to be particularly rapid. We know from fossil evidence and ice core analysis that climate parameters including the length of season available for photosynthesis have changed dramatically in the recent past. During the ice ages the winters were longer and colder. We also know that plant distribution patterns have changed considerably over time as past climate oscillations led to expansions and contractions of area suitable for different plants. This means that daylength variation is less important for plant distribution patterns than climatic conditions. Fossil evidence suggests that the larches used to be present in more lowland areas but that their distribution moved as the glaciers receded. It has been suggested that *Larix* would have been one of the first species to colonise areas formerly covered by glaciers, but that in the warmer periods when the ice retreated (including the last 15,000 years of 'interglacial' that we are still experiencing today) *Larix* became restricted to high altitudes (7, 5). This is probably not because it cannot survive lower down, but instead due to its low competitiveness at lower elevations. For example, the Japanese larch (*Larix kaempferi*, or Karamatsu in Japanese), has a narrow natural distribution range at higher altitudes in Honshu in Japan but can today be found across a much wider area where it has been planted by humans. The species grows well at the Arboretum of the University of Bergen close to sea level (Figure 11.2).

As the climate changes, and seasonal patterns change with it, we can expect to see species change, generation by generation, as individuals better suited to the new conditions reproduce more successfully (8). In *Larix* this could include earlier flowering, earlier emergence of new needles, and later yellowing and loss of needles. Future researchers will be able to track the impact on seasonal growth through changes in tree ring thickness. *Larix*, like other plants, will

---

Figure 11.2 (continued)
visible in both heart- and sap-wood. E) A young larch at the edge of the 'Blondehus' garden in intense autumn yellow. F) Dense stand of Japanese larches in the Arboretum in Bergen in the spring of 2022 with fresh green, newly sprung needles. (Photos by: Berit Gehrke).

hopefully continue to change its 'realized niche' – the area in which it is found – as it tracks human-induced shifts in its 'potential niche' – the area in which it would be able to survive if not outcompeted. If such changes occur faster than plants can disperse, then their populations – and potentially the species as a whole – may be threatened with extinction. Trees from across the world, including many species that are already threatened in the wild, are maintained at botanic gardens and arboreta. These diverse collections of species represent an insurance against disaster: a potential source for future reintroductions in the wild. They also enhance the show of beautiful seasonal variation for gardeners and visitors alike.

The authors

Berit Gehrke is head of the Bergen University Gardens in Bergen, western Norway. She has a doctorate in botany from the University of Zurich, Switzerland. She enjoys being outdoors in her free time and is a keen observer of plant life which she actively records using iNaturalist.

Michael Pirie is scientific curator of the Bergen University Gardens' Arboretum, with a PhD in plant systematics from the University of Utrecht, The Netherlands.

References

1.   Menzel, A. "Europe." In M. D. Schwartz (ed.) *Phenology: An Integrative Environmental Science*. Springer, Dordrecht, 2013 (https://doi.org/10.1007/978-94-007-6925-0_4).
2.   Oleksyn, J. & H. C. Fritts, "Influence of climatic factors upon tree rings of *Larix decidua* and *L. decidua* × *L. kaempferi* from Pulawy, Poland," *Trees* 5 (1991): 75–82.
3.   Yann, L. A. V. & K. Christian. "The interaction between freezing tolerance and phenology in temperate deciduous trees," *Frontiers in Plant Science* 5 (2014). (https://www.frontiersin.org/article/10.3389/fpls.2014.00541).
4.   Eamus, D. "Ecophysiological traits of deciduous and evergreen woody species in the seasonally dry tropics," *Trends in Ecology and Evolution* 14 (1999): 11–16. (https://doi.org/10.1016/S0169-5347(98)01532-8).
5.   Mamet, S. D., C. D. Brown, A. J. Trant, & C. P. Laroque, "Shifting global Larix distributions: Northern expansion and southern retraction as species respond to changing climate," *Journal of Biogeography* 46 (2018): 30–44. (https://doi.org/10.1111/jbi.13465).
6.   Motta R. & E. Lingua, "Human impact on size, age, and spatial structure in a mixed European larch and Swiss stone pine forest in the Western Italian Alps," *Canadian Journal of Forest Research*, 35 (2005): 1809–1820. (https://doi.org/10.1139/x05-10).

7. Wagner, S., T. Litt, M-F. Sánchez-Goñi, and R. J. Petit. "History of *Larix decidua* Mill. (European larch) since 130 ka," *Quaternary Science Reviews 124* (2015): 224–247 (https://doi.org/10.1016/j.quascirev.2015.07.002).

8. Pearman, P. B., A. Guisan, O. Broennimann & C. F. Randin, "Niche dynamics in space and time," *Trends in Ecology and Evolution 23* (2007): 149–158 (https://doi.org/10.1016/j.tree.2007.11.005).

Marit Ruge Bjærke

12 Unseen seaweed seasonalities

In April 2022, a new seasonal tradition started in a local square in Oslo, Norway. The year before, Japanese cherry trees had been planted in the square. Now the trees were about to blossom for the first time, and the local community wanted to celebrate this by arranging a Japanese *hanami* – a spring bloom celebration. In Japan, where hanamis are held every year, special forecasts estimate the time of blooming so that people can plan their celebrations accordingly. In Norway, the local community was not that experienced in hanami-celebrations. The date for the hanami was set long in advance. Luckily, however, there were still a few pink flowers left on the trees on the day of the celebration. The Japanese cultural attaché to Norway was there. The mayor of Oslo came. A Japanese-Norwegian choir sang. There was a display of Japanese martial arts and a Japanese tea ceremony. And to the local initiators' surprise, hundreds of people showed up to be part of this new seasonal celebration.

Meanwhile, in the fjord nearby, another species originating in Japan had just started growing into its spring form. It was the Japanese wireweed, a light brown seaweed growing in and below the tidal zone. It was not blooming. Brown seaweed like the Japanese wireweed do not bloom. Instead, new fronds were developing on its short perennial stem. Fronds that would turn the Japanese wireweed, now about 20 centimetres tall, into a bushy plant a couple of meters high.

Late in the summer, the Japanese wireweed grows small, brown structures called receptacles on the fronds. These contain its reproductive cells. Even later, the fronds detach from the stem. They float away and bring with them both female and male reproductive cells. The Japanese wireweed is able to self-fertilize. It can produce new Japanese wireweeds while floating.

The unwanted alien

Neither the Japanese cherry tree nor the Japanese wireweed are native in Norway. Instead, they are defined as *alien species*. Alien species are species occurring outside of their natural range. They have been moved to new places by humans, either intentionally or unintentionally. Since alien species often outcompete other species or change the ecology of the place they have been introduced to, they are considered one of the main direct drivers of biodiversity loss worldwide (1). To be defined as an invasive alien species, however, is not a property of the species itself, but of its relation to humans (2). Humans cause the introduction to new areas, humans define them as wanted or unwanted, and humans construct new understandings and practices around them. The Japanese wireweed was first observed in Norwegian waters in 1984. It had probably hitchhiked from Japanese to European waters with oyster spat that was used for culturing Pacific oysters in Europe. Thus, unlike the Japanese cherry trees, the Japanese wireweed arrived without being invited. Without human transport of oyster spat, however, it would never have managed it.

When the Japanese cherry tree introduced a new seasonal experience, the change initiated a celebration. The Japanese wireweed got . . . what? Nothing much, really. It was noticed in the newspapers as a threat, and placed on the Norwegian Alien Species List, categorized as having severe ecological impact (3).

Seaweed seasonalities

Oceans and their living inhabitants have been termed "the real lungs of the world". They produce more than half of the Earth's oxygen (4). Oceans and coastal waters are also subject to an enormous range of different environmental pressures, from pollution and climate change to land reclamation and overharvesting. Still, seascapes, except for the large mammals and fish living there, are largely unknown entities for many of us. The vertical and horizontal patchiness of coastal waters is different from what we find on land, the modes of transport are different and the species themselves are adapted to their environment in different ways. Do you, for instance, know the seasonalities of your local seaweeds? Would you know if they changed?

In Norway, the most common seaweeds, such as bladder wrack and toothed wrack, look similar all year round. That is, their size and number of fronds do not change with the seasons. They stand there, in the intertidal and subtidal waters and play hosts to a number of different algae and animals. Larger kelps like sugar kelp (*Saccharina latissima*) and oarweed (*Laminaria digitata*), have perennial stems, but grow a new blade every year.

The Japanese wireweed, on the other hand, shows large seasonal variations in form in Norwegian waters. In winter, it consists only of a small stem. In the summer, it is several meters long and extremely bushy (Figure 12.1). This means that, if a seaweed community changes from being dominated by toothed wrack and sugar kelp to being dominated by Japanese wireweed, it would also to a large degree change how seasons look to those who live in that community. Although few humans notice, the smaller algae using seaweed to live on and in, probably do. The same goes for the variety of animals using seaweeds as shelter and food.

Figure 12.1: Japanese wireweed. Left: Japanese wireweed in April. Jomfruland, Norway. Photo by Stein Fredriksen, used with permission. Right: Japanese wireweed in August. Stavanger, Norway. Photo by Ryan Hodnett. Licence: CC BY-SA 4.0 (link: Creative Commons – Attribution-ShareAlike 4.0 International – CC BY-SA 4.0).

Does seaweed seasonality matter?

Space is contested in coastal waters. Seaweed and other algae need light. They cannot grow too deep, and thus, there is not much seafloor of exactly the right depths available. Therefore, the larger seaweeds are important substrates for smaller algae. For small, marine animals, seaweeds are also places to hide and feed. This means that it could matter a lot whether the seafloor is covered by large seaweeds only during the summer season, or whether it is covered by large seaweeds all year round. But does it?

In a study from the outer Oslofjord, more than twenty-five percent of the macroalgae existing in the area seemed to be able to grow on the Japanese wireweed (5). Compared to the non-seasonal toothed wrack, there were more algae species living on the Japanese wireweed. Although some studies have shown that the Japanese wireweed harbors different animals than native species, others have shown that the composition of species and number of individual animals is mostly dependent on the structure of the seaweed, its number of branches and the distance between them, not on seaweed species (6). Researchers have discussed the possibility that the seasonality of the Japanese wireweed, and especially the fact that most of it will float away every year, will reduce its value as a stable habitat for the associated animals, both those that move and those that are sedentary. However, there is no certainty about this.

What do we see, what do we value?

Some ways of expressing seasonality are treated with awe and wonder, like blooming cherry trees. Others are treated with fear and loathing, while others again are rarely even noticed by humans. Invasive alien species are often unpopular. To humans, they represent change, and if outcompeting local species, they also represent loss. In some cases, like the Pacific oyster, they represent economic gain. And in others, like the Japanese cherry trees, they represent beauty. Japanese wireweed is neither of economic interest, nor is it considered beautiful. Although the Norwegian phycologist who spotted it floating past him in 1984 admitted to the local newspaper that "his heart beat a little faster" when he saw it, there are probably few other human hearts that beat for the Japanese wireweed (7).

As different species or individuals move from place to place, the understanding of them and of their ascribed value undergo changes. Should nature be understood as a set of economic resources? As something that ecologists should manage? Or maybe, as something that should not be changed by humans at all? Definitions based in the natural sciences are combined with aesthetic and economic valuations, but also with different degrees of attention. Who gets noticed? Not the ones lingering in the chambers of the sea.

Human interventions are changing the way seasons are expressed in nature, both through climate change and through moving species from place to place. The effects may be unintended, but we humans still decide how the changes affect our cultural expressions. I think we need to reflect on what determines our willingness to change and develop our cultural practices when meeting the new. Could we, for instance, celebrate and admire the achievement of the Japanese wireweed in the same way that we celebrate and admire the Japanese cherry? The Japanese wireweed has not been cultured, eaten, or used as medicine by humans. Still, it did manage to move. Could we celebrate the ability of a species to cling on to something, whether it is a Pacific oyster or a leisure boat? Could we admire the ability of a species to make algal babies with itself while floating? Could we set up a festival for the ability to grow metres and metres in one season, and then just let it all go? A spring festival called "The feast of the new fronds"? Just to make sure that more people knew what wonders are down there, and that even the ones we call invasives and aliens are worth a couple of extra heartbeats on our parts.

The author

Marit Ruge Bjærke works as a researcher in Cultural Studies at the Department of Archaeology, History, Cultural Studies and Religion, University of Bergen, Norway. Her background is in marine biology, history of ideas, and cultural studies. Her interests include the understanding and communication of environmental problems, with a special focus on biodiversity loss, temporality, and invasive marine species. Her relationship with Japanese wireweeds started in 1997.

References

1. IPBES. *Summary for policymakers of the global assessment report on biodiversity and ecosystem services of the Intergovernmental Science-Policy Platform on Biodiversity and Ecosystem Services.* Bonn: IPBES secretariat, 2019.
2. Frawley, J. & I. McCalman (eds.). *Rethinking Invasion Ecologies from the Environmental Humanities.* London & New York: Routledge, 2014.
3. Norwegian Biodiversity Information Centre. "The Alien Species List of Norway – ecological risk assessment 2018." Norwegian Biodiversity Information Centre, 2018. (https://www. biodiversity.no/alien-species-2018).
4. Buchanan, I. & C. Jeffery. "Towards A Blue Humanity." *Symploke* 27 (2019): 11–14.
5. Bjærke, M. R. & S. Fredriksen. "Epiphytic macroalgae on the introduced brown seaweed *Sargassum muticum* (Yendo) Fensholt (Phaeophyceae) in Norway." *Sarsia* 88 (2003): 353–364.
6. Sjøtun, K., C. S. Armitage, M. Eilertsen & C. Todt. "Fauna associated with non-native *Sargassum muticum* (Fucales, Phaeophyceae) vary with thallus morphology and site type (sounds and bays)." *Marine Biology Research* 17 (2021): 454–466.
7. Aftenposten. "Marinbiologisk sensasjon på Sørlandet [Marine biological sensation on the south coast]." *Aftenposten*, 4 August 1984.

Miriam Jensen

13 Feral swans and frightening encounters

During my fieldwork within and across the largest river system in Denmark, Gudenåen, and my participation in and observations of the first intermunicipal
planning process for the river, certain animals kept surfacing in conversations
and within my fieldnotes on the changing river system.

This is the story of one of them: the swan.

It's the middle of spring and I am facilitating a workshop in which a diverse
set of participants involved in the intermunicipal planning process for the River
Gudenåen are participating. Looking around, I see farmers, landowners, kayakers,
fishermen, archaeologists, public officials, local business owners, nature organisations and tourism associations. They are sitting in three groups: each group a mix
of participants.

It is completely silent in the room. Everyone is focused on an exercise in
which they draw their year, their seasonalities and their rhythms in relation to
the river system (Figure 13.1). After 15 minutes, I ask them to share their drawing
with the rest of the group. Walking around the room, I intercept the following
conversation when passing a group:

Was it not on this stretch of the river that the feral swan resides?
Yes, it is still here.
Is it the one who hisses?
Yes, we are not good friends with it.
Does it bite as well?

I become intrigued. What is the story of this particular feral swan?

Returning from the workshop, I go through the drawings and realise that
many of them include references to swans. One post-it note, placed on a drawing
of a landowner's year, mentions that swans might currently find it more difficult
by the river during the winter season and their breeding season. Listening in
more closely to the recordings from the workshops, I discover that the group conversations are filled with talk on animals, nature, and change. I hear reoccurring

Acknowledgements: I wish to thank Kyrre Kverndokk and Marit Ruge Bjærke (University of Bergen)
for hosting me at 'the Gardening the Globe' project in Bergen in the spring of 2022, where I first
started my investigation of the swan. Thank you for great discussions that led me to new ideas.
Thank you also to the CALENDARS project, and in particular Scott Bremer and Elisabeth Schøyen Jensen (University of Bergen), for their encouragement of my work and for widening my academic horizon. I also wish to thank the editors for their encouragement and for their helpful comments and
feedback.

Figure 13.1: Workshop participants discussing the frictions in timings they see between uses of the River Gudenåen. Jensen, M. (2022)

stories about mussels, birds, trees, and stream vegetation that have either been lost or increased in size within the river system.

Across these stories, the swan occurs once more. In one group conversation a landowner notes how the sight of swans and their cygnets by the river used to be a seasonal marker of the summer season for him. They are now gone, as previously dry areas are flooded. The landowner continues by saying:

> Now there is no room for the swans. They sit up on the trail with their cygnets and then people come running and cycling. Each time, the swans have to move and go into the water so people can pass, and then they go up again. This disturbance is not good for the swan.

I am struck by this loss of seasonal markers, but also by the intermingling of rhythms on just one hiking trail. I return to the drawings of participants' years and look for these rhythms. I realise that each participant's drawing consists of multiple rhythms, multiple seasonalities, multiple activities. No one's drawing is the same as another's. While at first sight it seemed like each person, each species, adhered to one specific rhythm, pattern or season, I instead find that people are navigating in several.

I decide to look further into the case of the feral swan and simply search online for 'swan' and 'Gudenåen'. I instantly stumble upon two Danish articles, both from 2018 (1, 2). The first is titled: "Aggressive swan attacked kayaker: overturned in the Gudenåen" (1), while the other is titled: "Kayaker attacked by swan" (2). They both explain frightening encounters between an "aggressive" swan and "peaceful" kayakers (Figure 13.2). But while the first article is short and mainly focuses on the aggressive swan, not the reason for the aggression, the latter includes a more complex story. In it, a biologist from the Danish association "DOF Birdlife" has been interviewed. He wants the municipality to put up a sign, where recreational users of the River Gudenåen are warned about swans in their breeding season. But within the article, there is one remark from the biologist that, for me, stands out as puzzling:

> He explains that swan eggs usually hatch from May until Constitution Day, which falls on Tuesday [5th of June]. However, due to the cold winter, the swans have started breeding late this year (2).

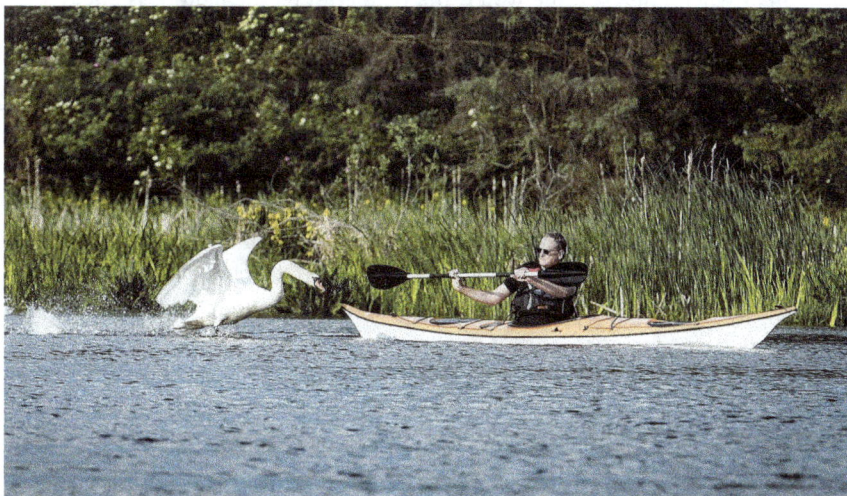

Figure 13.2: Picture from the article of the feral swan. Ballund, M. (2018)

The river system is changing and so are the known seasonal patterns of humans, animals and plants living by, in and with the river. This has implications for how animals such as the swan coordinates with the rivers rhythms, but also how human activities, such as the kayaker's boating season, are now becoming out of sync with the rivers rhythms. For me, this is an interesting example of a clash of times; the kayakers recreation bound to the Gregorian calendar on one hand, and the swan's rhythms, attuned to the environment in which it nests, on the other hand.

I return to the phrase from the group conversation about the feral swan: *"yes, we are not good friends with it"*, which was uttered by a local kayaker. Looking back at her drawing of the year, I see a drawing of the 'boating season' and realise that her calendar might be the same as that of the kayaker in the article. I find the recording of the group conversation in which the kayaker presents her year for the other group members, by saying that:

> The flag hoisting ceremony kicks off the boating year (. . .) that means that our interest lies within the summer, it is the temperature, it is the evenings, as we often paddle in the evenings and the length of the day means that we get more experiences on the water.

Another clash of times appears here for me too. While the kayaker is adhering to a specific, static date (the flag hoisting ceremony on the 2nd of April) that determines the beginning and end of the boating season, there is also something else going on. Within the boating season it is also a matter of being attuned to the environment when one is on the water, the temperature, the light; it is about sensing the season. As another group member remarked in the same conversation:

> It's the wind and weather that determines when locals go out in their boats. And more than anyone else, it is tourists that sail according to specific dates, whereas if you live out there you can say, 'well, it's raining on Monday, so I can wait until Thursday'.

The plot thickens. It seems to me that what the group member is implying is that locals are more temporally flexible as they are more attuned to the environment in which they are situated. This stands in contrasts to tourists, who might adhere to more static seasonalities bound to Gregorian calendar time. This is further supplemented by the fact that tourists have limited time on the river; limited temporal flexibility in their often pre-planned holiday schedules.

Returning one last time to the Danish article on the feral swan, I find a link to a different article from the BBC (3). It tells the story of a man who drowned as he was attacked by a swan. In the article, I find the following sentence:

> Two years later, there are still calls for it (RED: the swan) to be removed from the river, as the seasonal attacks go on. (2)

It seems to me that looking at river systems through the lens of a swan, and it's seasonal attacks, can open up for the complexity of reality. One animal can tell the story of changing seasons and rhythms, but it also tells a broader story of mismatches and clashes between times. It is in the encounters, sometimes the frightening ones, that time seems to be unravelled.

The author

Miriam Jensen is a PhD Candidate at the Department of Planning, Aalborg University. Her research interests lie within the temporalities of deliberative planning with a particular focus on temporal conflicts and mismatches between both human and more-than-human actors. Her PhD project investigates what role time and temporalities played in the conflicts and deliberative malfunctions that occurred within the intermunicipal planning process for the Danish river landscape of Gudenåen.

References

1.   Ballund, M. (2018). Svane angreb [Photograph]. Tv2 Østjylland: https://www.tv2ostjylland.dk/silkeborg/aggressiv-svane-angreb-kajakroer-vaeltede-omkuld-i-gudenaen
2.   Troelsen, S.B. "Aggressiv svane angreb kajakroer: Væltede omkuld i Gudenåen", *Tv2 Østjylland*, June 2, 2018.
3.   Jensen, M. & S. B. Troelsen. "Kajakroer angrebet af svane", *Tv2*, June 4, 2018.
4.   Nasaw, D. & T. Geoghegan. 'Who, What, Why: How dangerous are swans?', *BBC*, April 17, 2012.
5.   Jensen, M. (2022). Picture of group discussion in workshop [Photograph].

Tracy Kendall
14 Crimson Calamity

Introduction

Crimson Calamity is written from an individual Pohutukawa tree's perspective. The evergreen Pohutukawa, a member of the Myrtle Family, (Metrosideros excelsa) is a protected native tree of New Zealand. To the New Zealand people, the Pohutukawa tree is of particular significance in summertime, when its brilliant red flowers announce that the summer season and long-awaited Christmas holiday is imminent. This particular tree occupies a prominent position at Waitete Bay, where I live, and has become iconic. I wrote this piece as part of a local writers group, where we took up the theme of changing seasonality.

Figure 14.1: The Crimson Calamity tree at Waitete Bay, Coromandel, New Zealand. Left: tree in post-cyclonic flood over bridge, in January 2018 (Photo by: Deb Clark). Right: tree in January 2015 (Photo by: Peter Kendall).

I found myself here quite by chance. Blown by the whim of a gentle sea breeze I landed on the dry bank above the beach. My gaze is westerly out to sea at Waitete Bay on the Coromandel Peninsula, in New Zealand's North Island. It is here that I grew from a seed, into a sapling, then to a mature Pohutukawa tree Figure 14.1. My *iwi*[1] are all around me with many generations growing nearby.

---

1 *Iwi*: extended kinship group, tribe, nation, people, nationality, race – often refers to a large group of people descended from a common ancestor and associated with a distinct territory. (https://maoridictionary.co.nz/).

My adventurous roots are exposed, and frequently clambered upon by small children. My wood is dense and strong, shaped by generations of my forefathers to withstand wind damage and drought, even in the toughest of times. I'm tasty to introduced pests such as the Australian opossum and need to be protected from their hungry browsing. My light green leaves are velvet soft when young and mature to a tough darker green with a waxy finish. Although I am leafy green throughout the seasons, over time I shed my twigs in the wind, allowing my boughs to become long and slender. But it is my joyful red brush blossoms in summertime that earn me the affectionate title of the 'New Zealand Christmas tree.'

I've seen generations of people come and go from where I stand, like a guard, at the head of a humble, white picketed bridge. I observed the turn of a new century, and then another, in the face of relentless seasonal variability, the hammering of all weathers. The bank underneath me is dry and sandy, just as I like it. But the seasons are changing with the years in a way that is damaging and disturbing for me. I am a dynamic seasonal and cultural symbol at Waitete Bay on the Coromandel. My crimson flowering in the warmer months signal to the people in the Bay the start of the antipodean summer. But the patterns of summer weather are changing. More frequent sub-tropical depressions, combined with king tides, heavy rain and damaging winds are eroding my ability to stay upright on the bank. What will become of me?

I am sacred to the Māori people of Aotearoa and proudly represent a prominent place in New Zealand's indigenous Māori mythology. My flowers are symbolic of the blood shed by the Māori warrior Tawhaki in his endeavours to find help to avenge his father's death. Since this time, I've seen the waves of human colonisation, starting with the Māori eating shellfish in the shade of my branches, leaving their discards in middens sequestered in the banks nearby. Then came more waves of people, a kaleidoscope of cultures leaving chip packets, ice cream wrappers, and beer bottles among my roots. Now, as the four seasons lose their clarity, sliding and colliding into one another, without marked definition, the seasonal calendar is becoming blurred. Rising sea levels and storm surges have the potential to impact me. I may become a 'tree of the past,' to be treasured only in Māori legends.

I started out proudly, strong, true to form, and straight. Native birds, Tuis, Kaka, and Bellbirds stop to sip from my shallow bowls of nectar. I provide a habitat for the birds who nest in my hollows and feast on insects who take refuge in my gnarly bark. Bees are attracted to my fragrant nectar, from which creamy white honey can be made, by those who wish to profit. The *Bach*[2] owners in the houses above look down and admire my brilliant summer flowers, that scatter

---

2 *Bach*: Pronounced batch is a term Kiwis commonly refer to as a holiday home.

like fine red ribbons on the dusty gravel road in January, the New Zealand summer. Abandoned towels, sandals, car keys and kayaks are placed next to my trunk, as swimmers race into the surf. Sometimes people forget their belongings and I nurse a lost shoe, or sunhat for months. Older folk sit, seeking the respite of my boughs, grateful for the shade in these increasingly hot summer months. One year two defacing notices were impaled on my trunk that say: *"No parking here"* and *"boat ramp."* The angle of these notices gradually becomes tilted at 45 degrees over the years, a testament to my lolling bend.

In all seasons I am photographed. My sepia picture is featured by a Nikon NZ-Iconic Futures Exhibition, highlighting climate change, and sold to many for big money to grace their homes. My celebrated species is featured on New Zealand Christmas cards as a viable and antipodean alternative to the irrelevance of European holly and snow filled scenes. Proudly displaying my crimson cloak, I am the true meaning of a New Zealand Christmas 'down-under', where the locals take a picnic to the beach on Christmas day and sit under my twisty branches. They've even written songs about my genus *'Christmas on the beach'* (1): *"Christmas on the beach / pack your Christmas hamper / we're going to have a feast / underneath the old Pohutukawa tree / Christmas on the beach."* The fresh-faced school children sing in school assemblies, prior to the long summer break. But what will happen to the authenticity of our unique New Zealand Christmas if my species becomes compromised and loses our place on the coast? What would a true 'Kiwi' Christmas be without the Pohutukawa trees?

I am remembered not only at Christmas time. In shops all year round, the Pohutukawa species is depicted on placemats, curtain fabric, t-towels, and t-shirts for sale, all making their way to foreign destinations in tourists' suitcases, to be handed over as *Kiwiana*[3] to unwitting recipients. They coo and marvel at the brilliant red flowers.

"No way," they say, "a tree with red flowers, who would have thought?"

Here at Waitete Bay I am not a touristy gimmick from a t-towel, but an icon, a living rock-star tree, admired and revered by the homeowners who celebrate my style and grace. Little by little, year by year, I am leaning closer to the land that supports me. The ground beneath me is giving way, undermined by the tides, post sub-tropical events and increasing La Nina weather patterns. The Pacific Ocean has forever cycled between El Nino and La Nina, but scientists suggest that climate change is "weighing the dice toward La Nina" (2). When will the nodding heads react and rise to implement the changes needed to ensure my species, the

---

3 *Kiwiana* refers to collectable objects, ornaments, etc, esp. dating from the 1950s or 1960s, relating to the history or popular culture of New Zealand.

Pohutukawa, does not become a photographic memory, a remnant of the past? I am around 150 years old, I could and should live for several hundred years, even as many as a thousand years. This remarkable statistic is in jeopardy, and I may become a hapless victim of climate change.

The locals are increasingly fearful for the precarious way I loll and lean towards the road. There is talk of me being propped up, so that I will not fall and fail with these too hot summers, rising seas and increasing occurrences of post cyclonic weather, that may all contribute to my early demise.

"Shall we tie her up," one local suggests,

"Or stake her," says another?

They shake their heads perplexed, and do not seem to have the answers. The wagging heads make much noise, but where is their action?

"Remember the Pohutukawa," their great-great-grandfathers will say to each other, scratching their grey heads sagely?

"Why didn't we act sooner, how could we be so foolish?"

On the banks of Torehina Bay adjacent to my beach at Waitete, there is a leafy murmur of hope. The kaitiaki[4] of the surrounding area have thrown my species a lifeline, a korowai[5] of tree hugging love over the grassy bank. The nodding heads, both young and old, have planted a selection of sapling trees. The kaitiaki are nurturing these trees, which include Pohutukawa, to regenerate and establish the chance of new life, who hold wisdom in their young boughs. While I may fall and fail, become a woody skeleton on the beach, others may rise and thrive. This brings me hope. They say change rests with these smarter thinking animals, the humans. I'm in their hands, but will they act, and think like a tree?

The author

Tracy has a Bachelor of Arts in Education and English. She is a Teacher and Speech Language Therapist who worked in her private practice for 35 years in Auckland, New Zealand. Now she works remotely at Waitete Bay on the Coromandel where she and husband Peter have owned a beach house for 30 years. Tracy loves creative writing, gardening, hiking, Pilates, reading, and playing the piano. Tracy and Peter have three adult children, and several grandchildren.

---

4 *Kaitiaki* (Te Reo (Māori)): a guardian or trustee, typically of an environmental area or resource.
5 *Korowai* (Te Reo (Māori) for cloak): a traditional Maori cloak, decorated with tassels made from the flax plant.

References

1. Christmas At the Beach song: © Arif Usmani, 1989, kiwi kidsongs. (https://www.last.fm/music/Kiwi+Kidsongs/_/Christmas+On+The+Beach).
2. Armour, K. & D. Battisti. "Climate change seems to be favouring La Nina events." *Futurity*. 2022. (https://www.futurity.org/climate-change-la-nina-2809092-2/).
3. McKim, L. *Climate Change Impacts and Implications for New Zealand to 2100: A systematic review of recent research*. New Zealand Climate Change Research Institute, Victoria University of Wellington. Auckland: New Zealand, 2016. (https://niwa.co.nz/sites/niwa.co.nz/files/RA4-Review-of-recent-research.pdf).
4. Cronin, K., B. Doody, & A. Greenaway. 'Degrees of possibility': Igniting social knowledge around climate change: Workshop Report. Wellington: New Zealand, 2011. (https://www.academia.edu/1420090/Degrees_of_possiblity_Igniting_social_knowledge_around_climate_change_Workshop_Report).
5. NIWA. The impact of El Niño and La Niña on New Zealand's climate. Auckland: NIWA, n.d. (https://niwa.co.nz/climate/information-and-resources/elnino/elnino-impacts-on-newzealand).
6. NIWA. Seasonal Climate Outlook. Auckland: NIWA, n.d. (https://niwa.co.nz/climate/seasonal-climate-outlook)
7. NIWA. NZ's warmest and wettest winter on record. Auckland: NIWA, 2021. (https://niwa.co.nz/news/its-the-warmest-winter-on-record-again).
8. Tāne's Tree Trust. Website: https://www.tanestrees.org.nz/.
9. Project Crimson. Website: https://projectcrimson.org.nz/.

Part III Creativity and the arts

James Allan Muir

15 Tilting the frame: How the seasonal characteristics of light informs image

As a filmmaker my passion is to weave stories from light. I describe my craft as light chasing, I am a hunter of illumination and shadow. Looking for the fleeting interplay of light and darkness that speaks to the human condition. Knowing and understanding light is essential to this pursuit and it is in the seasonal language of light that I can find rhythm and code that guide my image making. Living in New Zealand this seasonal change can be acute. This is a place to experience light at its extremes.

Knowing light is a form of physics. The foundation of any image is made of light and its physical properties. Anyone who has learnt photography understands that the techniques to control light form the basis of required learning. Perhaps the greatest influence on changing light is our seasonal shift. Seasonal changes are caused by the earth tilting toward and away from the sun as it travels each solar orbit. The 23.5-degree tilt produces seasonal characteristics in the angle and quality of light as determined by the lower and higher incidences of the sun's zenith. These seasonal fluxes are most accentuated in the regions of the northern and southern hemispheres that extend from 23.5° latitude to 66.5° latitude. In these temperate regions, nature exhibits seasons which many define simply as, spring, summer, autumn and winter.

New Zealand has unique light characteristics because of its location in the temperate zone of the southern hemisphere with distinctive seasonal changes due to its latitude and landform. Clear air and dramatically variable landscapes enhance the characteristics of light in seasonal displays that have become widely appreciated by image makers all over the world.

For any image maker, be they painter, photographer, or filmmaker, all animate and inanimate character is shaped by light. Relationships to the viewer, relationships between characters and surroundings, are all affected by light. The visual characteristics of an image contain volumes of constructed meaning from the very angle and intensity of light contained. Through the lens we can manipulate the characteristics of light[1] and thus the meaning of image, however the origin is natural light, and this

---

1 Manipulation is generally technical adjustments such as aperture, shutter speed, white balance, and movement. Plus, this can include post production manipulation such as colour grading and graphics.

Acknowledgements: I would like to acknowledge everyone who has supported and been involved in the creation of the Calendars Project. In particular Scott Bremer and Paul Schneider as well as my partner Alison Titulaer and everyone who has kindly allowed me into their lives to film.

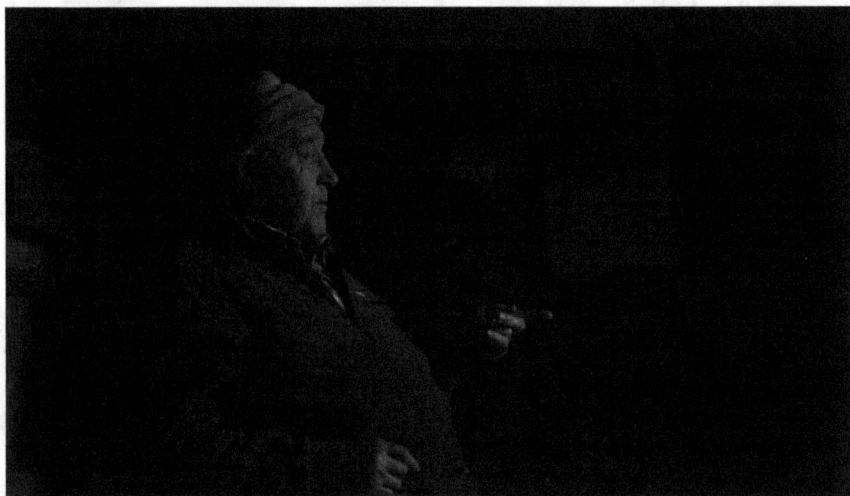

Figure 15.1: Winter in the Shearing Shed [Still from the upcoming film 'Seasons'] (Photo by: James Muir).

natural light is seasonally representative of the tilting earth. Wherever we are and whatever we are framing, whether we like it or not, our lens is tilted, and within this tilting frame are attached the visual characteristics of seasonal stories which situate our images through the quality, angle, and colour of light (See e.g., Figure 15.1).

How can light convey emotion? After all, it's just a bunch of particles and waves that don't appear to transmit any emotional information whatsoever. However, humans have managed to infuse some of their lush, sappy, scrumptious feelings into an otherwise omnipresent natural and indifferent phenomenon, giving all kinds of meaning to different lighting that we can use in our imagery. Light has come to play such an important role in how we tell stories and convey meaning through those stories that there now exists a highly complex and dynamic opus of meaning and emotional association that we can convey through how we light an image. A basic example of this can be seen in Figure 15.2. Here I have constructed a shot using natural light that gives the sense of fragility and even fear by subduing the character with green tones and backlighting at a low angle. This shot was actually taken in summer, but the framing, colour and light angle suggests a wintery birth is imminent.

The physical properties of light waves, their reflection and absorbance are manifest to our light sensing organs. However, the experience of light is transformed by our human perspective, our visual identity shaped by cultural cues which guide our conception of the world around us. Seasons hold such strong and indelible markers of time and place, drawing on intrinsic natural instincts for survival as well as more nuanced instincts for communication through storytelling, where light is metaphor.

Figure 15.2: Natural birth [Still from the upcoming film 'Seasons'] (Photo by: James Muir).

In New Zealand our image makers often use the low angle of winter light to portray the sense of isolation and otherworldliness of these islands. The light is cold, clear, grim, and short lasting. There is a melancholy that permeates art from these shores and the winter light gives context to the stories of colonisation and isolation that are deeply embedded in our psyche.

Figure 15.3: The colour of summer [Still from the upcoming film 'Seasons'] (Photo by: James Muir).

Through our shared knowledge and learned experiences we have developed an intrinsic set of light cues that relate to the seasonal rhythm through emotional context.

That rhythm becomes acutely important when editing images. Editing is the interface where we review images and there is a huge amount of decision making that solely focuses on the emotive context. The emotional journey guides our story and when constructed well, the seasons within a character will reflect the seasons without. This plays out in our lives every day, as the sun, the moon, weather, and temperature can all gently dictate our emotional state. Light is the main driving force that has the power to create emotion in four different and distinct ways: contrast, quality, colour, and direction.

Seasonal light, and indeed even the single diurnal cycle, offers light angles, quality, colour and direction enough to influence our experience of the character's journey that we project in our visual stories. Light angle can manipulate the context and emanation of an image; low key lighting with a lot of contrast is great for communicating fear, anxiety, distrust, and evilness, while high key lighting with little contrast is great for communicating happiness, peacefulness, joy, and contentment. Lighting is also used to portray different emotional states of a character. A wide prime lens, preferred by cinematographers, is ideal for picking up low contrast. If you direct your light to create less shadows, your subject will appear neutral and nonthreatening, but the more you adjust it to create shadows, the more your subject will appear dubious, untrustworthy, scary, or unbalanced.

Natural light conditions change over the course of the year both with respect to spectrum, intensity, and photoperiod. Due to variation in solar elevation angle, atmospheric water vapour content, and ozone column thickness, photon ratios change according to the season. The maximum solar incidence angle is 90°, at which point the Sun is directly over a target area which results in a lower incident area, thus a higher intensity. In summer the high zenith means that the light is projected downward illuminating the frame from angles which create a strong differential between light and dark spaces (high-key lighting). Summer light is bold, harsh, and bright. The shadows are dark and concealing. Summer is not subtle, the quality of light is brazen and direct, the colour is yellow and gold (Figure 15.3). Summer light makes heat which brings haze and dust, heated air disturbs the clear lines and summer images become an expression of maturity, lust, and adventure. Yet the summer light both conceals and reveals; rendering the characterisation of image as raw and powerful, a gratuitous display that can be powerfully memorable for its fun, its intensity, and its potential to go horribly wrong.

At a lower angle of incidence, solar radiation lands on a larger area, resulting in more diffuse light conditions and a lower intensity on the surface. The angle of light refracts in the camera's glass, sending off dancing spheres of light or bokeh across the frame, the difference between light and dark spaces is less defined. This (low-key) winter light is more characterised by grey, diffuse light and with cool silver edges, sometimes the winter light has a crisp quality because of the clear air. Longer wavelengths are accentuated as they travel through leafless trees or across ocean plains. Back lighting subjects using low angles helps give an even tone with a dreamlike appearance. In winter light we can see more of a character, feel more intimate and connected through the need for closeness and the ability to see into shadow Figure 15.4.

Figure 15.4: Matarangi beach in summer and winter [Still from the upcoming film 'Seasons'] (Photo by: James Muir).

Over the course of the day the solar elevation angle has further implications on light quality as it influences the preferential diffusion of different wavelengths. The phenomenon of Rayleigh scattering through which light is scattered by atmospheric molecules has a great effect on light in images. Rayleigh scattering more effectively deflects short wavelengths towards the Earth at high solar elevations, giving the sky its blue appearance during the day. This phenomenon also explains the dominance of red during sunset and sunrise as the lower solar elevation angle results in a longer path which, combined with Rayleigh scattering, results in more deflection of blue wavelengths away from the surface.

The diurnal variation in angle of incidence adds another dimension to how light conveys meaning and we can use the morning and evening light to capture images similar to the quality of light experienced throughout the winter season. Hence many image makers choose to capture their scenes in the 'Golden Hour' which is the time for low-key lighting.

The nuance of meaning extolled from light in image is extensive and at times unexplainable. I have only touched briefly on the basic ideas that shape how we use light to convey meaning and how that use of light is shaped by our experience of seasons. The camera captures light, but the mind interprets it. To experience the flux of seasons is to experience the breadth and depth of humanity's emotional state. The earth tilts and we tilt with it leaning into our stories with a yearning for the consistent reflection and projection of the human state.

Now we are confronted by a phenomenon which is disrupting our ability to read light. Our seasons are changing and our images will change with them. How much longer can we reliably associate imagery of seasons with the seasons themselves? The context is being lost and the codified meanings embedded in our cultures are becoming muddled. Yet imagery and story will assist us to adjust. We are required to learn new narratives and to implement new paradigms that will ensure survival. That light chasing instinct which drags me out of bed at 5am to spend hours in the cold and semi-dark filming the mist rising off rivers, listening to the calls of animals echoing through the land, welcoming a silver dawn. That instinct is the investigation of light that keeps us in tune with seasons. Because the seasons are still there and will always be there as long as the earth is tilting.

Being a cinematographer (light chaser) is a challenge because the camera does not adjust for contrast as smoothly as the human eye. So, we must choose our light carefully. We draw on seasonal light as a metaphor and emotional guide to create images that are effective at conveying meaning. Each frame is tilted by the seasons, as the physicality of light and our experience of it weaves meaning into our lives during our circumnavigation of the sun, over and over again.

The author

James Muir lives in Matarangi, New Zealand. He is an award-winning Director/DoP/Editor and natural history cinematographer. Before becoming a filmmaker, James was a biologist specialising in behavioural ecology and conservation. He has a master's degree in science communication. James's award winning films are available to view on Vimeo and include: River Dog, Love in a Little Town, Antarctic Waters, Mauri o te Kauri and Pigman.

Eamon O'Kane

16 The nature of art: Working with changing seasonalities

I have been a practicing artist working with painting, drawing, sculpture, installation, photography, animation, and video for the last 30 years. I am Professor of visual art at the University of Bergen and have been teaching alongside my artistic practice for over 25 years. In this text I will examine how seasonality is a recurrent theme that has inspired and shaped my artwork.

The house I grew up in, Cavanacor House, is in the northwest of Ireland and is surrounded by ten acres of garden and forest, and the estate would have been much more extensive in its heyday. These surroundings were a huge influence on me as a child and the rhythms of the seasons affected me greatly.

Whilst preparing my portfolio for entering the art academy, I had been very influenced by Claude Monet's studies of time in his paintings of Rouen cathedral, the haystacks, and his garden. I made several painting series which developed my interest in the changing seasons and transitions from day to night during the first year at the art academy. In my paintings 'The Studio in the Woods', begun in 2003, I explored the desire to find the perfect space in which to work creatively whilst also acknowledging that the perfect space is unattainable. The works are based on real buildings, but they become sort of a fantasy or occupy a liminal space between the fantastic and the real. There is also the undercutting idea that they're not completely ideal. The work explores that myth of the artist working in creative isolation, which I also worked with in 'Overlook', a project based on Stanley Kubrick's film 'The Shining'. Jack Nicholson's character thinks that all he needs is to get away from it all to write, but he doesn't realise that it's going to drive him mad. I painted from stills taken from the film which depict the Overlook hotel in the autumn and winter, and I extrapolated them into fifty-two small paintings, one for each week of the year. The paintings depicted spring, summer, autumn, and winter, and reflected the sequences in the film where the entropy of the descent into the darkest snow blizzard is echoed by the main protagonist's descent into madness.

Seasonally uncanny: The panorama and the shopping centre

As a student in Dublin and later Belfast, I made numerous large scale panorama paintings, into which I tried to incorporate a sense of seasonality. My interest in the 19th century phenomenon of the panorama grew out of experiencing the immersion of standing in front of Monet's panorama paintings of his garden at Giverny, and his panoramas have continued to be a fascination throughout my art career. For a project entitled 'Panorama: I Like Shopping Centres and Shopping Centres Like Me' at an art centre outside Dublin in 2006, I chose to mix the phenomenon of the panorama with another 19th century construction, that of the 'Kaiser Panorama' (Figure 16.1). The panorama is about looking from the centre out whereas the Kaiser panorama is about looking from the circumference in. The panorama is an experience of something very large scale and the Kaiser panorama is an experience of viewing through lenses to something quite small scale. For me, there was a paradox in hybridising the two. I wanted to present a panorama of the area to the people living there, using the shopping centre and other buildings. Victor Gruen, who invented the shopping mall, was an émigré who pre-war went to America via England. He envisaged the shopping mall as a utopia, turning the arcade or the street inwards so one is surrounded by all the shops, and he wanted it to form communities. By creating an interior space where people could go from shop to shop without experiencing the weather outside, Gruen created a seasonless space. A space where people could shop uninterrupted by the elements and the outside context. Paradoxically, the internal space of the shopping centre developed into a destination for seasonal activity where people go to buy their Christmas shopping, their Easter eggs, or their summer holiday clothes.

The context for the first iteration of this piece was Blanchardstown, which was a working-class suburb of Dublin, a type of satellite town with the largest shopping centre in Ireland at the time. It was shown in Dublin in the autumn and into the winter, the second iteration was shown in London in the summer, and the third in Paris in the early spring. In all three versions I incorporated influence from the outside space and the climatic conditions in the artwork. Trees with leaves, trees without. In Paris this was taken to a new level with the interaction between the existing trees coming into bloom and the painted tree silhouettes. These tree silhouettes pointed back to the large charcoal wall drawings that I did on the gallery walls in the art centre in Dublin, one of which could be seen shedding its leaves (which were depicted in the drawing) in real time through the window directly outside the gallery. I have continued with this approach in other exhibitions and am interested in drawing attention to seasonality by bringing them into these public spaces through

Figure 16.1: Panorama: I like shopping centres and shopping centres like me, 2006–2009 Dublin, London, Paris. Wooden panels, door lenses, sandbags, paintings and models. Variable dimensions with 30 metre x 2.5 m painting on plywood.
Source: Eamon O'Kane, *Panorama: I like shopping centres and shopping centres like me*, 2006–2009 Dublin, London, Paris. Photography by Eamon O'Kane.

drawing and animation so that the audiences can experience a type of seasonal uncanny.

And time begins again: Inside and outside the greenhouse

In 2009 my family and I took over a bankrupt plant nursey complex just outside Odense, Denmark. Here I embarked on a site-specific project to explore humankind's fragile relationship with and dependence on the natural world. For ten years I documented the derelict plant nursery before it was finally demolished and returned to nature. During this process I traced and retraced my steps around the complex over and over, reflecting on the changes over time. The location could be seen as a place in decay but also as the beginning of a transformation back to nature. I noticed the greenhouse seasonalities in relation to the contrast between the outside seasonalities and how a greenhouse can change rhythms and interact with the outside. These contrasts were especially evident because of the complex becoming more and more derelict, and the flora and fauna interacting with the spaces in unplanned ways.

Figure 16.2: Where There Are People There Are Things and Greenhouse Archive, 2009–2019. Mixed media installation, photographs and video.
Source: ane, *Where There Are People There Are Things* and *Greenhouse Archive*, 2009–2019. Photography by Eamon O'Kane.

Gradually I built up an archive of thousands of photographs and many hours of footage of the interiors and exteriors of the greenhouses (Figure 16.2). The photographs have been displayed on light boxes made from recycled and adapted light components used in the nursery and installed on sculptural structures echoing the spaces in the nursery. They have also been used in video and sound installation detailing aspects of this very particular place and the seasonal changes occurring across the years that were documented. The context of the derelict greenhouse complex, past and present, is useful in considering seasons as polyrhythmic. The 'natural' rhythms of the flora and fauna engaged with rhythms occurring within the semi derelict greenhouses creating hybrid intersections of seasonality. For example, a branch from an outside apple tree grew through into the greenhouse and produced apples of a much larger size which ripened much earlier than the apples on the outside, but which were tasteless compared to their smaller 'natural' counterparts. Through these photographs and videos, I was looking into the encounters between different seasons occurring concurrently inside the greenhouse and outside, and exploring how they clash or sync, and how animals and plants adapt to these sometimes-contradictory environments and the seasons of nature regenerating in unexpected ways.

Walking and drawing: Trees and a changing seasonality

When the Covid pandemic lockdown began in March 2020, I started taking daily walks with my wife and two sons near our house, and I always brought my camera so I could photograph the trees in the area. I was able to continue teaching in Bergen using Zoom and I set myself the task of making one tree ink drawing per day based on the photographs I was taking. The trees in a way became a marker of time for me and as they accumulated, I was able to comprehend the passage of time but also my place in the world, which had previously been governed by other interactions with the society. One of these drawings, a cherry tree in blossom, was influenced by van Gogh's paintings The Pink Peach Tree (1888) and The Flowering Orchard (1888). Vincent van Gogh had a big influence on me in the years leading up to applying for art college, especially his paintings of chairs, his bedroom, and the almond blossom. It is well known that he was influenced by Japanese prints, and he may have known Hokusai's depiction of cherry blossom branches in the 1833 woodblock Bullfinch and Weeping Cherry.

The architect Frank Lloyd Wright was also hugely influenced by Japanese culture. He visited Japan on several occasions and was a big collector of Japanese prints. Wright was also keenly aware of the rhythms of the natural world. Back in 2008, I made the painting Falling Water Seasons Remix of Wright's iconic building whilst on a residency at the Irish Cultural Centre in Paris (Figure 16.3). In the painting I was attempting to depict a world out of sync, exploring notions of utopia and dystopia, and how humanity has disrupted the natural equilibrium and brought the planet to the brink of dystopian chaos. The seasons are out of balance, and the painting attempts to present this imbalance by depicting all four seasons in one painting. Global warming has caused changes in climate patterns and atmospheric circulation, both of which disrupt the natural seasonal calendar that we have always lived by. Trees sprout earlier, and flowers appear weeks earlier than usual. Spring comes earlier and gets shorter every year. These disturbances affect wildlife, which is dependent on a series of interconnected events for survival. I have noticed these changes at our home in Denmark where we now often see snow falling in autumn while some plants are still bright green whilst others are shedding leaves in autumnal colours.

In my exhibition Seasons in 2021, the drawings, the paintings, the wood blocks, and actual trees all came together. I presented a new series of sculptures with architectural models and wooden structures. Large trees that needed to be removed during the process of demolishing the greenhouses were placed in the middle of the gallery space, and wooden blocks and sticks were systematically arranged on the floor. The wooden blocks were inspired by the educationalist Friedrich Frö-

Figure 16.3: Falling Water Seasons Remix (painted whilst listening to In Utero by Nirvana), 2008. Oil on canvas 223 x 274 cm.
Source: Eamon O'Kane: Falling Water Seasons Remix (painted whilst listening to In Utero by Nirvana), 2008. Oil on canvas, 223 x 274 cm. Photography by Eamon O'Kane.

bel's building sets for children. Fröbel's ideas about block constructions as part of the child's natural development have inspired the rapidly changing man-made landscapes that appear in my animations which show seasons out of sync. The paintings in the exhibition depicted modernist buildings at different times of the year, Casa Bo Bardi in winter, The Farnsworth house in autumn, Villa Mairea in summer and Tempe à Pailla in spring. The sculptural elements in the exhibition interacted with the paintings and drawings on the walls through their projection of shadows and colour from the plexiglass panels inserted into the large wooden screens. This also pointed to the world outside the gallery and the passing of time.

My artworks are shaped by contemporary culture and society, and the place or site in which they originated. Reality exists in the processes that attempt to make them happen. The modernist period in architecture and design was an interesting period in that respect in that so many people attempted to achieve different types of utopias and quite often failed nobly in the process. I often use colour (or the lack of it) to heighten certain emotional states in the paintings and to, in turn, point to seasonal changes and time passing. In my paintings I am interested in setting a stage for something to happen. Fields like science, architecture or engineering can have a much bigger impact on society than artworks. I see artistic practice as one viewpoint from which to look at the longer-lasting consequences of emerging technological environments, by (to coin Marshal McLuhan's term) creating 'anti-environments' or ruptures for critical reflection. Much of my artwork might be understood in relation to contemporary society and the innovations that have transformed humankind's place in the natural world. Donna Haraway (1) says that "stories are much bigger than ideologies, in that is our hope". In the artworks where I highlight the topic of changing seasonality, there is a focus on drawing attention to how our actions as humans are causing changes to the environment and hopefully the viewers will reflect on this and their own relation to the themes. I see my artworks as open-ended stories and I recognise them as objects with their own agency and potential to point towards a future where imagination and creativity can be a driving force for ecological care and empathy.

The author

Eamon O'Kane (born 1974, Belfast, Northern Ireland) explores the ideological tropes and visual forms of modernist architecture in his paintings and immersive sculptural installations. He is Professor of Painting at the Art Academy, University of Bergen and lives and works in Norway and Denmark.
He received his B.A. in the History of Art and Fine Art at the National College of Art and Design in Dublin, Ireland in 1996 and went on to earn his M.F.A. at the University of Ulster, Belfast in 1998 and later an additional M.F.A. in Design Technology at Parsons School of Design, New York in 2001. He has had over 80 solo exhibitions internationally, and his work is held in the public collections of Burda Museum, Baden Baden, Germany; Lentos Art Museum, Linz, Austria; Museum of Fine Arts, Brest, France; and The Arts Council Collection, Ireland. He is the recipient of grants from Culture Ireland, the Norwegian Arts Council, the EV+A Biennial Award, a Fulbright Award, the Pollock Krasner Foundation Award, and the Tony O'Malley Art Award. His monographs include Oneriric Nature (University of Bergen, 2022); And Time Begins Again (University of Bergen, 2018); Hybrids (Academy of Art and Design, Norway, 2013); Eamon O'Kane: and Case Histories (ArtSway and Rugby Art Museum, UK, 2009).

Reference

1. Haraway, D. J. *The companion species manifesto: Dogs, people, and significant otherness.* Chicago: Prickly Paradigm Press, 2003.

Magnhild Øen Nordahl

17 Simulating seasons in virtual reality

Two Rocks do Not Make a Duck is a sculpture and Virtual Reality (VR) artwork made by the artists Cameron MacLeod and Magnhild Øen Nordahl. It was first shown at the Munch Museum in Oslo and will later be presented at the Arboretum in Bergen in connection to an art exhibition and research symposium on seasonality (Figure 17.1). When a person puts on the VR headset, they will see a simulation of the landscape outside the space where the artwork is exhibited. In Oslo, the river, the fjord and other geographical landmarks were there, but no buildings or objects made by humans (Figure 17.2). A simulated nature-version of the cityscape remained. In Bergen the scene will be recreated to immerse the users in a virtual version of the Aboretum gardens. The user can move through this simulated landscape by moving around in the space where the piece is shown, with the walls of that physical space functioning as movement boundaries also in the virtual world. By lifting and moving around rock-shaped sculptures the user can experience changes in the virtual environment, such as different weather conditions, different times of day and times of year. We called the rocks the weather-rock, the day-rock, and the year-rock. In this text I will describe parts of the process, challenges and some of the technological affordances and limitations in developing a virtual landscape where seasonal changes occur.

We realized early on that to make a virtual environment which *looks* real is something quite different than trying to simulate the complex natural world in a scientifically accurate way. Our knowledge, budget, time, and the point of view from where the user was standing limited what was possible and meaningful to simulate. We had to simplify, to make abstractions, to choose which environmental events to simulate, and to build a whole from those parts with the added building blocks and tools provided by the VR technology.

The exercise of trying to imitate something made us look closer at and learn about what we were imitating. First, we had to think through how the environment changes during a year, what these changes look like, and which changes were possible to simulate. We became aware of things we had not thought of before, such as how the sun makes an analemma (a figure eight shape) on the sky, when observed regularly at the same time of day from the same location. I realized that I knew very little about how the night sky changes throughout the year, and the developers who were tasked with simulating all these things were surprised at how irregular and complex tidal variations are. We were able to include some of these intricate movements and changes in the simulation for free, by using existing software functionality and plugins. Others required more work.

The environment in the scene would change according to different kinds of time, such as the actual points and speed of clock time in the user's world, compared to the simulated time in VR. When the user starts, the actual and simulated time correspond. The VR scene is thus set up so that the sun is in the same place in the virtual sky as in the actual sky outside the windows of the museum. When the user starts moving the day-rock or the year-rock the simulated time starts to differ from actual time and starts to affect the VR environment accordingly. If a user built a cairn with three rocks (a duck), the VR scene would shift back to actual time so that the simulated and actual time again corresponded. The VR developers had to make a blueprint for the scene that allowed the control over the environmental events to shift between the different kinds of time, depending on the user's interaction with the rocks.

We had to consider how the environment should respond to the movement of the user. Which elements should change, and how fast should those elements change, for example when moving the year-rock? If we simply sped up time and included all the movements in the VR environment, the seasonal shifts would become obscured by all the visual effects of the fast-forwarded landscape timelapse. The sky would switch from bright to dark like a blinking strobe light, with clouds rushing over the sky at enormous speed. We had to reduce the number of things happening in the environment, and to split up the scene so that some elements would be affected by one temporality, and others by another. For example, we decided to keep the time of day unchanged when passing through the year. This meant that while moving the year-rock, the movement of the sun on the sky, and the changes in daylight, were created by seasonal change, and not by the day passing. That is why the previously mentioned analemma appeared on the VR sky. Seeing this figure eight shape appear in the simulation was an indication that the software plugin used for the sky simulation was accurate.

It was challenging to find the right speed for seasonal changes. If too slow, the user would not understand that anything was happening and would not be compelled to move the year-rock. If too fast, the experience would become overwhelming and feel out of sync with the human body and sensory apparatus. We tried many different settings with different test users and realized that the user's experience of the interaction was most intuitive when the speed of the changes in the environment corresponded with the movement of the user's body. If someone moved the rock fast the changes happened quickly, if they moved slowly, they happened slowly. A resynchronization of the body and landscape's time and movement meant that most people understood that their interaction triggered some event, while it allowed them to also just stand still or sit down and contemplate the view.

The museum hosts kept a logbook in which they wrote down how people interacted with the art installation. They also included some of the visitors' comments.

Figure 17.1: Two Rocks do Not Make a Duck, at the Munch Museum in Oslo in 2022.
(Photo by: Magnhild Nordahl).

People seemed to really like the starry nights and the changing of seasons, and some spent a long time sitting down on the floor, moving the rock just incrementally. One girl reacted to the piece with a laughing-fit, while two ladies in their 50s called the experience boring and wanted something more action-packed. A man in his 70s and his son experimented a lot with the piece. They lay down, sat on one of the rocks, moved multiple rocks simultaneously and built several ducks. A couple from Italy in their 50s were intent on balancing on top of the rocks, which they both managed to do on top of the day/night rock.

Many people asked about the technology behind the nature-simulation and commented on how being in the simulation made them feel. Several people mentioned that the virtual landscape reminded them of their place of birth. Some people did not recognize that the landscape in VR was a simulation of their current location, outside, while others enjoyed identifying the surrounding landmarks. One woman in her 50s expressed her disbelief at how much time this had taken to film and was even more astonished when she learned that what she was not in a film but a computer simulation. Another woman felt scared and alone, while others were less convinced, noting for example that the fjord should freeze over in the winter. One person commented that it is interesting to think about how much the landscape is affected by humans, and in a review of the show a critic wrote that "all of a sudden the digital world appears more natural than the real".

The digital world was made up of layers of 3D models, many of which were downloaded from the online 3D assets library Quixel. To build them from scratch would require an unmanageable amount of manual computer-work, and common practice is therefore to combine objects from such archives of virtual ready-mades. The 3D models we used were made from 3D scans of nature, capturing only a brief moment in the lifecycle of a plant. To make this plant grow its leaves from buds to full size, to let the leaves fall off and blow in the wind, and to make other elements in nature move in a realistic way, we used existing software functionality and plugins. Using the 3D computer graphics game engine Unreal Engine, 'Ultra dynamic sky' simulates the movement of clouds, 'Volumetric Clouds' makes it look like the clouds interact with sunlight, 'Fluid Flux' is a plugin simulating water in motion and interaction with objects, and 'Speed Tree' is a system simulating a virtual plant's growth. Some of these we could use, others were not compatible with the other parts of the simulation. Speed Tree for example did not have high enough resolution for VR, and its seasonal variation was not detailed enough. Our developer explained that the 3D model of a tree is typically built up by three layers: a stem, branches, and leaves. These are programmed to respond differently to time passing. In fall, a gradually expanding 'invisibility texture mask' on the leaves make them disappear, while the branches and stem remain unaffected. In some cases, it was challenging to make all these parts behave separately and together in

Figure 17.2: The view of the area in VR in different seasons.

the way they should. In an earlier stage of the scene, the stem of the tree was affected by the wind in the same way as the leaves, which made it look like the tree was swaying in some material much denser than air, like a large underwater plant.

Two Rocks Do Not Make a Duck (2022) is a collaborative artwork made by Cameron MacLeod and Magnhild Øen Nordahl. The Oslo-version of the VR scene was developed by Jonathan Nielssen and Jørgen Steinset. The production of the work was supported by The Munch Museum, CALENDARS research group, Bergen Kommune, Billedkunstnernes Vederlagsfond, Kulturrådet and Vestland Fylke.

The author

Magnhild Øen Nordahl is a visual artist living in Bergen, Norway. She is currently doing a PhD in artistic research at University of Bergen and is the co-founder of Aldea Center for Contemporary Art, Design and Technology.

Video of the artwork (video credit: Kunstdok): https://www.youtube.com/watch?v=v4FyRTbYCwk

Laura op de Beke

18 Dark seasonality in videogames

I live for the change of seasons. My favorite one is the transition from summer to fall, when I don my red coat to match the yellows and oranges of the parks, forests, and tree-lined streets of Oslo. The shortening of the days, and the drop in temperature also gives me an excuse to hole up in my apartment and play videogames all day, which for a person who studies the cultural meanings and contexts of games, like me, fortunately counts as research. What games I reach for depends on many things, but I often find myself looking for an experience that matches the conditions outside. For example, when the temperature plummets in the winter I crave wintery titles like *Subnautica: Below Zero* (Unknown Worlds Entertainment 2019), in which you explore an icy ocean planet; whereas in the summer I opt for the lush English countryside of a game like *Everybody's Gone to the Rapture* (The Chinese Room 2015). But I wonder, these days, at a time when familiar seasonal associations and practices have fallen out of sync with the Earth's increasingly disrupted weather patterns, what are the games that resonate with this new climate-changed reality?

In Tom Apperley's book *Gaming Rhythms* (1, page 19), he writes that what is central to the "experience of everyday life is the negotiation between the cyclical rhythms of nature and the linear, mechanical rhythms imposed by contemporary society." At first glance—given gameplay conventions invested in progress and the accumulation of points, levels, and resources—videogames seem more closely attuned to mechanical, linear temporalities than they are to ecological rhythms. On the surface gamers do not experience much seasonality, computer-bound as they are; and when they do, the kind of seasonality they engage with often follows a more commercial, profit-driven logic that has very little to do with the Earth's changing weather patterns, but which is punctuated by holiday sales and new releases.

When looked at a little more closely, however, gameplay and game culture *are* sensitive to seasonal shifts in temperature. For starters, gaming consoles and PCs produce heat as their main external output. In frosty Norway, during winter, I often warm my hands on the keypad of my ancient, blazing laptop. This same outpouring of heat poses a challenge for players in warmer climates who have to resort to many creative means to cool down their rigs, from high-tech liquid cooling systems to bags of frozen biryani (2). But there comes a time when even such measures may fail as Benjamin Abraham points out in his book *Video Games After Climate Change*. Growing up in Australia and gaming from his poorly insulated attic room, he remembers that "playing during summer holidays meant periods of gruelling physical endurance punctuated by retreats to cooler parts of the house" (3, page 1). Sometimes it's just too hot to play videogames; and with global temperatures rising the repercussions of such dangerous seasonal spikes in temperature are increasingly on my mind.

Perhaps as a response to the dawning realization that the world will be facing more extreme weather events more frequently, seasonality has achieved a certain thematic prominence in videogames, especially in farm-themed titles. The farming simulator has become one of the biggest game-genres in the last decade, demonstrated by the continued popularity of the *Harvest Moon* series (1996, renamed *Story of Seasons* for English release in 2014), and the many games like it, notably *Stardew Valley* (Barone 2016) and the *Animal Crossing* franchise (Nintendo 2001–2020). The latter, since it is synced to a localized real-time seasonal calendar, provides an especially apt example. In the game players tend to a little community that they check up on every day: weeding, gardening, and socializing with the other villagers. To keep such long-term play interesting, each season has its prospects in terms of fishing, gathering, farming, and social events. For example, *Animal Crossing* anticipates some seasonal celebrations with special gameplay opportunities, which in the case of the Japanese cherry blossom festival are always planned in the first week of April. However, these days cherry blossom festivals in Japan are held earlier every year because due to warmer temperatures cherry trees start blooming as early as March. In other words, there is a growing gap between the representation of seasonal events in videogames and their actual timing. This gap is all the more pronounced because seasonality in farm-themed games emphasizes the regularity and properness of the seasons, which in the temperate regions of the Northern hemisphere are loosely associated with snow, flowers, bountiful fruits and vegetables, and falling leaves respectively. Such predictable rhythms intersect neatly with the game-genre's other temporalities of progress and resource accumulation because predictability allows players to maximize their productivity in-game, leaving no stone unturned, and no opportunity wasted (4).

By playing these kinds of farming simulators, it has become clear to me that the seasons players delight in can be read with a certain sense of nostalgia, especially in juxtaposition to their new associations with drought, flooding, forest fires, and toxic algae blooms. However, there are also videogames that engage with seasonality in a way that speaks to these new experiences of less predictable —and more dangerous weather. These games make use of what I would call 'dark seasonality,' which looks like an emerging trend in videogames. The strategy game *Endless Legend* (Amplitude Studios 2014) features alternating summer and winter cycles, where the winter lasts for an unpredictable number of turns, drastically limiting the moves you can make; in *Rain World* (Videocult 2017), lethal torrential showers punctuate play, driving you underground to find shelter; *Death Stranding* (Kojima Productions 2019) also features a dangerous kind of rain shower called 'timefall' that speeds up decay and degradation; in the city-survival game *Frostpunk* (11 Bit Studios 2018) players have to weather a dramatic snowstorm without knowing exactly how long it will last, or if their stores will be sufficient; the post-apocalyptic beaver-town simulator *Timberborn* (Mechanistry 2021) hinges on a recurring dry season that lasts longer each cycle, and that a player's industrious beavers have to prepare for by damming enough water; the game *Season: A Letter to the Future* (Scavengers Studio 2023) tells the story of a girl on a quest to record the sounds and sights of the last season before a mysterious cataclysm washes away everything; and the recently announced *Diluvian Winds* (Alambik Studio 2023) involves preparing for and rebuilding after a recurring flood.

Engagement with dark seasonality in videogames echoes the emergence of similar themes in climate fiction. For example, N.K. Jemisin's *Broken Earth* trilogy (2015–2017) is about a world that is geologically destabilized as a result of harmful resource extraction. Its people now experience an unpredictable but recurring 'fifth season' in which volcanic eruptions, tsunamis, droughts, pandemics and all manner of natural disasters threaten the longevity of human civilization. Similarly, Karen Thompson Walker's *The Age of Miracles* (2012) asks what would happen if the globe suddenly slowed spinning on its axis, creating much longer days and nights. Stories like these might not immediately read as climate fictions since they do not engage with global warming explicitly, but as depictions of "global weirding" they create a space for the reconsideration of our relationship to a changing environment (5).

Videogames can get us to do the same. Moreover, as I argue in my PhD dissertation, while videogames sometimes flirt with the imagery of disaster movies, by grace of their temporally protracted and interactive nature, many of the games mentioned above offer an emphatically durational experience of dark seasonality. They do not posit 'the storm' as something to be overcome, assuming a fresh start on the other side. Rather, they simulate tumultuous weather-worlds as new realities that we need to become habituated to—worlds where small decisions accrue considerable consequences over time, which means that if anything, videogames dealing with dark seasonality may impart valuable qualities like caution, long-term planning, and grit.

The author

Laura op de Beke is a media scholar and creative practitioner with a PhD from the University of Oslo. Her dissertation looks at 'Anthropocene temporalities' in videogames, asking how they give us access to the ways in which our conceptions and experiences of temporality have accrued new meanings and feelings in an age deeply impacted by climate change. She is also the founder of the online reading group un-earthed (www.un-earthed.group.com).

References

1. Apperley, T. *Gaming Rhythms: Play and Counterplay from the Situated to the Global*. Amsterdam: Institute of Network Cultures, 2010.
2. Chang, A. *Playing Nature: Ecology in Videogames*. Minneapolis: Minnesota University Press, 2019.
3. Abraham, B. *Digital Games After Climate Change*. London: Palgrave Macmillan, 2022.
4. Op de Beke, L. "Pastoral Videogames: Industry, Entropy, Elegy." *Ecocene: Cappadocia Journal of Environmental Humanities* 2 (2021): 177–191.
5. Canavan, G. & A. Hageman. "Global Weirding." *Paradoxa* 28 (2016): 7–14.

Barbara Adam

19 Seasons in time: Bases, threats and opportunities. A triptych of poetic theory

https://doi.org/10.1515/9783111245591-019

Living
Planetary
Rhythmicity

I live rhythmicity
I experience rhythmicity
I synchronise the rhythmicities
of the world and those that I embody
which set the diurnal & seasonal patterns
of existence in my personal & social life
I live and coordinate those rhythms
without having to consider them
until they collide in conflict
and normality turns
to stress and
illness
These
rhythms
of our planet
are ancient and
extend from the dawn
of time to its imagined end
while body rhythms have evolved
with each species and demarcate them
Adaptable within strict limits, they
enable change & development
enhancing our cultural life
and our social existence
Crucial is therefore
knowing of our
rhythmicity
for now
and the very
long term future
Pulsing to the symphony
of the planet's rhythms within
ensures not just our individual but
also the planet's thriving and survival
which we ignore or supress at our peril
The layered complexity demands our
engagement & commitment in all
spheres of daily life: in family
school and work, in health
business & in politics as
nothing can escape
its commanding
ubiquity &
reach

Seasons for our temporal relations
Annual repeating patterns afford predictability
enable us to know how to plan and go on
provide overall predictability
with delimited variation
Change within certain bounds
allows for stable & flexible responses
and opens up futures beyond seasons & years

Seasonal rhythmicity is repetition with change
Approximate & similar in its repetition
it can never be exactly the same
Time is formed in interstices
of change & essential flexibility
The emergence of life depends on it
and evolution requires it for any mutations

Embodied Rhythmicity – planetary motion in us
means a symphony of seasonal patterns
deeply contextual and tied to place
is constituting our identity
This embodied memory of evolution
has its cultural patterning superimposed
in relations of habituated negotiated conflicts

Non-stop life of everything, anywhere, at all times
is the antithesis to seasonal embeddedness
seeking different forms of predictability
in sameness & bland uniformity
irrespective of context and difference
But will it enhance global unity and empathy
or be an appropriate response to the anthropocene?

Changing approaches
to the seasons:
Threats and Opportunities

Who still celebrates rhythms?
Seasons are so very yesterday!
Sameness is the order of the day
Irrespective of season and context
the same temperature for inside living
the same food offered in shops at all times
globally sourced & distributed in supermarkets
with just-in-time supply chains sidestepping context
producing ever expanding food miles and fuel demands
creating increasing sensory disconnection from the planet
and decreasing sense of effects on our world and communities
Many of the world's young people recognise the damage caused
and call to account their leaders from politics, economics & science
To achieve desired social transformations requires temporal analysis
of ancient planetary rhythmicities and their open future extensions:
spatial effects & symptoms accompanied by understanding of time
where complex, multi-layered processes implicate single moments
and vice versa: the one is in the whole and the whole in each one
with all processes extended in and over open time ad infinitum
Rhythmicity and seasonality shared with our fellow creatures
confronts us with the unity of all life & its key precondition
allows for recognition and visions of a common heritage
that encompass as central the physicality of our being
and transcend the dualities that currently guide us
towards boundless either-or dead-end solutions
Knowing ourselves implicated in futures not
of our making creates responsibility for
intended actions with unintended
outcomes, affecting untold
others yet to be born
Seasonality
temporality
rhythmicity
foundations of life
continuity and thriving in
the human-created anthropocene

The author

Barbara Adam is Emerita Professor at Cardiff University's School of Social Sciences. The social temporal has been the primary intellectual project of her academic career, resulting in five research monographs and a large number of publications in which she sought to bring time to the center of social science analysis. This focus facilitated a unique social theory, whose relevance transcends disciplines and is taught across the Arts and the Humanities as well as the Social and Environmental Sciences. On the basis of this work, Adam has been awarded two book prizes as well as numerous theory-based research grants and fellowships. She is founding editor of the journal *Time & Society*.

Part IV **Rhythms of daily life**

Sarah Strauss

20 Time is out of joint: Disruptive seasonalities of the AnthropoScene

The time of Covid was marked as much by its monotony as it was by its global scale, and that is an odd combination indeed. The cataclysmic fear and uncertainty that the pandemic unleashed in 2020 brought our worlds to a halt, sending people out of school and work and into isolation, just as the season was turning to spring in the northern hemisphere and people had begun to emerge from their winter lethargy.

We who had been researching the markers and impacts of a changing climate for decades saw in the rise of Covid-19 a parable for the climate crisis and hoped that the global efforts to turn the Covid tide would translate to a renewed enthusiasm for engagement with the longer climate crisis that had been unfolding for decades. We saw blue skies as planes were grounded and jet contrails all but disappeared, and we hoped it would help communities imagine a world in which fossil fuel residues were reduced and our human impacts on this planet could begin to reverse. A research project called CALENDARS—an inquiry into the ways we mark seasons through time, and how these cultural forms are implicated in our management of the impacts of a changing climate, among other things—began that same year. And so, my opportunity to rethink our seasons and the uses of seasonality to navigate our shifting climate and landscape was embedded in these Covid times. In this chapter, I consider how we might use our memories and emotions as they connect with our lived experiences of the changing seasons to imagine a way forward through the AnthropoScene, the ever-transforming landscape we have wrested from carbon and water and wind and sun.

Although I now reside in New England, I lived for 24 years in Wyoming, in the high desert of the Front Range of the Rockies. There, the local mountains were called the Snowies and the Never-Summer range, because since the colonizing of the American West, these had never completely lost their snow cover. But in recent years, with severe drought, they have become bare in summer, and that marker has contributed to the circumstances of the winter of 2022, with wildfires along the Front Range in Boulder and Colorado Springs—in which a local politician remarked that Colorado no longer has a 'fire season' because it lasts all year long. Similarly, in November of 2022, three different hurricanes rolled over Florida and Puerto Rico. The 'hurricane season' runs mostly from July to October, with only three other hurricanes (and ten tropical storms) hitting the US in November since 1851—until 2022. The edges of these patterned seasons have blurred, and the ability to exhale and feel safe from such severe wind or firestorms for a few months has been removed. The 500-year floods have become 100- to decadal scale events (1), with intensities and/or frequencies of these events bumping into one another in ways that we lack words to describe, and therefore also have difficulty in designing policies to manage. In the Arctic, thunderstorms have become a part of the forecast, where before they had no word. ThunderSnow is a new term that is becoming commonplace in the Rockies. And I think too of the seasonalities of salmon, tied so closely to the seasonal cycles of meltwater coming down from the mountains to the sea, providing the cold temperatures needed for these fish to spawn successfully and thereby also contribute to the important work of sediment transport in these rivers. We have been attending to the physical challenges of dammed rivers and hydropower production removing the salmon's upstream migration options, but only now can we see that opening the rivers is not enough if they are now too warm for breeding.

Solastalgia (2) is the term given to the emotional distress generated by environmental losses. Initially, this term was applied to sadness for scars on the land caused by mining, or the existential dread brought by severe drought; lately it has been applied to climate change more broadly. But here, I invoke it to describe the sadness for the losses of season and cycle, of the rhythms of the earth as it turns, and the months and years bring their cycles of growth and decay. It is not the change itself that is disturbing. In fact, that is what we expect: certain changes at certain times are both expected and anticipated, helping us organize our lives and communities. We have also gone through cycles before, in which those annual cycles vary widely, showing us times of drought as well as ice ages. As a species, we have always moved when the climatic conditions made our adaptive strategies insufficient to the task of survival. What differs today is the fact that while our fossil-fuelled modes of rapid transit have made it possible to migrate more easily than ever before, our cultural, economic, and political structures of borders and passports and walls have made it impossible for most people to leave safely or legally. And animals and plants are also on the move across state and national borders, making management of the rich and shifting biodiversity also a challenge. We are now locked in place, but the place has itself changed as the seasons have shifted. Adaptation becomes more challenging, invoking a sadness for our lost seasons and a sense of tragedy for the lost future of the place where we are fixed; this sentiment holds especially for those who are the most vulnerable, lacking the resources or capacity to move on. The changing climate forces us to make decisions that must be addressed locally, but that also create conflicts and conundrums at scales far beyond.

We know that climate change is a global problem. Yet, it is one thing to say that we share the atmosphere, and the damages that occur to it are damages to ourselves, our very being, as well as to the planet. It is another thing entirely to recognize the specific and differential impacts that almost always harm the most vulnerable the worst. We know too that only through collective counteraction— for which we have lost many of the stories and most of the skills—can we attempt to right the ship. As an academic anthropologist, the tools I have deployed are mostly teaching and writing, but the writing has, by virtue of a system that values speaking to fellow academics more than it values speaking to wider publics, largely been limited. The time has come to integrate my own academic and everyday lives, and to write and practice in tandem, with intentionality. And so this small contribution—an effort to bring together threads and help me respire with purpose and fortitude for the transition ahead.

To 'respire' is to breathe. In my earlier work on 'oasis regimes' (3), I discuss how a deep breath empirically demonstrates our dependence on this planetary system. The archaic definition of respire, however, takes that notion one step further— "to recover hope, courage, and strength." I have been contemplating the visceral as well as metaphoric aspects of these practices as I seek ways to engage a wider variety of publics into action on both mitigating the root causes of climate change and the necessary adaptive strategies to address the changes that are already upon us. Arjun Appadurai uses the "capacity to aspire" (4, page 282) when considering how the imagination can move us from one way of being in the world to another; the transformations we seek must be envisioned before we can experiment. Using the lens of seasonality is one way to help us focus on our relationships with the planet and each other, as a strategy for bringing the broad strokes of climate and atmospheric shifts into focus at a more human scale.

What brought me to anthropology in the first place was the stories. As an undergraduate who had imagined becoming a biomedical researcher, I took premed courses while stumbling from philosophy to comparative religion to anthropology in search of people and their stories, and eventually landed, as a senior, studying the Bhagavad Gita in Sanskrit at Edinburgh University, and interning with a supplemental nutrition program at Navajo Mountain, in the Utah strip of the Navajo Nation. The clarity of the west, and the fragility of life in that thin, brittle air, with water scarcity a constant threat, breeds fatalism or faith, and sometimes it's hard to tell the difference. But in that clarity and fragility is great beauty and complexity. In the past, such landscapes were used seasonally; the most marginal would not have been occupied year-round, but only when game or other conditions allowed, and when times got tough, people moved. Always. We still do, but the political and economic regulation of such environmentally driven mobility is a significant part of the current predicament. If we must stay, and the land has changed, then adaptation to the new conditions is our only hope. And so, we respire.

My time in Scotland during that same senior year that I lived at Navajo Mountain seeded a connection that has threaded through my life, culminating most recently in teaching a study abroad course on climate and energy that took us back to Edinburgh, and onward to the two experimental communities of Findhorn and Eigg. These are places where sustainability, community, and respiring together with the diverse assemblages, human and beyond, that comprise these locales has continued to inspire others. Findhorn, an agricultural and spiritual countercultural commune founded during the 1960s, and Eigg, a 21st century success story about throwing off the yoke of an absentee landlord, building habitat, and developing a model for low carbon living in a place of scarce resources, are both inspirations to new generations of seekers who want to experiment with living comfortably and communally within a carbon budget. These are not places where isolated individuals can make decisions that ignore the well-being of the community in favour of their own ideals. Humanity has a vast repository of ways to remake, repair, and build relationships anew across our worlds as we move toward a lower carbon society. In Leslie Marmon Silko's book *Ceremony*, the Singer Betonie observes that:

> 'The people nowadays have an idea about the ceremonies. They think the ceremonies must be performed exactly as they have always been done, maybe because one slip-up or mistake and the whole ceremony must be stopped and the sand painting destroyed. That much is true. They think that if a singer tampers with any part of the ritual, great harm can be done, great power unleashed.' He was quiet for a while, looking up at the sky through the smoke hole . . . . 'You see, in so many ways, the ceremonies have always been changing. . . . At one time, the ceremonies as they had been performed were enough for the way the world was then. But after the white people came, elements in this world began to shift; and it became necessary to create new ceremonies. I have made changes in the rituals. The people mistrust this greatly, but only this growth keeps the ceremonies strong. She taught me this above all else: things which don't shift and grow are dead things.' (5, page 126).

In both the Scottish and Navajo textile traditions (see Fig 20.1), we see strategies for pattern-making and also accommodating flaws, following old methods but with new designs. Weaving and knitting are tied to the wider ecology beyond humans and permit an awareness of seasonal rhythms in life. Making and remaking our material and physical lives, whether with yarn or in architecture, for ritual or relaxation, with intent to heal or entertain, generally happens according to blueprints for a start, but then is open to invention and fancy. While many assume that tradition means "the way it used to be," with an implication of stasis, we know that traditions are always invented, and it is when that flexibility is lost, that death begins.

Figure 20.1: Storm pattern rug, Navajo Mountain, Utah, 1983. (Photo by: Sarah Strauss).

So far, 2023 has brought the warmest Massachusetts January on record, with average temperatures nine degrees Fahrenheit higher than normal. The cycles of freeze and thaw seem to be moving at a frenzied pace, accelerating the sense that our seasons have become so disrupted as to be indefinable. We are adrift, ricocheting from ice storm to heat wave in ways that have been rare in this part of the country; the centre does not hold. But if we can hold our own roots firm, while swaying and bending with the wild-eyed tempests of the AnthropoScene that we have ourselves wrought through our energetic quests, we will find new paths and signposts to guide us through these times of change to a fresh rhythm and pace. We will adapt; we always do.

The author

Sarah Strauss is professor of anthropology and directs the graduate program in Community Climate Adaptation at Worcester Polytechnic Institute. Her research focuses on the intersection of environmental and health issues, values, and practices, especially related to climate adaptation and energy transitions. Professor Strauss has conducted ethnographic fieldwork in Rishikesh and Auroville, India; Leukerbad, Switzerland; and the Rocky Mountain West. She has been a visiting scientist at the National Center for Atmospheric Research (NCAR) in Boulder, Colorado, visiting professor in the Department of Geosciences of the University of Fribourg, Switzerland, and the Department of Anthropology at Pondicherry University, India, and Interdisciplinary Fellow at the Rachel Carson Center for Environment and Society in Munich, Germany. Her books include Weather, Climate, Culture (2004, edited with Ben Orlove), Positioning Yoga (2005), and Cultures of Energy (2013, edited with Stephanie Rupp and Thomas Love).

References

1. Reed, A.J., M. E. Mann, K. A. Emanuel, & J. P. Donnelly. "Increased threat of tropical cyclones and coastal flooding to New York City during the anthropogenic era". *PNAS* 112 (2015): 12610–12615. (https://doi.org/10.1073/pnas.1513127112).
2. Albrecht, G., G-M. Sartore, L. Connor, N. Higginbotham, S. Freeman, B. Kelly, H. Stain, A. Tonna, and G. Pollard. "Solastalgia: the distress caused by environmental change." *Australasian Psychiatry* 15 (2007): S95–S98.
3. Strauss, S. *Positioning Yoga*. Oxford, UK: Berg Publishers Ltd, 2005.
4. Appadurai, A. *The Future as Cultural Fact*. New York: Verso, 2013.
5. Silko, L. M. 1977. *Ceremony*. New York: Penguin Books.

Gordon Walker

21 The seasons of a new home: Learning with heat and light

Seasons are many things, but at least in material terms they are most fundamentally about cyclical shifts in flows of energy, moving patterns of sunlight and sun-heat that enter into places, environments and ecologies, and into our lives. When we relocate where we are living these seasonal patterns in heat and light become newly encountered and experienced. In moving to a different part of the world this change may be profound. But even in moving to a new house just down the road, there are new energy rhythms to encounter, to learn and adapt to.

Nine months ago, I moved house. Only about a mile or so, from a late 19th century Victorian terrace with a form and layout typical for Lancaster, a small city in northern England. A house that is longer back to front than side to side, squashed between its neighbours and with just a small yard at the back. Over the last six years I had become used to living in it to a certain pattern, including to how the rhythms of sun-heat and sun-light penetrated its variously porous walls, doors and windows, in a predictable way for an east-facing, terraced house. Rhythms shifting through the seasons, responded to and supplemented by my use of energy for light and heat in the home, my wearing of more or less clothes, my drinking of hot cups of tea, my filling of the deep-winter hot water bottle, my opening and closing of windows and curtains. A learnt, sedimented rhythm of making it work well enough, a 'lay thermodynamics' (1) of managing flows of heat, light and bodily warmth.

Where I have now moved is to a building designed long ago to contain cows and horses, agricultural equipment, muck, and straw. Dating from maybe the 18th century and falling into disrepair by the mid-20th (see Figure 21.1).

In the 1990s, this derelict remnant of stone, slates, rafters, and cobbles, was transformed into a collection of buildings for humans to live in. Three co-joined houses, one of these making my home with a very different layout and orientation to where I had lived before. Its plan is L-shaped, it turns a corner, it has rooms jumbled on top of one another, windows on four sides and in various parts of the roof. It has gardens at front and back, trees on rising land to the front and left side. It's a lovely place to live. I am fortunate to be able inhabit its character, its quiet, its proximity to non-humans.

When part of a farm, this stone-built structure used to have seasons that were felt practically and sensually, with little mediation by technology. Inhabited by a rhythm of agricultural practice that shifted with the coming and going of light and dark, the growing season and the not-growing season. A building into which the

Figure 21.1: Derelict farm buildings before they were converted into dwellings. (Photo by: Gordon Walker).

cold and damp deeply penetrated, with little moderation of its season-by-season thermal rhythms through artificial means of lighting or heating. Only the breath and bodily heat of its animal and sometimes human inhabitants mixing into its temperature. A local history says the farm was never much of a success, its animals struggling and sickly because of its cold and frosty orientation to the north.

So far, within its new form as house and home, I have lived with some of its winter, into its spring, through its summer and into autumn. In so doing I have been attentive to where and when flows of outside light and heat enter its space. Noting when shafts of light first penetrate into the corners of windows where they didn't before, extending further day by day, as the sun moves over-head and spring sunlight intensifies (see Figure 21.2). I have enjoyed the morning warmth that poured through the kitchen window and onto the upstairs landing. I was surprised by how a shaft of sunlight found its way through a ceiling window, illuminating and soothing the start of the day.

I have watched leaves bud and emerge on the trees to front and side, adding shade into solar pathways that were once open; wondering if that will obstruct the planned addition of solar panels on the garage roof. I have been learning the

Figure 21.2: Images of sunlight inside and outside of different parts of the house. (Photo by: Gordon Walker).

rhythms of the internal domestic warm spots and cold spots, how different spaces in the house gain and lose their energies, working out what is needed and not needed in animating patterns of artificial lighting and heating, window opening and curtain closing. In so doing I have been managing, as best I can, through experimentation and mistake-making, the set of already installed energised technologies and the costs of running them. As the autumn cold appears I am feeling the beginning of a return to when my inhabitation began, both light and warmth diminishing, a closing in.

In the garden I have followed how the photosynthetic energies of spring have brought life into borders, beds and pots, discovering what had been over-wintering, ready to emerge. And what may or may not be newly planted in the sun, shade and semi-shade. I have been recurrently delighted at a new arrival, a new flowering, even late in the year, that stayed quiet for so long, waiting for its moment in the seasonal parade. This season saw a good crop of tomatoes, but it also left leaves scorched by a summer heat wave never-before imagined this far north.

I have been learning what I expect, from now on, to know better. Learning how to anticipate the cycling rhythms of the house, its daily patterns through each of its seasons. Over time my home's energetic rhythms will become more deeply entwined with my rhythms, my beats and pulses and the temporal structure of my living at home. But those rhythmic relationships will not stay still and fixed in place, for repetition is always with difference (2). My house will age, deteriorate and weather, performing differently as the years pass. As I also age, as my circumstances change, my relation to the seasons and their energies will also evolve, maybe with some struggle as my habits try to fossilize and stay in place. And the northern temperate seasons of Lancaster will never repeat identically, never allowing a pure anticipation of what has come before, even more so as we force them into an ever more uncertain climatic and energetic future.

The author

Gordon Walker is Professor at the Lancaster Environment Centre, Lancaster University, UK. He is a human geographer with expertise on the social and spatial dimensions of environment, energy and sustainability issues. This includes work on environmental and energy justice; energy and rhythmanalysis; social practice, transitions and energy demand; community based renewable energy; and vulnerability to climate hazards. His most recent book is 'Energy and Rhythm: Rhythmanalysis for a Low Carbon Future'.

References

1.   Walker, G. *Energy and Rhythm: Rhythmanalysis for a Low Carbon Future*, London: Rowman and Littlefield, 2021.
2.   Lefebvre, H. *Rhythmanalysis: Space, Time and Everyday Life*. London: Continuum, [1992] 2004.

David Macauley

22 Outside-In: Restor(y)ing the Seasons

In this chapter, I share my personal reflections on changing seasonality through observations in and around the house and home. I relate these thoughts to the subject of domestication, which loosely involves bringing the exterior (outside) world to the more interior (inside) human realm, and along the way transforming the stories we tell about the seasons. I arrive to my views through years of walking, gardening, photography, and travel as well as teaching and writing about philosophy and environmental studies, including the recent publication of a book entitled *The Seasons: Philosophical, Literary, and Environmental Perspectives.*

I grew up outside of a sleepy college town situated along the Susquehanna River near the eastern seaboard of North America. Here, in this rural setting, the seasons have tended historically to be marked by relatively clear transitions and dramatic transformations. Spring emerges in a lush green fullness from the more subdued winter whites and earthy browns. The blues of summer skies and streams grow more pronounced as heat and light expand their presence. Autumn, in its turn, contracts and "falls" back as warmth and daylight recede, giving way to the golds, reds, and oranges in the woods, parks, pastures, and fields. In this swath of the country, the close correlation between the seasons, the primary colours, and the classical elements—earth, air, fire, and water—captivates the eye and seduces our imaginations.

In my youth, I associated family tasks around the house with the reliable arrival of distinct periods of the year: raking leaves and chopping wood for the fireplace in autumn; shovelling snow in winter; preparing the garden or cleaning out the house in spring; and cutting grass or picking strawberries and blueberries in summer. I also learned to appreciate cultural aspects of seasonality: for me that meant cross country season in the fall; wrestling season in winter; track season in spring; and baseball season in summer.

There appeared to be a larger unwritten but trustworthy calendar that informed me it would soon be the appropriate or pre-appointed time for ice skating on the frozen ponds and sledding on the snow-ballasted hills (winter); hiking the newly thawed stream and waterfalls adjacent to our scouting retreat (spring); swimming in and canoeing on the tributaries of the river (summer); or camping out in the cooler nights under the changing leaves (autumn).

As I look back through time now, I believe these recollections are not mere wistfulness on my part, a painful search for a lost home as the word 'nostalgia' suggests. Rather, there were—and still are—broad rhythms and deep ecological forces at work that have generated seasonal continuity and tethered the meteorological and calendar years together.

Nevertheless, seasonal disruption has been occurring at an alarming rate over the last several decades, and the cyclical or simple story of seasonal change is being called into question. Like many others, my bodily senses have been picking up on and becoming attuned to the warning signals in the local environment.

One modification to my understanding of seasons has come with the realization that this 'New England model' of the four seasons – with its deep, vibrant, colourful, clear-cut, and sweeping changes in weather patterns, plant and animal ecology, and dramatic alterations of light length and intensity – has limitations in its extension and application elsewhere. I had grown used to this theatrical view of the four seasons, where "each one enters like a prima donna, convinced its performance is the reason the world has people in it," to borrow the words of novelist Toni Morrison. But the diverse calendrical years that I have witnessed through travel, since my adolescence, signal to me that the traditional and conceptual 'pail' (or framework) of the four seasons is either porous or not always portable to distant places. We can't easily move this four-season model and its orderly four-part story—cold earth (winter), warming water (spring), radiating fire (summer), and cooling air (autumn)—across the country or around world and, when we do, the pail may yield a leak.

While the Asian poet Kyoshi Takahama observes in his haiku that "walking around an early spring garden [is] going nowhere," travel beyond the domestic sphere and one's homeland does offer lessons about seasonal change. Through journeys to foreign countries like India and Indonesia, I experience wet and dry seasons, a monsoon season, and the allure of seasonal spices and foreign foods in ways that challenge and metamorphose my vision of four distinct periods of the year. Through visits to less distant places such as San Francisco, Hawaii, Los Angeles, and the Pacific Northwest, I encounter micro-climates and seasonality with wholly different dimensions and ambient or emotional "feels" than I have grown accustomed to on the East coast. These trips are reminders that complex stories and intersecting narratives about seasonal change co-exist.

Another personal change came through my evolving understanding that the once 'wild'—largely independent and external—seasons have been increasingly 'domesticated' and internalized *within* my home world and *inside* human culture more generally. Sometimes in surprisingly unnoticed ways. Tasty summer tomatoes, for example, are now preserved year-round in mason jars or tin cans on my kitchen shelf while fresh strawberries are frozen like rhinestone gems in the refrigerator freezer ready to be enjoyed during any chosen month.

Similarly, through walking and distance running I've learned that I carry the seasons with me on my outings and often bring them back home, where they are domesticated—sequestered within the hold of the house (*domus*)—and sometimes preserved for short interior 'visits' (Figure 22.1). I track the winter snow into my Victorian home after a hike to the food co-op; cockleburs adhere to my socks in summer and wind up on the living room floor following a walk in the woods; and autumn leaves hitch a quiet ride on the base of my boots into the sunroom off my back porch. Luka, my grey cat, perks up his nose, ears, and tail and takes note of these uninvited but still welcome seasonal visitations. He also daily indulges in the slowly migrating pockets of warm light that move through the house, curl up in the corners with the spider webs, and make themselves silently at home; further revealing the porosity of my house as the changing seasons slip through the cracks.

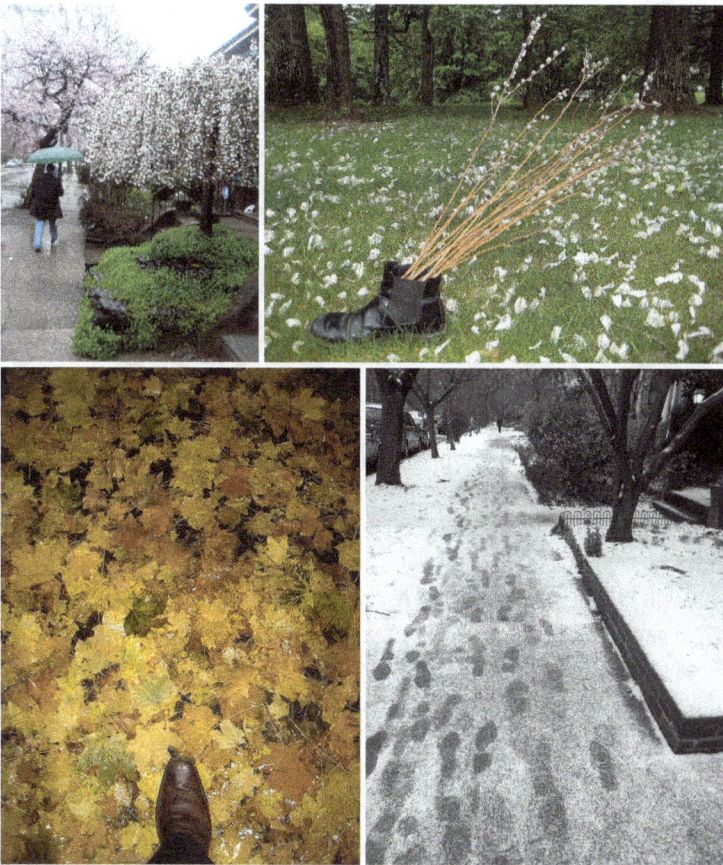

Figure 22.1: Walking in spring, summer, autumn and winter. (Photos by: David Macauley).

This movement by foot across the landscape is best accompanied with and guided by seasonal knowledge. For me, there are appropriate winter walks, autumn ambles, summer strolls, and spring excursions, whether to the local cemetery, a Philadelphia park, or the Appalachian Trail. I now set forth on these jaunts with the expectation—and half-conscious hope—of encountering something new or unfamiliar about seasonal change: birds that oddly delay or even defy their long southern flights in autumn; flowers that pop their curious heads out of the ground way too soon in winter; pedestrians unprepared for sudden stormy tumults from gathering clouds above or fickle fluctuations in the sun's energy during mid-summer; the unexpected snowstorm in May; or a too-warm-for-comfort afternoon in early spring.

Awareness of the seasonal dimensions of bird watching, medicinal plant gathering, and animal observation—knowing their migrations, hibernations, or breeding seasons—is valuable to this enterprise and practice of learning about the local environment through walking, and, of course, coming home to share stories about such journeys.

While writing these reflections, I glance around the house to spot other signs of the season's subtle entrance into the confines or comforts of domesticity. I spy several framed postcards of paintings by the 16th century Italian artist Arcimboldo resting atop the old bureau in my guest room. In these works, one finds human portraits composed entirely of seasonal motifs: winter's face is artfully constructed of gnarled roots; spring's visage consists of colourful flowers; summer's expression is fashioned out of harvested vegetables; and autumn's countenance appears through the shapes of plucked fruit and fallen leaves that are cobbled together (Figure 22.2).

I pause and take in the warm 'Indian Summer' breeze sliding invisibly through the screen in my bedroom window and sense its coiling intersection and co-mingling with the slowly rotating ceiling fan overhead. The seasonal atmosphere outside blends calmly with the interior air. And while I resist the lure of air conditioning in my house, I acknowledge that it is employed widely as means of comfort through which we attempt to overcome seasonal forces and phenomena while at the same time transfiguring them to our own luxurious demands or perceived needs along the way.

Outside my house, gardening teaches me pragmatic and aesthetic ways through which to collaborate with seasonal time, which is no longer so predictable given the capriciousness of the planet's climate. My Weeping Snow Cherry Tree, which I planted in front of my home, bursts into white flowers to mark the shifting yearly arrival of spring. My climbing rose bush, which stretches skyward off the front porch, both amazes and gently disturbs me by blooming late into November or, alternatively, extra early in mid-February. Vegetable gardening allows me to transport

Figure 22.2: The Four Seasons, Giuseppe Arcimboldo (1560).

the fruits of my outside labour into the house, where home grown food can be cooked and eaten, or temporarily displayed as an emblem of seasonal change.

A transformative learning experience has also occurred through the influx of the seasons into my own maturing character and the home of my body. The external *temperature* and my own more internal *temperament* are often wedded in interesting and challenging ways through *temporal* changes in the recurring wheel of the year. I regularly battle Seasonal Affective Disorder in the winter months when the light of the sun wanes and my mood drops in tandem with it.

I've come to realize as well that the seasons may be meaningfully grasped as phases of a vibrant and complete human life. In this regard, I find wisdom and solace in Yoko Ono's observation, "Spring passes and one remembers one's innocence. Summer passes and one remembers one's exuberance. Autumn passes and one remembers one's reverence. Winter passes and one remembers one's perseverance." Such insights lead me to recall the Zen Buddhist notion that when one has fully and deeply experienced the seasonal changes in the world that one is ready to die, a point beautifully illustrated in the Korean film, 'Spring, Summer, Fall, Winter . . . and Spring,' which explores the seasonal cycle through the life of a Buddhist monk who lives on a rotating wooden island in a mountain lake.

Writing is a final way I transport the seasons indoors—like unpacking luggage full of enchanting souvenirs from faraway lands—and then carry it with me as I try to metamorphose the meteorological world into meaningful words. Poetry could well be said to be the original language of the seasons, but it remains a primary tongue and voice through which I and many others comprehend and conduct an intermittent dialogue with the permutations of spring, summer, fall, and winter.

I read Wallace Stevens, Bashō, Robert Frost, James Thomson, and John Keats to listen to a broadened and nuanced vocalization of seasonal change. When I am inspired by this ancient craft or perhaps surprised by a sublime weather event, I might dabble myself in generating haiku-like descriptions, short meditative reflections, or photographs of seasonal outcroppings. Such pursuits permit me to express the changes I perceive in the wilderness or feral world and to domesticate, tame, or trick them into stories or other culturally accessible forms of communication. "Spring too, very soon! They are setting the scene for it—plum tree and moon," writes Bashō.

Through these developments, the seasons themselves are altered, amplified, and given new cultural shapes, and narrative forms. The rhythms, cycles, and atmospheric dimensions outside in 'first nature' are thereby transported inside and thus domesticated as a kind of 'second nature' (culture), providing them with greater accessibility and new meanings for us.

I understand the current ecological challenge, then, as involving an imaginative rethinking and aesthetic *re-story-ing* of the seasons to critically retrieve and creatively *restore* a semblance of their once symphonic and magisterial place in the world. Doing so can aid us in rediscovering their relevance for a diversity of cultures and communities around the globe as well as enlarging our understanding of our individual homes and homelands. New social stories and embodied narratives might help transition us to more sustainable relationships with seasonally influenced phenomena ranging from regenerative agricultural practices and environmental art to architectural design and ecological tourism.

I suspect we will continue to witness immense changes in the idea and experience of the seasons as they enter the domestic, cultural, and human spheres and then, in turn, colour the way we view the more-than-human world. "Storytelling," the philosopher Hannah Arendt once declared, "reveals meaning without the error of defining it," a point we should keep in mind as we engage in the important environmental tasks before us.

The author

David Macauley is Professor of Philosophy and Environmental Studies at Penn State University, Brandywine. He has taught at Oberlin College, Emerson College, and New York University. His books include *Elemental Philosophy: Earth, Air, Fire, and Water as Environmental Ideas*; *Minding Nature: The Philosophers of Ecology*; *The Seasons: Philosophical, Literary, and Environmental Perspectives*. David is completing two books, *Walking: Philosophical Foot Notes* and *The Wisdom of Trees: Thinking Through Arboreality*.

Scott Bremer

23 Telling the year by the rugby season, and getting confused

Let's be clear, I'm terrible at rugby, but I have always been a rugby player. When I was five, in those formative years, my grandad signed me up for a team in my hometown of New Plymouth, on the cold, wet, western tip of New Zealand's North Island. On Saturday mornings, he'd fill me up with porridge and drive me to games all along the coast, in bare feet on the frosty grass. We kids turned those fields into mud baths, and afterwards grandad would drive me home for a hot bath and we'd watch rugby on the TV, with chips and lemonade. The rugby season signified winter for me, and it lasted three or four months, from around June.

Back then I never questioned why rugby was a winter sport, it was tradition. But writing this chapter, I alighted on an on-line chat board hosted by the Guardian newspaper in the United Kingdom about 12 years ago (1). On there, a group of (I imagine to be) grizzled and battered ex-rugby-players interrogated this tradition. There was some agreement that rugby's winter status derives from its origins in British 'public schools' in the 19th Century, where it was organised according to school terms and timed so as not to clash with the cricket season, which is a decidedly summer sport (demanding a hard-packed, sun-baked surface). Rugby, by contrast, could certainly be played in wet conditions. Indeed, for many it is preferable, *"It is infinitely less painful to be dumped on your backside in a wet soft goo than to be driven into summer's rock hard earth"* noted a certain Jeremy Scott on the chat. And New Zealand's cold, wet, and windy winters ensured that that tradition persisted.

So it was that the codified time schemes of British elite schools came to affect the timing of New Zealand's year, which likewise lived from summer cricket to winter rugby, but by an inverted southern hemisphere seasonal pattern. Sport seasons – especially rugby and horse racing – were some of the most deeply ingrained social rhythms setting a tempo to life. This is exemplified in Rod Derrett's iconic 1965 album, named for the three R's that culturally shaped the male population's lifestyle at that time: *'Rugby, Racing and beeR'* (2). My grandad grew up in that epoch, and I guess he was determined I'd live by at least one of those pillars.

Back to me, and a few years later I was at high school, still playing rugby badly. It was a boys' school with an army of rugby teams, and I reached my sporting pinnacle in the 5th best team. School rugby was regimented, the season organised into the winter terms. We played home games on the exposed racecourse cross the road and got buffeted from the cold wind coming off Mount Taranaki. I still associate the smell of muddy grass mixed with sweat and liniment with those winter months. But by then – the mid-1990s – the game was changing. Talented schoolboy players started to practice in autumn and kept training in the spring and summer 'off-season'.

The 1990s saw New Zealand rugby detach from winter, for several different reasons, and this was a bit disorienting for me. It was even the focus of a study, 20 years ago, from Higham and Hinch (3). Like many sports, rugby was professionalised, and the best players became devoted to that game year-round (4). At the same time, promoters saw rugby not only as a sport but also an income-generating source of entertainment and tourism. Higham and Hinch's paper is all about how the tourism industry sought to "overcome the seasonality" of the sport. This coincided with processes of globalisation; with advances in plane travel and communications technologies meaning teams could just as easily play overseas as domestically, and the match could be beamed to the public back home. The national competition was augmented with a 'Super-12' rugby league, filled with professional players from New Zealand, Australia, and South Africa. Add to that the international fixtures, and now there was a lot of rugby to watch. When I started playing in 1986, first class rugby was played from June – October. But by 1999, the top-level players were playing from January – October; 10 months of the year!

By the turn of the century, elite rugby was about the spectacle. New stadiums were built, which flashed with advertisements, and the players ran out through fountains of sparks. Tourists flocked to the cities where the Super teams played and filled the motels. I should know; as a student job I moonlighted as a mascot, running up and down the side-lines buoying up the crowds. The rugby unions changed the rules too. Before, a rugby match could deteriorate into a muddy, grunting scrummage that would shuffle around the field. But the public wanted fast-running play with the ball in hand, so a raft of new regulations was put in place to change the style of play (4). But this style is hindered by wet slushy conditions, and so it was no accident that the Super-12 league started earlier and earlier; by the late 1990s it kicked off in January – mid-summer – when the ground was hard and the ball dry. Rugby was cutting its ties to the cold and dark months of the year, and in so doing changing its very nature. In some ways, it was not the same game.

In the early 2000s, having finished school, I bounced around a few university social teams. But it was apparent that men's rugby was for the devoted and the talented, and I was neither. Then, as I entered the drudgery of office work, I was confronted with a new trend in rugby that was gathering momentum, the world of mid-week social sport. The office put together a mixed-gender 'touch rugby' team – an almost-non-contact version of the game – which played in the domain on the sunny Wednesday evenings of summer; puffing around against the police team, or the printery, or a ragtag band of 16 year olds. This sport had few ties to the rugby I grew up with. It was temporally displaced – from wintery weekends to summery weeknights – and it missed all the seasonal cues like the wind, the mud, the smells.

By then, as 2010 approached, the cycle was closed, and now international rugby was televised the full year-round. The World Rugby Sevens series – an even faster game packed into 14 minutes – picked up where the New Zealand national tournament finished, beginning in November, and running over our summer. And there were the European unions and the Six Nations tournament. When I visited my grandad, I found him overwhelmed. His Saturday afternoon ritual had taken over his whole week, his whole year! In retirement there was always a match to watch or listen to on the radio. Always something to have a flutter on. I think he reorganised his life around rugby, and those cherished winter activities became diffused throughout the year. I wonder what winter meant to him in the end?

That was all years ago. Today I live in Bergen, in the weather of Norway's west coast fjords. Rugby is a niche sport here, but globalisation means it ekes out a following in even the most unlikely places. In many ways it's a social club for expats yearning for something from the home country, though its perceived brutality also draws curious Norwegians. There's an Irish pub in town that plays all televised international matches in a backroom, and there's always something to watch, and someone to watch it with. I started playing again, though these days it takes me a fortnight to recover from a game. The irony is that I'm back to playing from May to October – like I did in the 1980s – but in Norway that maps onto the warmest and driest months; the 'summer'. The snow drifts and long dark of the winter months can be prohibitive. And sadly, I've lost the muddy smell I associated with rugby on the racecourse in winter. Now we play on artificial grass.

In New Zealand in the 1980s, the rugby season gave people like me or my grandad as indelible a set of temporal reference points as the farmer's harvest, or hunter's 'roar'. The sport – the activity – more clearly signalled the period of the year than any meteorological or phenological values. When we said "rugby", winter broke. And these cues got buried deep. Though I've lived outside New Zealand for 14 years now, I still find it discombobulating to prepare for the summer rugby season in Norway. But, having transformed according to processes like professionalisation, commercialisation and globalisation, sports like rugby no longer function the same as seasonal markers. I no longer tell the year by the rugby season.

The author

Scott Bremer is a senior researcher at the Centre for the Study of the Sciences and the Humanities at the University of Bergen, and research associate at NORCE Climate. His research focuses on governance for environmental challenges – especially climate adaptation – with a focus on the different ways of knowing and acting that guide peoples' decision-making. He is the project leader of the European Research Council 'CALENDARS project', uncovering the often-overlooked influence of seasonal cultures on patterning peoples' thoughts and actions.

References

1. https://www.theguardian.com/notesandqueries/query/0,5753,-23854,00.html
2. https://nzhistory.govt.nz/media/photo/rugby-racing-and-beer
3. Higham, J., & T. Hinch. "Tourism, sport and seasons: the challenges and potential of overcoming seasonality in the sport and tourism sectors". *Tourism Management, 23* 2002): 175–185.
4. https://www.world.rugby/news/582543

Deborah Hide-Bayne

24 Apps and me: How apps are shaping my experience of the New Zealand environment and seasons

Deborah Hide-Bayne is an English artist and writer who moved to rural New Zealand in 2003. As part of a Coromandel writers' group, she became involved with the CALENDARS Research Project and this book. These are her personal reflections on how phone apps and the environment intersect in her life, and how those apps shape her experience of the environment and the seasons.

These days we rely a lot on technology. My family bemoan the fact that my iPhone and I go everywhere together. We take it for granted, but isn't it incredible that in my pocket I've got a supercomputer connecting me to the world at the swipe of a screen? 'App' is a word that has crept into commonly used language over recent years. Who needs a torch, a watch, a telephone or a road map when there is an app to do it for you?

I consult a weather app most mornings; I hope it gives me a better understanding of my environment – an overview – but I wonder if this really is the case? I'm sure weather modellers have lots of training but does history and the estimates and assumptions that those men and women use really produce something worth having? As a child, I was taught how to judge the weather by looking at the clouds, but this seems to be an arcane form of knowledge these days. Do you know the rhyme, "Mackerel scales and mares' tails make lofty ships carry low sails"? I have memories of sailing with my father and him pointing out the different shaped clouds and what they meant. I learned that both the high clouds that look like they have been combed out into long strands and the ripples or repeated patterns that look like a sky full of fish scales, are accurate predictors of rain coming.

I have an app too that tells me when it is high tide (an important consideration in a town dominated by fishing and boating). Our boat can only come up the creek on a 'king' tide (in Spring and Autumn) so having this data to hand is critical for which day to book Darius and his tractor to pull the boat trailer up onto the hard stand. We pace around in the petrol station (Darius' main occupation is a garage mechanic) all looking at our phones and comparing information. "What about 5:30am on Tues 26th? The tide will be 3.3m that morning . . . should be enough water under her."

My attention is inevitably pulled back to my phone, and I think about an app called *Calm*, a meditation app that I also use on a daily basis. Every morning I have the option to listen to a 10-minute guided meditation and there are several word authors or perspectives to choose from. While I'm on the main home screen or waiting for the app to load I can choose from a large range of soothing background noises (39 in all; I just counted them). It's interesting to realise that they're all natural sounds: waves lapping on the shore, cicadas chirping, rain, birdsong, a waterfall, a gently flowing stream . . . I'm sure you get the gist.

Today I thought two things about that: one is that I don't know much about these sounds. I don't know which type of bird is entrancing me with its song; I don't know where the waterfall is that endlessly flows; I don't know the name of the stream that gurgles over pebbles on its way to the sea and yet I still find it grounding to hear those sounds. The second thing I realised is that I could listen to these sounds anywhere: in a paddock in New Zealand (where the real cicadas are loudly competing for my attention) or in the city of Auckland on the top storey of a soaring tower block . . . or New York or Tokyo. Technology has allowed me a disconnect between the sound and the actual location where the sounds was recorded. So, is that a good thing or a bad thing?

The obvious benefit of bringing these sounds to people who wouldn't otherwise be able to hear them is that it supports people's mental health and wellbeing, and that's a good thing.

However, I do worry that we are starting to rely on an imagined nature rather than going out for a walk or wandering through a forest or being by a stream. A fully immersive experience in nature brings with it smells, sounds, the wind on your face and the sun moving across the clouds. Or a dripping fringe, stinging cheeks and wet socks – they aren't always positive sensations. But either way, I think we can all agree that an authentic experience is what we are truly craving and the recorded sounds from a phone are only a poor imitation.

A negative consequence that occurs to me is that I don't know if those birds still have a habitat to live in; I don't know if that waterfall still has enough water in it to flow; I don't know if that stream is now polluted and choked with plastic. Will we be able to notice the changes that are happening around us if we are not truly immersed in and engaged with nature? I suspect not. Friends in Auckland haven't noticed the recent summer droughts in the same way as I have. Yes, the pavement is dry and dusty but it isn't that different from how the pavement looks the rest of the year. If there is nothing growing near you to see regularly and witness its progress or health, how can you tell if there is a drought? The water still comes out of the tap, doesn't it? The volatility that farmers and growers are witnessing as a result of climate change is disconnected from the consumer. Insulated from these changes, the average joe won't realise that things are changing until he is hit in the pocket at the grocery store or when the tap runs out of water.

There are new apps coming on stream all the time that give more detailed information about the earth as a whole (like Earth Now and the UN's Climate Change app). I find Earth Now a bit scary to be honest. There is such an incredible amount of data at the touch of a button, but I don't have any real understanding of what I am looking at. Apparently, I can check the Earth's vital signs (just like a patient in a hospital) but this nurse has no idea what air temperature New Zealand should have, or how much carbon dioxide should be present. I imagine myself with one of those upside-down watches that pins to your uniform, holding the earth by one hand to check its pulse, and the watch in my other.

As a climate scientist it must be amazing to have all this information at your fingertips though. It seems that technology is bringing us closer to an understanding of climate change in some ways but further away in others. Is lots of data more useful than a lived experience of something? Does it have more validity? I don't think so; I think the data can supplement lived experience and as someone who has an interest in the democratisation of science, the potential of science to contribute to a sustainable world is huge. I think the more people who have access to and an understanding of scientific methods and data, the better.

In my small rural world of Coromandel, the turn of the seasons and the specifics of each day's weather remain key factors in my day. Right now, on the Coromandel Peninsula in the dry of a New Zealand summer I absolutely know that we're having a drought. Trees that have been in the earth many years are drying up and dying; vegetables and new plantings need constant watering to survive. I don't remember it being like that even 20 years ago when I first moved here.

Is there an app for rainfall on the Coromandel? I should find out.

Generations of my forebearers have depended on rain to grow their crops, relied on the sun to ripen them and counted on good harvests to sustain them through the fallow months. The weather also dictated whether there was surplus food that could be traded or sold; the weather being the factor that most decided whether it was a good year or a bad one. I know that this is no longer the case; other factors have taken priority. Governments and individuals make decisions every day that potentially impact climate change for everyone, for better or for worse.

Perhaps by insulating people from the consequences of these actions, we do them and the world a disservice . . . if you can't see the physical effects of climate change in the world around you, will you be aware enough and motivated enough to change your behaviour or to vote for people who make this their priority?

The author

Deborah Hide-Bayne is an English artist and writer who moved to rural New Zealand in 2003. When she is not painting, drawing or writing, she relishes growing and cooking really good vegetables then eating them with other fresh seasonal food in gorgeous surroundings with family and friends.

Jake Stenson

25 Fire and snow: The changing nature of seasonal work in a Canadian mountain town

Nelson, British Columbia is a small town of around 10,000 people nestled in the Selkirk Mountains. Nelson is defined by hot, beautiful summers and cold, snowy winters creating a labour market where many residents will work two jobs: one for the summer and one for the winter. Our changing climate is disturbing this rhythmic seasonality, bringing less predictable winters and longer hotter summers that cause destructive wildfire seasons. This piece draws on my experience as both a wildfire fighter and an employee in the local ski industry to explore how the loss of predictable seasonality is impacting the lives of seasonal workers in Nelson and disturbing the duality of employment.

A town of seasons

I moved to Nelson five years ago. One of the first things I noticed was how the locals would talk in differentiated seasons, "Are you having a good summer?" or "Are you all set for winter?". This was in stark contrast to my dreary home island of the United Kingdom where I remember a universal season. Always some brand of grey, damp, and rainy. Nelson is a mecca for outdoor adventure sports and the changing seasons are signified by people's hobbies. The falling leaves see mountain bike racks swapped for ski racks and baseball caps are traded for toques (Canadian lingo for 'Beanie'). You'd laugh at how many times people ask, "Are you excited for Ski Season?" in October whilst it is still 20 °C outside. But Nelson's population is quite obsessed with the changing of seasons. The excitement around town is palpable as the first snowfall dusts local mountain tops, or the first sunshine warms our faces after a long winter.

The pronounced seasons in Nelson are evident in employment, leading many locals to have two separate jobs. In the summer, outdoor jobs are popular as people work as tree planters, wildfire fighters, tradespeople or in the tourism industry. As winter draws in and snow covers the mountains, people transition to working at the local ski resort, as avalanche forecasters, ski guides or at one of the many local ski lodges. Summer jobs typically run from April to October, and winter jobs from December to March, allowing some well-earned time off in the 'shoulder season'. These seasonal jobs are intense, physically demanding, and require long working hours. Moreover, they regularly require travel to remote locations and time away from home and loved ones. Despite the hardship, people take pride in their seasonal jobs and revel in the fact that they don't tick the societal boxes of a typical "9-5, Monday to Friday". People are also very much defined by their jobs during the season, schedules dictate your friendship circle or ability to make plans outside of work. You know very well that your wildfire fighter friend can't commit to a summer trip, and maybe won't respond to your texts as they grind away deep in the forests of British Columbia.

Hotter summers

The well-tuned seasonality of work in Nelson is beginning to be interrupted as we see the everyday impacts of climate change in our community. Traditionally, the core wildfire season would run from June to August giving firefighters three tough months of work. During this time, the work schedule would be 14 to 16-hour days for two weeks continuously, followed by three days off. However, hotter and drier summers are extending this core fire season from May through October. Firefighters' contracts are being extended to match this and there are plans to implement a year-round wildfire service. In 2022, an unusually warm fall saw fires burning through to the end of October. The common belief amongst firefighters that, "Once the rains come in September it will all be over" no longer rings true and creates unpredictability and seasonal confusion.

Working with such intensity for extended periods of time is having negative effects on firefighters, creating increased burnout and physical exhaustion. Moreover, October and November often provided a much-needed respite between seasonal jobs giving time for rest and relaxation, but the extended seasons are eating away at this time. Alongside this, fire seasons are becoming more destructive; the three worst fire seasons in British Columbia have been within the past five years (1). 2021 saw an extended period of temperatures above 45 °C across British Columbia creating exceptionally difficult working conditions and greater destruction to communities and homes. Watching hundreds of houses in a community burn to the ground brings a far greater emotional toll on firefighters than some trees in a remote area.

Unpredictable winters

If you're lucky enough to catch a chair lift ride with a local veteran at the ski hill, they will assure you that the winters here aren't like they used to be. There is a collective memory of colder winters with never-ending snowstorms bringing perfect light, fluffy snow that was a dream to ski. I am told that the snowbanks in town would reach 10 feet high and stay all winter long. In my five years in Nelson, it is rare to see such a sight even for just a day. Whilst it is hard to decipher what is exactly true and what may be rose-tinted memories of a bygone era, it is clear that our winters are becoming warmer. The ski industry is a huge revenue source for Nelson, with a ski resort and dozens of heli-skiing operations in the area that brings tourists from across the world. With less predictable snowfall and warmer winters, there is growing uncertainty around these stable winter jobs. Moreover, a volatile climate creates greater avalanche danger in the region leading to higher risk for seasonal workers. Avalanche professionals, ski guides and ski patrollers must navigate working in higher-stress positions. Climate unpredictability creates greater dangers in both summer and winter work for locals, adding stress to these already intense seasonal jobs.

Reflection

The impacts of a changing climate are evident in Nelson; seasonal workers face burnout and exhaustion as jobs become increasingly dangerous. Furthermore, unpredictable seasons mean certain jobs may be lost, whilst others run longer making it difficult for workers to plan time off to rest and recover. This begs the question: is the long-standing dream of sustainable seasonality coming to an end in Nelson? As it is across the globe, climate uncertainty is creating an unsettling epoch in Nelson where locals are having to question their working identities and renegotiate lifestyles that have been built around seasonal work for many years. The familiar seasonal pendulum is being disturbed in Nelson, and whilst this may provide future opportunities, it will not be without great unease and disruption to seasonal workers and existing ways of living.

The author

Jake Stenson grew up in the UK and moved to British Columbia, Canada in 2017 to spend a winter skiing. Five years later he found himself still enjoying the Canadian mountains and has worked as a wildfire fighter and ski resort employee. In his free time, you can find Jake revelling in one of his many outdoor passions; skiing, climbing, trail running, mountain biking, hiking, or camping. Jake is currently studying for a Bachelor of Geographic Information Systems and works flying drones to map forest fires.

Reference

1.   Report: BC Wildfire Service. "2021 Wildfire Season Summary." Province of British Columbia, 2022. (https://www2.gov.bc.ca/gov/content/safety/wildfire-status/about-bcws/wildfire-history/wildfire-season-summary).

Part V **Professional practices**

Paul Schneider
26 How seasonal is gin?

No spirit is as seasonal as gin, from its ingredients to its consumption. Culturally, gin is tied to summer. The ingredients used to make gin can only be harvested at a certain time of the year: juniper, coriander and angelica are three key ingredients used by distillers to distil Classic Gins. The raw ingredients are harvested in autumn while citrus, including the oranges and lemons most commonly used in the distillation of gin, are a winter fruit. The harvesting of more tropical ingredients on the other hand, including cinnamon, cardamom, or grains of paradise tend to be governed by seasonal rainfalls. As the seasonal conditions for the raw ingredients, also referred to as 'botanicals', shift under new climate regimes it is worth shedding some light on how the seasonality of gin may be impacted. Exploring this topic makes sense from social, economic, and environmental perspectives.

I distil gin. It began as a pastime pleasure, or maybe even an obsession, and then almost overnight turned into a success story. The judges at the 2022 World Gin Awards awarded Awildian Coromandel Dry Gin, which I developed with my partner, with the prize of the World's Best Classic Gin. The ability to capture and combine seasonal flavours and aromas through distillation fascinates me to this day. These days this is something I do several times a week using a traditional 150L copper still. I use fresh ingredients as the seasons permit, many of which I grow in our distiller's herb garden. Others are foraged, or we work with small-scale growers. Harvesting sometimes takes me to exciting places. Two of my favourite activities are picking citrus and blackberry. At the beginning of September, the end of winter on New Zealand's Coromandel Peninsula, I tend to pick Seville oranges. According to the owner of my favourite tree, this is one of the original Seville trees brought to New Zealand after WWII. Over the years it has evidently withstood many weather events. It is old and gnarly yet strong and beautiful. I am grateful to have permission to harvest these oranges. In a couple of months, it will be time to collect honey before the Tutu plant (a New Zealand native) flowers, as this can lead to tutin poisoning of the honey. At the peak of summer, once the morning dew has lifted and the leaves are dry from the night, I pick enough blackberry leaves to last me through the year. Many see this plant as a pest and people prefer to get rid of it, but for me it is a highly prized seasonal resource. As I pick the leaves, I make sure to enjoy as many berries as I can, as this is a relatively short seasonal time window. Soon the insects and the birds will take over and there will be none left.

Gin botanicals and the flavours they create in a gin must be carefully structured, somewhat like an orchestra. There is a beginning and a middle and an end to a great flavour profile. Each of the over 20 raw ingredients that I use plays its part in this symphony. Not too loud and not too much in the background but "just right". For this, the seasonal harvest must be carefully organized. The flavour composition in gin is in many ways the sensory wonder that nature has to offer. Each of the botanicals has a seasonality to it, albeit in many cases in different parts of the world. One secret' lies in knowing exactly when these botanicals are at their best, when they are ready to be harvested to be used either fresh or to be dried or otherwise preserved. The list is long and there is always some seasonal gin-related activity over the course of the year. If it is not harvesting and curing, then it is gardening and caring for the plants.

The ingredients are not the only seasonal parts of gin. When it comes to its consumption this is highly seasonal too. This has been shaped by the cultural pillars on which gin was built. A quintessentially British colonial drink, a gin and tonic which is probably the most popular way to enjoy gin, simply tastes best in summer. This is a crisp and refreshing beverage with hints of bitterness, sweetness, floral notes and some heat that surprises the drinker's taste buds, especially in combination with the chilled liquid. To some extent, for a boutique distillery, this can represent a cash flow challenge. With peak sales over the summer months, winter can be a different story. Leaving export ambitions to the northern hemisphere aside, we managed to overcome this by developing a 'winter gin': a fire-side sipping gin experience that is characterized by warm, woody and spicy notes. What is more, this manuka wood-aged gin is rounded off with manuka honey, just enough to add a hint of comforting sweetness.

As with natural products in general, but more so in this case given the dependency on seasonal produce as well as seasonal consumption, it is already clear that there will be climate-related impacts. What will become of the availability and the quality of its raw ingredients? Also, from a business perspective, how will sales change as the seasons change? For an industry that was globally valued at $14.03 billion in 2020 and is projected to grow both internationally and in New Zealand (1), these are all questions worth asking. Will consumers turn to other spirits if, for example, the traditional summer holidays in New Zealand are dominated by colder and wetter weather?

As I am writing these lines, we have just lived through Cyclone Gabrielle, a severe weather event that has caused widespread damage and destruction resulting in a National State of Emergency. "The severity and the damage", New Zealand's Prime Minister Hipkins pointed out, "[. . .] has not been experienced in a generation". While severe, Cyclone Gabrielle was not the only extreme weather event on the Coromandel Peninsula this summer. In just two months, we experienced six extreme and unseasonal weather events. Apart from the devastation, this has a significant impact on people's lives and on seasonal produce. For the Coromandel this continues to mean that locals, visitors, and tourists are impacted in their travel because roads have been heavily impacted, and parts of the peninsula have been cut off. This is unfolding on the back of the Covid Pandemic. This may or may not be the new normal, but it certainly feels like change is happening rapidly. An impact on what we do and what can be done at certain times of the year is inevitable. Given the geographical spread of where gin botanicals are sourced as well as where the spirit is enjoyed, a shift in climate regimes will impact both small-scale producers as well as the gin industry as a whole. Cyclones like Gabrielle are projected to occur more frequently and more severely in my back yard as part of a drastically different climatic future on New Zealand's Coromandel Peninsula. A future that is dominated by uncertainty and impactful events leaving its mark on the way we grow, harvest, process, and enjoy natural products such as gin. For now, I cherish every season that I can visit the old Seville orange tree and I am grateful for the honey that our bees are still producing, as well as for all the other seasonal ingredients that go into making Awildian Gin. But already I am beginning to adjust the way I do certain things, because it has become necessary. I have become more aware of change and its ripple effects on my immediate and wider surroundings. Uncertainty has maybe become the order of the day but what is certain is that gin is highly seasonal, and this is unlikely to change.

The author

Paul Schneider worked as postdoctoral researcher in the CALENDARS project based at Massey University, New Zealand, while being based remotely on the Coromandel Peninsula. Schneider's research background is in climate change adaptation, coastal risk, and resilience governance. The social and physical setting of the Coromandel Peninsula, where he continues to live and work, has been a key aspect of his research for over a decade. Recently, he switched careers and now focuses his time on distilling gin (https://www.awildian.com/).

Reference

1.   https://www.alliedmarketresearch.com/gin-market-A11469

Manuel Hempel

27 Losing seasons in the landscape: When the bee season falls out of synchrony

By day I work with climate change science, but my other job is as a beekeeper. I've started to think what a changing climate might mean for me and my bees, including how it might alter 'the season', when everything comes together; when the weather, the fruit trees, the bees, and the people – beekeepers and horticulturalists – all work in synchrony. I've had conversations with beekeepers from all over, including a chance encounter with a French beekeeper recently, and many seem worried that this seasonal pattern is falling apart. But it's not only a changing climate that is to blame. There are linked changes in land use and landscape that likewise influence a change in bee season.

As a climate scientist, my workday structure is mainly socially constructed. Meetings, deadlines and working hours are in principle flexible, made up, set and defined by interacting with other people rather than nature, and this brings with it a certain degree of autonomy. As a Bergen-based beekeeper, however, I periodically have to give up autonomy over my own time and respond directly to nature. What I do and when I do it is no longer up to myself, or other people. I respond to the bees and their needs, which in turn respond to the local vegetation, which is tuned to weather conditions depending on the regional climate and meteorological seasonality of the year. All because our young planet randomly collided with a rather large asteroid, resulting in a 23,5° tilt between the earth's rotational axis and its orbital plane around the sun. Some 4.5 billion years later we can still feel the side effects: long bright summer days followed by long, dark winter nights during the Norwegian 'mørketid' – the dark times. A rhythm that we Nordic beekeepers have adapted to in unison with the bees.

The winter period is dedicated to honey sales, maintenance, and preparation. As spring approaches, we beekeepers from all over the country begin to follow the local flora very closely and share our observations. We do so joyously, exchanging observations across Norway about the first snowbells, willow buds, crocus sprouts. Early or late? Which region is ahead? Our excitement grows as the long-anticipated hazel bloom in early March marks the start of the Nordic beekeeping season. These trees provide the first substantial pollen – protein – of the year. This stimulates the queen to resume reproduction and start growing the colony just in time to be ready (meaning a strong colony population) for the fruit bloom about 6 weeks later.

The west coast of Norway where I live is characterized by its rough terrain, deep fjords, rocky islands, and steep mountains. When the mountains meet with the humid western weather approaching from the Atlantic Ocean, this can bring plenty of precipitation. As a result, Bergen, the largest city in the county, experiences an average of 239 rainy days a year. All these factors make the region rather unsuitable for most forms of commercial horticulture, with one exemption: fruit production along Hardanger Fjord. Stretching about 80 km in-land, the local microclimate, in combination with relatively gentle and fertile slopes along the shorelines, provides favourable growing conditions for fruits and berries, ranging from apples to plums, cherries, pears, raspberries and cassis. All these crops require active pollination to achieve a rich, high-quality yield.

The fruit bloom is an annual event which brings together various 'actors' – bees, trees, beekeepers and fruit farmers – as hundreds of honeybee hives are moved into Hardanger Fjord orchards for pollination services in late April Figure 27.1 (l). The more bees, the better for everyone involved. Strong colonies can take advantage of early blooms and thrive. Excess honey can be harvested by the beekeeper. High fruit pollination rates might translate into high yields for farmers. And, generally speaking, their success is our success, as about 35% of our food is directly or indirectly dependent on animal pollination, with the majority by insect and bee-species (1)

Figure 27.1: Beehives during spring in the Hardanger Fjord; Camille in one of his apiaries in the Alpes close to Peyresq. (Photos by: Manuel Hempel).

But local weather conditions are decisive for success. Honeybees do not fly below 10 °C or in rainy conditions, most local blooms do not provide much nectar below 18 °C, frosty nights can damage the flowers (future crops), and even short rain showers can wash nectar out from the blossoms. A lot of factors need to play out simultaneously to make things work out for everyone. Hence beekeeping, and pollination, is particularly sensitive to weather conditions and vulnerable to climate risk.

The Nordics are often mentioned as one of the regions that might partially benefit from the global climate change trends we are experiencing today. Rising temperatures and an extended growing season might increase yields and arable land area, opening for new opportunities for horticulturists and beekeepers alike. Fruit production in the previously unsuited northern Trøndelag region is increasing, some Hardanger fruit farmers started growing apricots, and the northernmost commercial vineyard can now be found on the slopes of the Sognefjord at 61,16 °N, a mere 668 km below the arctic circle. But there is a major downside: increased climate variability. Extreme weather events are not only predicted to occur in higher frequencies but are expected to increase in intensity. As of today, western Norway has already experienced a more than 1 °C temperature rise since the 1970s, but at the same time precipitation has also increased by about 15%, trending upwards (2). Previously-rare extreme weather events, such as the infamous 2018 summer drought, or the extremely wet west coast summer of 2017 – both of which caused substantial losses to agricultural yields – are becoming more and more common.

The climate is also changing in southern Europe, but unlike the Nordics the future scenarios include all of the risks but none of the rewards, as there are very few prospects for long term positive effects on agriculture and ecosystems. The Mediterranean region has been warming up 20% faster than the global average. The water demand is expected to double by 2050, yet a 10–15% reduction in rainfall is predicted in the likely scenario of an average global warming of 2 °C (3). This is nothing new. We have seen the trickling rivers and raging wildfires in the media over the past 20 years. But climatic changes can often be perceived as abstract, far away, and hard to grasp. So, what does this mean for people's daily lives in the affected areas?

About 1800 km south of Norway, in Peyresq, a small village 1500 m above sea-level in the Alpes de Haute Provence, I met Camille in late summer 2022. He has been living in Peyresq since the early 90s and has been keeping bees and growing fruit in the surrounding mountains ever since. Now, at age 66, he has retired as an Engineering Professor and is fully dedicated to farming the land and caring for his honeybees Figure 27.1 (r).

Looking back at the past 30 years Camille has experienced substantial changes in the climate, affecting the landscape and livelihoods of all human- and non-human inhabitants. And his story is typical for many places in the area. Livestock farming and pastoral activities have traditionally shaped the landscape, architecture, and societies in the region. Just a few decades ago the local economy was mainly driven by agriculture, with sheep farming being omnipresent. Hay meadows and winter stables in the valleys and vast summer pastures on the mountain tops, separated by forests along the mountain slopes, have defined the region's typical cultural landscape, equally appreciated by the locals and an increasing number of tourists.

Today, due to a combination of uncertain prospects in agriculture, population dynamics and a rapidly emerging tourism industry, agricultural activity is gradually giving way to tourism. This trend is being amplified by recent changes in the local climate, which imposes new risks to agriculture, often making it economically unsustainable. Southern France has seen severe summer droughts in the last couple of years, and when I met Camille in early September 2022, the region had just experienced one of the hottest and driest summers on record. The combination of changing climatic patterns and land-uses is reshaping the landscape and its seasonal rhythms, affecting the foraging grounds for the bees. The traditional pastoral practice relies on growing hay for winter feed in the valleys and taking advantage of the mountainous wild meadow resources during the summer months. Over the years, an altered hydrology, with diminished water resources for the livestock, has meant these reservoirs had to be manually resupplied, significantly increasing the effort and operational costs. Then, as extended droughts progressively diminished the meadow resources themselves, on which both bees and livestock forage, the traditional practice faded out and local farmers stopped herding sheep in the mountains. They either give up the activity altogether and turn to tourism, or shift to intensified agricultural practices in the valleys, which depends on supplementary feed and competes with the tourism industry over scarce land and water resources.

The effects of this development are clearly visible in the landscape. Camille showed me old pictures of the mountains across the valley. Formerly covered in a diverse cultural landscape of farms, pastures and hedges, the mountain slope is now fully overgrown by various fast-growing conifers, originally introduced for wood production. With the departure of the grazing livestock from the mountain meadows, which previously kept the trees in check, the meadows are in a steady decline as the ecological balance shifts from grasslands to forests.

As for Camille, the consequences of this development – the connected changes in climate and landscape – are not only of an aesthetic nature but have directly impacted his life as a beekeeper and fruit grower. It might seem counterintuitive when dealing with cold blooded insects, but in beekeeping long stable winters are your friend. Longer summer seasons and shorter winters have increased the pressure of certain pests, such as the parasitic Varroa mite, which requires bee brood to multiply. Long stable winters have helped keep these mites under control, as the queen does not lay eggs during wintertime. Under a thick insulating layer of snow, the beehives used to also be well protected from wind and extreme temperatures. But as the snowline gradually retreated up the mountains, the apiaries are increasingly exposed to wind and high temperature fluctuations. As a result, the bees need more energy in the form of honey to keep their temperature stable and face the risk of running out of supplies before spring arrives. This has substantially increased winter losses over the last few decades.

The changing vegetation has also affected nectar sources, as the biodiverse mountain meadows were overgrown by thick conifer forests that provide comparably little value to pollinating insects. And the remaining nectar sources now often dry up during the increasingly hot summer months, cutting honeybees and other wild pollinating insects off from essential food sources. Today, Camille harvests about 50% less honey per hive than he used to back in the 90s. To compensate, he has increased the number of hives he has in the valleys, but the overall workload and effort has also scaled accordingly. To gain the same results, he now needs to put in far more resources and time than he used to. Time he could have been spending with family and friends in an already tight growing season.

But honey yield, effort and time is not what concerns him most. As a fruit farmer, who depends on pollination for his crops, he is very aware of the interspecies relationships that have evolved over millions of years and form the basis that many ecosystems are built upon. But the calendars of bees, trees and farmers seem to be getting more and more out of sync. Early warm periods trigger early responses within the systems. But plants and bees have different response times and rhythms. As a result, the honeybees now often fail to keep up with the trees and meet the blooms at full strength, missing out on an important nectar flow and resulting in poorer pollination results. And five months later, when its eventually time to harvest, the temperatures often remain so high that it's hard for the farmers to perform fieldwork during the day and get the harvest done in time. What Camille does and when he does it is not up to himself. He responds to the bees and the trees, which respond to the local vegetation, which is tuned to the weather depending to the regional climate and meteorological seasonality of the year.

Back in Norway, we are still far from the conditions in southern Europe, but we can already catch early glimpses of the challenges we might have to face in the future. It is uncertain how we will be able to adapt. But one thing is for sure, no matter what: When the Hazel starts to bloom, thousands of beekeepers all over the country will be getting excited and start preparing for 'the season'. The rest will follow.

The author

Manuel Hempel has a background in aerospace engineering and after several years in the industry transitioned to human geography with a focus on climate risk in agriculture and food systems. He is based in Bergen, Norway, where he is affiliated to the Bjerknes Center for Climate Research and currently works in the Climate and Environment department of Norce Research. His research focusses on the co-production of climate services for a better handling of climate risk in society. He has also been working as a semi-commercial beekeeper for many years, providing pollination services and producing honey in and around Bergen.

References

1. Potts, S. G., V. Imperatriz-Fonseca, H. T. Ngo, J. C. Biesmeijer, T. D. Breeze, L. V. Dicks, L. A. Garibaldi, R. Hill, J. Settele, & A. J. Vanbergen. *The assessment report on pollinators, pollination and food production: summary for policymakers.* Secretariat of the Intergovernmental Science-Policy Platform on Biodiversity and Ecosystem Services, 2016. (https://www.ipbes.net/assessment-reports/pollinators) (accessed on 17 March 2023).
2. Meteorological Institute of Norway. *Vestlandet since 1900.* (https://www./met.no/vaer-og-klima klima-siste-150-ar/regionale-kurver/vestlandet-siden-1900). (accessed on 17 March 2023).
3. MedEC, *Mediterranean Experts on Climate and Environmental Change: Climate and environmental change in the Mediterranean basin – First Mediterranean assessment report MAR1*, 2020.

Simon Meisch

28 I have bee-s/-n up there

Wo die Schwalbe das Nest mit den törigen Jungen umflattert,
Und die Schmetterlinge sich freun und die Bienen, da wandl' ich
Mitten in ihrer Lust; ich steh im friedlichen Felde
Wie ein liebender Ulmbaum da, und wie Reben und Trauben
Schlingen sich rund um mich die süßen Spiele des Lebens.[1]

When you are invited to reflect on how beekeeping changes your perception of the seasons, you see some well-trodden paths before you that your train of thoughts can follow. Obviously, depending on where you live, your year has a certain number of seasons that come with specific plants and thus honey and pollen sources. When you start beekeeping you become aware of, and keep paying attention to, these natural rhythms, its botanical manifestations, and phenological interactions. Furthermore, beekeeping as a social practice is temporally structured and has its own seasons, i.e. recurrent times when specific actions usually need to be done such as preparing the hives, swarm control or varroa treatment. As these seasons are co-produced by the bees, the beekeeper, and their natural environment, you can ponder on your own beekeeping seasons. Finally, also beehives have their seasons, e.g. colony build-up, drone rearing, swarm time, honey production, driving out the drones or rearing winter bees. Of course, all these seasons hang closely together and all of them are influenced by processes such as climate change or globalisation (e.g. in terms of emerging novel species such as the Varroa mite or the Asian hornet). Next to these well-trodden paths, there are less ostensible ones, and my reflections took an unexpected path.

When contemplating on how I as a beekeeper perceive seasons, I soon realised that this chapter needed to be about me keeping bees at a specific place and about being seen as a person who does this practice at this locale. For, often when I come from the bees, I would pass my friends' house to see if they are in their garden. Depending on the direction I come from, they ask me if I had been "up there". With this, they refer to the piece of land where I keep my bees and which I rent from the city of Tübingen. The city owns many agricultural lands and lets out some to citizens for a small sum. This way, the municipality does not have to maintain these

---

1 "Where the swallow flutters around the nest with the foolish young, and the butterflies rejoice and the bees, there I walk in the midst of their delight; I stand there in the peaceful field like a loving elm tree, and like vines and grapes the sweet games of life wind around me." (From Friedrich Hölderlin: Muße; own translation).

plots and citizens have their green space. In fact, many citizens try to get hold of such land, so I consider myself lucky to have obtained one.

The patch is about 800 square metres big and an ancient vineyard. Today, three of four terraces are covered with mixed woodland, the two upmost ones with broadleaf species such as oak and beech and the one below with pines and hazel. The lowest and biggest terrace is covered with dry grassland, some fruit trees (cherry, pear, and plums) and an old apple tree completely overgrown with ivy. The patch is enclosed by hedges (blackthorn, hawthorn, elder, hazel, brambleberry, and privet). Some of the neighbouring lands are still used for growing grapevines, others as orchards. I believe it is a good place to keep bees as they find pollen and nectar sources in all outdoor seasons of the bee year.

My piece of land is part of the Hirschauer Berg, a landscape and nature protection area' on the south slopes of the Spitzberg which is a free-standing ridge between the Neckar and Ammer valleys and which extends over eight kilometres west of Tübingen.

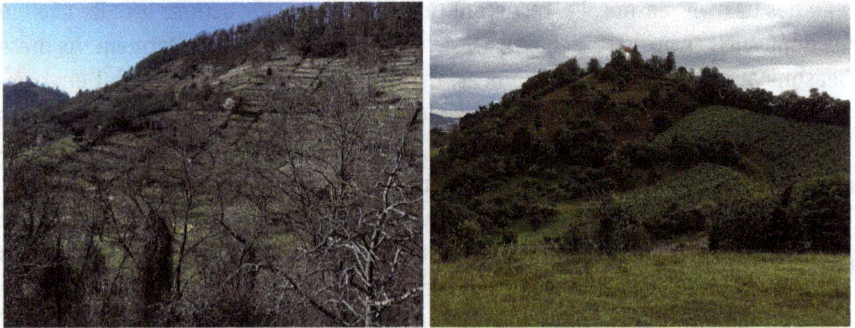

Figure 28.1: The Hirschauer Berg with its heritage of vine growing, taken in March (left) and July (right) (Photos by: Simon Meisch).

The slopes of the Hirschauer Berg consist of a mosaic of dry grasslands and bushes. Visitors can easily recognise how the area was used for growing grapevines. The landscape is still characterised by terraces made of dry-stone walls built of Keuper sandstone (for both, see Figure 28.1).

In the Middle Age, the forests on the steep, climatically favourable southern slopes were cleared, and vineyards were planted. In its heyday, the area was an important wine-growing region. Yet, with the Little Ice Age, the climatic conditions for growing wine in this area deteriorated; with the Reformation, the monasteries as organisers of local viticulture disappeared; and with the Thirty Years' War, the regional population collapsed dramatically. Increasingly, people began to use vineyards for sheep grazing and growing fruit or hops, and hence continued to keep the landscape open and free of woods.

Today, many plots of land are no longer used, and a natural succession of shrubs and trees is progressing. From a biodiversity perspective, though, this is an undesirable development. With centuries of agricultural cultivation, a special habitat for heat-loving plant and animal species has emerged. In summer, the soils of exposed areas can warm up to 70° Celsius. Limiting woody plant encroachment thus requires constant maintenance – also from me, as it is one of the conditions of the lease to keep the land open.

Figure 28.2: Blackthorn in spring and autumn (Photos by: Simon Meisch).

While agreeing to this nature conservation rationality, parts of me regrets its consequences, as some of the shrubs are my favourite seasonal markers, especially blackthorn. In spring, its white flowers froth the slopes, exuding a sweet fragrance, and providing a rich bee pasture. In autumn, its fruits, the sloes form clouds of dark blue and violet, and because of its astringent tannins, make a remarkable jam (see Figure 28.2).

For me as a beekeeper, it is relevant that my bees live on a former vineyard as its microclimate can be different to other spots close-by. For instance, on the internet, you find all sorts of useful tools informing you about bees' flight days in the flowering season or the best periods to treat against the varroa mites. Although these webpages tailor their information to a specific place based on the postcode, they often do not match with my own observations. I still need practical wisdom to contextualise such information and incorporate it into my practices and as such learn how to create knowledge fit for beekeeping at this place.

Thus far, my narrative is consistent with the experiences of many beekeepers and can be comprehended by what the social anthropologist Sara Asu Schroer called 'weathering': "The concept [. . .] describes the weather as an ongoing activity that has a transformational force on how air currents and landforms interplay and co-create each other. It is further pivotal for mediating the movements of humans and other living beings that sense, perceive and experience in the midst of a weathering world." (1, page 194). As a beekeeper, I am subject to the same elements and as such try to perceive them – albeit imperfectly – through my bees' eyes.

Acknowledging this, I begin to regard myself in a bigger picture, as an inhabitant of what Barbara Adam called a 'timescape': I do not only become aware of the "spatial features of past and present activities and interactions of organisms and matter" within this unique landscape of the Hirschauer Berg, but also its "rhythmicities, [. . .] timings and tempos, [. . .] changes and contingencies" as results of processes of reproduction within the beehive, the pollinating bees, natural succession and the very specific interactions of land and air. And I see myself as part of these "complex temporalities of contextual being, becoming and dwelling", and try to make sense of it and find my way through (2, page 10).

Contemplating seasons from a beekeeper's perspective proved to be a good exercise as it broadened my perspective. To my surprise, I began to think about the academic seasons for the first time. Obviously, life in academia is also temporally structured, and for all national differences, terms and term breaks alternate everywhere. The term usually feels longer; its time is more condensed and races by as one meeting follows the next. Moreover, academics often live in fear that some other person will do more and better in less time, turning academic life in a virtual race with invisible competitors.

It might be an interesting empirical question to what extent national academic seasons are in sync with the many other temporal patterns to which the minds and bodies of academics belong. With some certainty, we can say that academic seasons tend to be decontextualised – and here I noticed an inconsistency with me as a beekeeper. Approaching my bees with the temporal mindset of an academic always creates problems. Bees are peaceful, but they suffer no fools. In my experience, working with bees as if they were on a 'to-do list', squeezed into a tight schedule, does not lend itself to good experiences. Conversely, I feel I am a better beekeeper if I first locate myself in the overall system of the Hirschauer Berg, feel, smell, and observe what is happening around me before engaging with the bees.

Basically, this is a familiar conceptual insight, but one that feels different in practice: to produce knowledge well, the separation of subject and object does not work. After all, being amongst or in the middle of things, is what we literally mean by having an interest in something ('inter-esse'). So, being "up there" with my bees taught me how it *feels* to be someone who produces good knowledge fit for a function at a given place and time. Thus, thinking about bees and seasons showed me a way not only to be a good beekeeper, but possibly also to become a better academic. A first step has been taken . . .

The author

Dr. Simon Meisch, ethicist and political scientist, is a senior lecturer for interdisciplinary ethics at the International Centre for Ethics in the Sciences and Humanities of the University of Tübingen. There, he is responsible for coordinating interdisciplinary ethics teaching. His research topics include climate change adaptation, approaches and methods of application-oriented ethics (especially water ethics), ethics didactics and the environmental humanities.

References

1. Azevedo, A. & S. A. Schroer. *"Weathering: a graphic essay"*. *Vibrant 13* (2016): 177–194.
2. Adam, B. Timescapes of Modernity. The environment and invisible hazards. London/New York: Psychology Press, 1998.

Bruce Glavovic

29 A new season for climate change science and praxis?

Introduction

I write these reflections at the end of the 27th Conference of Parties meeting of governments (COP27), held in Egypt in November 2022, at which governments sought to progress climate action. COP27 was informed by the Sixth Assessment Report (AR6) by the Intergovernmental Panel on Climate Change (IPCC). Established in 1988, the IPCC provides UN member nations with comprehensive assessments of the state of climate change science and its implications.

I spent much of 2017–2022 devoted to AR6. I was a Coordinating Lead Author of the chapter on sea-level rise in the IPCC's *Special Report on the Ocean and Cryosphere in a Changing Climate* (1), Lead Author of the chapter on Climate Resilient Development, and co-lead for the Cross-Chapter Paper on Cities and Settlements by the Sea, in the Working Group II report (2). How can I convey the gravitas of the climate predicament outlined in AR6? Moreover, where do we stand now – after more than three decades of intensive climate change science-policy interactions? What does this portend for climate change scientists, policy advisors and elected politicians? What does it mean for you and I? And how might answers to these questions inform our understanding about seasons; and how we might navigate impending dangerous climate change?

Heading towards an epochal winter for the climate science-policy-praxis nexus

The notion of epochal seasons is apt because the nexus of climate change science, policy and praxis dates back well over three decades. One could say that the IPCC's First and Second Assessment Reports marked spring with the 'birth' of the IPCC and COP meetings. The Third, Fourth and Fifth Assessment Reports were the summer for the climate science-policy-praxis nexus. Global awareness and climate action came to full bloom. The 2015 COP meeting in Paris was noteworthy for agreement to limit global warming to below two degrees Celsius (above pre-industrial levels), aiming for a rise of no more than 1.5 degrees Celsius by 2100. Global warming beyond this level is dangerous. IPCC Assessment Reports paint a progressively dismal picture of the state of the climate, but governments procrastinate at successive COP meetings.

A new season is upon us. We are entering a world of dangerous climate change. This is a present reality for many. A recent World Meteorological Organisation report finds there is a 50:50 chance of global near-surface temperature crossing the threshold of 1.5 °C above pre-industrial levels by 2026 (3). Six out of 10 respondents to a 2021 *Nature* survey of leading climate scientists expect global warming to reach at least 3 °C above pre-industrial levels by 2100 (4). Climate-compounded disasters – more intense and frequent extreme hydro-meteorological events and disruptive change – manifest this new season of climate turbulence.

Past approaches to climate science, policy, business practices, and consumer behaviour no longer suffice. A new climate praxis – transformative ways to translate climate knowledge and understanding into action – is urgent and imperative. It might seem counter-intuitive but, in charting new pathways into *terra incognitae*, we can look to the past and be guided by ancient wisdom and insights from indigenous people about how to navigate uncharted waters.

Climate turbulence, anxiety, fatigue, and (in)action

Climate-compounded disasters are commonplace. They cause devastation. Many people are frightened about humanity's prospects. Climate anxiety and climate fatigue are pronounced. Calls for urgent climate action are growing. But many people are emotionally drained by having to contemplate difficult moral choices when plausible actions they might take don't seem likely to make a difference.

Progress at COP27 was dubious, despite the UN Secretary General's stark warning at the start of the meeting: "We are on a highway to climate hell with our foot still on the accelerator" (5). Post-COP27 news headlines are very disappointing: "COP27 ends with historic win and dismal fail" (6); "COP27 outcome: fossil fuel progress criticised, historic climate fund cheered" (7). Dismal progress at COP27 compounds the failures of prior COP meetings. Prospects for better outcomes at COP28 – to be held in the United Arab Emirates in 2023 – are grim given the undue influence of oil producers and lobbyists at COP27 (8).

Climate inaction by world leaders is confounding – especially when hope is raised by apparent progress at COP meetings, and fresh promises made to translate climate change science into action.

The UN Secretary General's clarion call echoes myriad long-standing calls to action by the youth, scientists, Indigenous People and citizens around the world.

Yet, governments and world leaders have failed to translate robust climate change science into action at the requisite pace and scale – despite having approved each IPCC AR since 1990. How many more COP meetings will it take before human-induced global warming is arrested and those most at-risk are enabled to take transformative adaptive action? How might we mobilise action in the face of the climate impasse?

The coming winter for the IPCC and new pathways for climate action

I have had to reconsider my involvement in future IPCC work. Should I and my fellow climate change science colleagues roll up our sleeves after AR6 and prepare for a new AR cycle – AR7? Will more science make a difference in this new season of climate turbulence? Challenging moral questions about the role of science are raised. All of us – whether citizens or policy analysts – face vexing choices.

There is an unwritten social contract between scientists and society. Public investment in science is expected to lead to better understanding about our world and help achieve beneficial societal outcomes. Dismal progress at COP meetings and weak political action around the world indicates that the science-society contract is broken, not only with respect to climate change but the raft of intersecting socio-political-environmental crises that humanity faces. It is time for climate change scientists to pause and ask: how we can restore the science-society contract?

This question underpinned a journal article I wrote with Tim Smith and Iain White, entitled *The Tragedy of Climate Change Science*, published at the close of 2021 (9). We identified three main courses of action: First, continue "science as usual" – which has been dominated by the natural sciences and documents the state of climate change and its impacts. The findings of successive IPCC reports, and AR6 in particular, coupled with tepid mobilisation of climate action by successive COP meetings, demonstrates that persisting with this course of action is untenable.

Second, bolster social science contributions to climate change research, and intensify advocacy and activism, to identify and address political barriers to climate action. In practice, this course of action has been underway for well over a decade. Despite concerted efforts, the political impasse is entrenched; most palpably reflected in the outcomes of successive COP meetings. This option is also untenable given the narrow window of time left to avert dangerous climate change.

Third, albeit unpalatable, we argue that it is time to stop research that merely documents global warming and its impacts. We propose a moratorium on climate change science-as-usual. This more radical course of action focuses attention on exposing and mending the broken science-society contract. We reached this conclusion reluctantly. In doing so, we recognise the remarkable success of the IPCC and the climate change science community. In the space of three decades, the IPCC has provided robust evidence about the nature and root causes of climate change and identified the actions necessary to tackle global warming. Public and political awareness has been raised. The time has come, we argue, for the climate change science community to hold governments and world leaders to account. They need to act on the IPCC findings they endorsed, distilled in the closing statement of the 2022 Working Group II *Summary for Policymakers*: "The cumulative scientific evidence is unequivocal: Climate change is a threat to human well-being and planetary health. Any further delay in concerted anticipatory global action on adaptation and mitigation will miss a brief and rapidly closing window of opportunity to secure a liveable and sustainable future for all (*very high confidence*)" (2).

Our article provoked a polarised response – from open hostility to strong support. Unsurprisingly, some scientists argued that science is an objective undertaking and has no place for advocacy. Politics should be left to politicians, they say. Others welcomed our fresh case for addressing long-standing political inaction. Many recognise that science does not exist in splendid isolation of the *realpolitik* of public decision-making. The science-society contract needs to be restored.

We did not elaborate on how to operationalise the moratorium. That would have been presumptuous. Rather, we called for serious introspection and robust deliberation amongst the climate change science community about how best to implement a moratorium. At the very least, I think, the 'architecture' of the United Nations Framework Convention on Climate Change (UNFCCC), IPCC and COP cycles need to be critically evaluated and fundamentally reconfigured.

This does not mean that scientists should stop all climate change research. There is much that can and should be done with local communities and governments to enable more targeted and timely climate action. There are many ways to expose political inaction and restore the science-society contract. This will unfold in diverse ways in different settings. What is clear is that climate change science-as-usual should not continue. Halting the next IPCC assessment cycle to critically evaluate the best way forward is essential if we are to break the climate change impasse. Hence the coming winter for the IPCC.

Just as climate change scientists need to pause and reflect on how best to navigate these uncharted waters, so too do others – citizens, policymakers, business leaders, politicians, and others. What inspiration and guidance might we draw upon to weather this new season?

Ancient foundations for charting climate resilient development pathways

The World Meteorological Organisation (2022) recently published a multi-organisation synopsis of climate change science. Entitled 'United in Science', it finds the planet is in "unchartered territory of destruction" (10). How do we chart climate resilient development pathways in this *terrae incognitae*?

Introspection and deliberation amongst climate change scientists alone will not suffice. Scientists, citizens, policy advisors, business-owners, labour, government officials and politicians, the youth and many more need to be brought together in new ways to build shared understanding about our predicament and how to mobilise collective action. We can lean on traditional knowledge and ancient wisdom as we face turbulent futures.

Te Ao Māori, the worldview of the Indigenous People of Aotearoa New Zealand, provides a robust foundation for charting climate resilient development pathways in Aotearoa – enabling people and nature to prosper. Māori draw on mātauranga Māori (their ancestral knowledge), te reo Māori (their language) and whakapapa (ancestral lineage) to articulate their deeply spiritual, intertwined relationship with nature. There is an extensive and robust body of knowledge and scholarship that describes Kaupapa Māori (Māori-centred) approaches relevant to Western constructs like climate resilience and sustainable development.

We can draw on many other ancient wisdoms – e.g., from the Great Law of the Haudenosaunee Confederacy in what is now the northeast USA in which decisions were guided by considering outcomes for the seventh generation. The concept of ubuntu, an Nguni Bantu term from southern Africa, encapsulates the relatedness of our shared humanity: "I am because you are." Among other things, ubuntu is a celebration of interdependence, fellowship, reconciliation, community and harmony – including unity between the physical and spiritual worlds.

Religions have diverse creation stories but concur about the divinity of nature which needs to be treated accordingly. For example, in 2015 Pope Francis published the *Laudato Si'* – entitled *Climate change & Inequality: Care for Our Common Home* – an encyclical that centres on caring for nature and all people. The ancient Chinese religion, Taoism or Daoism, is founded on divine harmony between nature and people.

Ancient wisdoms, indigenous knowledge and praxis, and the world's religions, provide nautical charts and navigation tools for making our way through uncharted, turbulent waters. They are celestial reference points for navigating this new epochal season. They light a pathway to counter the dark side of humanity. They outline spiritual, ethical, and moral imperatives that can be distilled as a duty of care and respect for each other, across generations, non-human species, and nature. They are foundational for restoring the science-society contract and enabling climate resilient development for human and planetary well-being.

The author

Bruce is a Professor at Massey University, New Zealand. His research centres on making societal choices in the Anthropocene, focusing on coastal governance, climate change adaptation, and natural hazards planning. He held leadership roles in the IPCC Working Group II contribution to the Sixth Assessment. He is co-Editor-in-Chief of *Ocean & Coastal Management*. He led the team that produced South Africa's *White Paper for Sustainable Coastal Development* in 2000.

References

1. Oppenheimer, M., B.C. Glavovic, J. Hinkel . . . & Z. Sebesvari. "Sea Level Rise and Implications for Low-Lying Islands, Coasts and Communities". In H.-O. Pörtner, D.C. Roberts, V. Masson-Delmotte, et al. (eds.), *IPCC Special Report on the Ocean and Cryosphere in a Changing Climate*. Cambridge: Cambridge University Press, 2019. (https://www.ipcc.ch/srocc/).
2. IPCC. *Climate Change 2022: Impacts, Adaptation, and Vulnerability. Contribution of Working Group II to the Sixth Assessment Report of the Intergovernmental Panel on Climate Change*. Cambridge: Cambridge University Press, 2022. (https://www.ipcc.ch/report/ar6/wg2/).
3. Tollefson, J. "Top climate scientists are sceptical that nations will rein in global warming". *Nature* (2021). (https://www.nature.com/articles/d41586-021-02990-w).
4. Frangoul, A. "We're on a 'highway to climate hell,' UN chief Guterres says, calling for a global phase-out of coal". *CNBC*, 2022. (https://www.cnbc.com/2022/11/07/were-on-a-highway-to-climate-hell-un-chief-guterres-says.html).
5. Oram, R. "COP 27 ends with historic win and abysmal fail". *Newsroom*, 2022. (https://www.newsroom.co.nz/sustainable-future/cop-27-ends-with-historic-win-and-abysmal-fail).
6. Stuff. "COP27 outcome: Fossil fuel progress criticised, historic climate fund cheered". *Stuff*, 2022. (https://www.stuff.co.nz/environment/climate-news/300744509/cop27-outcome-fossil-fuel-progress-criticised-historic-climate-fund-cheered).
7. The Guardian. "Fears over oil producers' influence with UAE as next host of Cop climate talks". *The Guardian*, 2022. (https://www.theguardian.com/world/2022/nov/22/fears-over-oil-producers-influence-with-uae-as-next-host-of-cop-climate-talks).
8. Glavovic, B. C., T. F. Smith, & I. White. "The tragedy of climate change science". *Climate and Development* 14 (2022): 829–833. (https://doi.org/10.1080/17565529.2021.2008855).
9. Stuart, L., J. Lüterbacher, L. Paterson, R. Deviller, & S. Castonguay. *United In Science 2022: a multi-organization high-level compilation of the most recent science related to climate change, impacts and responses*. WMO, 2022. (https://library.wmo.int/index.php?lvl=notice_display&id=22128#.Y35grXarFPZ).

Mathias Venning

30 Forecasting Seasons: Using seasonal forecasts to decide agricultural rhythms in East Africa

Introduction

Seasonal forecasting in East Africa is nothing new. The practice of predicting the likely average weather conditions for a particular area, over a coming season, has been around for centuries. However, with major advances made in the atmospheric sciences and associated technology, *how* we forecast seasonal climate information has changed significantly. While seasonal planning used to be a matter for local agricultural systems, instead I've seen that seasonal forecasting is now the domain of climate science. Climate science aims to carefully predict metrics such as temperature and rainfall for a given time period, and therefore determine the "most correct" seasonal practices of local farmers across East Africa. In turn, this shift has introduced a whole new range of stakeholders to local agricultural decision-making processes; many of whom are far removed from the rural communities in which these decisions are expected to be carried out. This chapter draws on my research experiences in East Africa, focused on the development of seasonal forecasts for agriculture. Here I have been working with many of the new stakeholders introduced across agricultural decision-making and witnessed the increasing complexity in seasonal rhythms.

Expecting climate

The working definition of 'climate' commonly used in meteorology and many other atmospheric sciences is, "the average weather conditions for a given area over an extended period of time", typically a thirty-year period (1). Beyond the world of natural science, science fiction writer Robert Heinlan (2) coined the popular adage, "climate is what you expect, weather is what you get". And whilst the above characterisation is often mistakenly attributed to Mark Twain, the famous American humourist did remark that, "climate lasts all the time and weather only

Acknowledgements: My thanks go to those people across East Africa who have shared with me their thoughts and experiences. Local voices are more valuable than ever as we navigate a changing climate.

a few days" (3). There are of course many different understandings of climate, yet these quotations do show that climate has often been understood as a relatively stable natural phenomenon. As such, it is normal that a level of societal expectation for the climate of a place depending on the time of year, or season, has formed. There is then also a logical expectation for the type of activities that can be undertaken at a particular point in time, activities that are deemed seasonally appropriate for a local climate.

This expectation is very visible amongst those rural farmers in East Africa I have worked and spoken with across the research projects I am involved in. In Ethiopia for example, farmers across generations have prepped, planted, nurtured and harvested their fields, cycle after cycle, according to normally expected seasonal weather patterns. Many describe how the *meher* growing season, hugely important for the success of their long-cycle cereal crops like maize and sorghum, relies upon the cyclical arrival of the *kiremt* rains every June – September. The *meher* growing season is itself made up of a diverse bundle of practices that take place before, during and after the *kiremt* rains; including soil tillage, crop selection, planting, seed sewing, irrigation, fertilisation, weed and pest management, crop harvest and crop drying. This is by no means an exhaustive list, but it does make obvious the complex relationship between the rhythms of local agricultural practice and seasonal weather.

Changing expectations

There is of course natural variation in seasonal weather patterns – the *kiremt* rains mentioned above differ in their onset (start), cessation (end) and intensity year-on-year. One historic way of predicting this natural variation has been the use of indigenous forecasting knowledge. Communities across East Africa have long observed various seasonal indicators, such as animal intestines and migration patterns, plant and insect life, and celestial bodies like the moon for seasonal weather prediction. I listened at length to one rural farmer in Tanzania describe how he knew when to plant his crops each year based on whether he had heard a particular birdsong, knowledge that had been passed down from his father before him. However, he then told us how at first the birdsong had become less and less reliable as a seasonal indicator, before eventually it had faded altogether. He had not heard the birdsong in three years, which he attributed to the changing local climate causing a change in the birds' migration.

It is abundantly clear that anthropogenic, or man-made, climate change is having a significant impact on seasonal weather patterns. Season-on-season weather is differing more frequently and more significantly from the average, or from what is normally expected.[1] Past experience and traditional seasonal indicators are thus becoming less and less reliable for seasonal forecasting and agricultural decision-making. How now should farmers decide when an activity is appropriate for the time of year? How do they know they are making the best decisions? Who is now involved in making these decisions?

Climate science to the rescue?

One response has been to turn to climate science and associated technologies. General Circulation Models (GCMs) first emerged in the 1950's, yet it is only really within the last two decades that scientific and technological advancement has enabled the production of relatively reliable seasonal forecasts using these models. Despite this recency, science-based forecast information now has an increasing role in agricultural practice across East Africa. It is easy to see why.[2] Think of providing a ministry of agriculture or a local farmer in East Africa with forecast information, derived from GCMs that capture the increasing variability of the climate, letting them know when, where and how much it would likely rain over an upcoming season. Ministries could then make decisions on seed and fertiliser distribution, while farmers could decide when to plant and harvest their crops.

Climate informed decision-making theoretically improves agricultural outcomes, and science-based seasonal forecasts are a common topic of conversation in agricultural climate adaptation. This is backed up by an extensive literature highlighting their ever-improving accuracy, reliability and potential benefits. Various organisations around the world are now routinely producing seasonal forecast information derived from GCMs for decision making. Maybe then, this is an easy answer to our earlier question. Farmers should now use these new seasonal forecasts for agricultural decision-making as it enables them to make 'better' decisions. Right?

---

1 What is perceived as normal obviously differs from person to person. But this is less important than recognising the fact that everyone does have a 'normal' that defines their climate expectations. Increasing variation in seasonal weather due to anthropogenic climate change is therefore still undermining expectations.

2 This is certainly compared to the role of indigenous forecast information in regional and national agricultural policy making. I am hard pressed indeed to think of a time that I have heard indigenous forecasting meaningfully included in an agricultural policy discussion in East Africa, and that one would be chosen over a science-based forecast in such a forum is scarcely believable.

More stakeholders, less autonomy

New ways of producing seasonal forecasts have brought new stakeholders into agriculture, re-distributing power in decision-making processes. Whereas before decision-making was mostly the prerogative of individual farmers, now the landscape covers a large network of international, regional, national and/or local organisations. One example of this is the Greater Horn of Africa Climate Outlook Forum (GHACOF), which is intended to connect seasonal forecasts to local farmers in East Africa through regional and national organisations. The GHACOF occurs three times per year, and brings together climate scientists, meteorologists and experts from multiple sectors, including agriculture, to discuss the potential impacts of the forecasted seasonal weather in the Horn of Africa region. It also facilitates the production of policy recommendations and practical preparatory advice. The intention is that the seasonal forecast and advisory information are then communicated via national networks to local communities.

Agricultural advisories, facilitated by the GHACOF and produced nationally, contain direction on what to plant, when to plant, where to plant, how to plant and when to harvest – according to a neatly defined 'meteorological season'.[3] Clearly then, agricultural decision-making has shifted somewhat, from the fields to the boardrooms and offices where this advisory information is produced. What counts as agricultural best practice throughout the season is now decided upon by a collective of experts, sitting far removed from the contexts in which they imagine decisions will be made.

It would be easy to say that no one is forcing farmers to use the forecast information or agricultural advisories, but this restructuring in agricultural decision making should not be underestimated – the effects are very real. Local farmers in Ethiopia speak about following the advisory information given to them because of a perceived trust in the expert system and a lack of alternative sources of information. Additionally, ministries of agriculture across East Africa make decisions about the national resource distribution of agricultural inputs such as seed and fertiliser based on this forecast information. Many local farmers I've had conversations with specifically say that they feel the ministries of agriculture now have a sizeable stake in their farms because of their role in the distribution of these resources. As such, the new science-based seasonal forecasts are changing local agricultural calendars and seasonal rhythms.

---

3 The GHACOF produces seasonal forecasts for March-April-May (MAM); June-July-August-September (JJAS); and October-November-December (OND).

Scientific promise vs. reality

Reduced autonomy may not in itself be such a bad thing. You could say it is just a natural adaptation of agricultural rhythms to reflect a changing climate, especially if the new seasonal forecasts result in improved agricultural outcomes. However, there are several other issues that complicate the matter. I will touch on just a few.

Communication networks between national and local actors are shaky at best, and the timeline of forecast information production, dissemination and local use are often misaligned. In many cases, rural farmers are unaware of forecast information, or receive it too late to make use of it, or do not understand it, or mistrust it and do not want to use it. Even if a farmer receives the information on time, understands it and wants to use it there is no guarantee they will have the resources to do so. For example, access to the seed recommended by the advisories is not always possible.

Additionally, understandings of seasons are often different, with local definitions of a particular season varying widely. The GHACOF itself issues forecast information for the entire East Africa region at points during the year that mediate between the rainfall seasons of eleven countries – sacrificing local seasonal relevance for a regional best-fit. Complex seasonal timeframes with huge variation across countries are packaged into neat parcels of 3 to 4-month intervals. Of course, forecast information is tailored by national organisations but local complexity is still not well captured. The same farmer in Tanzania who used local birdsong as a seasonal indicator described how each rainy season typically started one to two weeks earlier in his district compared to the neighbouring district where his brother lived, and that his valley had received much more rain than a neighbouring one despite both being within the same forecast area.

Finally, and very importantly, GCMs are inherently uncertain and only deal in probability. They cannot predict the future perfectly so there is no guarantee that what is forecast will come to be. What constitutes the best decision is therefore subjective and raises the possibility of mis-action. For example, if a local farmer is told the rains are delayed when in fact they arive 'on time', entire agricultural calendars may be disrupted. The consequences of which are very serious for the farmer if specific windows for planting or harvesting are missed. Inevitably, the consequences of an incorrect forecast are also less serious for those who produce the forecast; themselves often sitting in an office far detached from the season as it plays out 'on-the-ground'.

Is there an answer?

So, are seasonal forecasts the future of agricultural decision-making in East Africa? They are certainly not perfect. But if traditional seasonal indicators are being eroded and seasonal weather is changing beyond what is normally expected, what is the answer? In a perfect world, I do believe science-based seasonal forecasts can be beneficial. But there are a few prerequisites that involve navigating and solving the issues over utility, reliability and legitimacy described above. Prerequisites that unfortunately remain unfulfilled in many agricultural contexts across East Africa. Nonetheless, I believe we will continue to see a shift in dependency to science and technology for making sense of new seasonal patterns under a changing climate. As such, new stakeholders will enter many decision-making processes with unforeseen and potentially harmful consequences, despite the best of intentions. Increasingly, we may see local seasonal agricultural decisions being made by people sitting far removed from local contexts. We must be cognisant of all that this involves.

The author

Mathias Venning is a PhD candidate in the Climate & Environment Department at NORCE Norwegian Research Centre AS, affiliated to the University of Bergen, Norway, through the Centre for the Study of the Sciences and the Humanities (SVT). His PhD project explores how climate forecast information, as an example of science and technology, interacts with society for climate adaptation.

References

1. Royal Meteorological Society. "Glossary of Meteorology. Ed., R. E. Huschke. Boston, (American Meteorological Society), 1959. Pp. viii, 638." *Quarterly Journal of the Royal Meteorological Society*, *86* (369), 431–431. (https://doi.org/10.1002/qj.49708636919).
2. Heinlan, R. *Time Enough for Love*. New York: G. P. Putnams & Sons, 1973.
3. Le Row, C. B. *English as She is Taught*. New York: Cassell and Company, 1887.

Part VI **Planning & engineering**

Vilja Larjosto

31 New seasons on a tropical island

Itaparica

Itaparica is an island in Brazil, facing the city of Salvador. The island is situated in the biologically, physically, and culturally diverse Baía de Todos os Santos – the Bay of All Saints, or Kirimuré by its indigenous name. With 45km of beach, Itaparica's coastal zone is dominated by walled resorts with holiday homes around old fisherman village cores. Although artisan livelihoods modernize and lifestyles urbanize, the island has a rich Afro-Brazilian cultural tradition associated with natural resources.

On Itaparica, the Atlantic Forest, the mangroves, and the abundance of marine habitats provide biodiversity and livelihood opportunities. However, urban expansion and land speculation have fragmented many ecological habitats. Due to accelerated coastal erosion and storm surges, the rising sea level is making its way into islanders' consciousness. It will directly impact coastal livelihoods, settlements, and the coral reef ecosystem. The linked effects of climate change, urban development, and environmental degradation may expose a growing population and their livelihoods to future hazards.

In my doctoral research (1) I explored how seasonal phenomena and their spatial influence could be integrated to build ecological and social resilience on Itaparica island. Based on the island landscape, the research aimed to plan for more sustainable seasonal rhythms on the island.

Seasonal phenomena and livelihoods

Seasonal phenomena on Itaparica range from tourism to ecological cycles, jobs, and cultural practices (Figure 31.1). To a large extent, seasonality occurs in the *maré* space that is the tidal interface between sea and land: people gather on the beach, animal species migrate and breed, and the tides too act seasonally, with the spring tide rising higher than the regular tide in March and September.

From December to February, the peak season of tourism stresses many coastal habitats, but it also increases income opportunities. The tropical winter is characterized by increased rainfall and rougher sea between April and August, the 'off-season.' Ferries and boats continue to transport commuters and goods, but a ghost-town atmosphere takes over. Many locals appreciate the off-season as

Figure 31.1: Mapping seasonal phenomena on Itaparica island.

a pleasant time. It is the season of uninterrupted tap water, calm, wetland habitats, and school uniforms.

Many islanders support their families with artisan fishing and clamming. Their livelihoods are highly dependent on the island's coastal biodiversity. The activities decline during winter but are carried out throughout the year. Seasonal and tidal rhythms affect the variety of the catch and hence the fitted fishing and clamming practices, and locations. Demand increases in summer when many tourists are on the island, but over periods of closure fishing is restricted to protect the breeding of certain species. Locals also have knowledge about the seasonality of other natural resources. The traditional extraction of plants and plant-based materials for boats, fishing equipment, household items, musical instruments, food, medical uses, handicrafts, and religious practices may vary seasonally.

The seasonally limited income from tourism, and low access to other jobs, causes income insecurity. Tourism is heavily concentrated on the beach during summer months, and almost no other offers exist. Over the tourist season, congestion, noise, and waste peaks stress coastal ecosystems and local inhabitants. Coastal development, contamination of beaches, coral bleaching, and oil spills can have severe impacts on community livelihoods based in the marine zone. Furthermore, most food is imported from the mainland, and it is expensive. In the high season, the water supply from the mainland has shortages. Facing these challenges, some locals have counted on natural springs and subsistence agriculture, but these resources too face threats, from contamination to extreme weather. Alternative sources of income and protection of coastal biodiversity are necessary. To build resilience, a diversity of livelihoods and tourism offers could be developed based on the island's rich nature and cultural heritage, and seasonal rhythms.

Projecting new seasons

'New Seasons' is a landscape architectural strategy that addresses livelihood security and biodiversity on Itaparica. It develops ideas from the seasonal phenomena that are characteristic of the island. Part of doctoral research conducted on site and remotely in 2017–2019, it is a pilot plan experimenting a seasonal approach to resilience building. Although the research did not include a participatory process, the proposal aims to be sensitive to the local social and cultural context. The project combined literature research, maps and drawings, photography, and some interviews. The concerns and wishes of local communities were considered through the planning reports of participatory workshops held by Instituto Polis, Oficina and Demacamp for another project in 2015. The goal of the strategy presented here is to diversify livelihoods and facilitate a move from the unsustainable beach-tourism model towards environmentally and culturally sensitive forms.

To diversify income and tourism opportunities hand in hand, this strategy draws from the Afro-Brazilian cultural tradition and nature-based livelihoods of Itaparica Island. These cultures are, in many ways, founded in seasonal dynamics. The proposed spatio-temporal strategy identifies and integrates cultural heritage sites and stories, fishing practices, nature reserves, springs and fountains, horti-culture, Candomblé temples and their associated green areas,[1] and other potential sites and practices (Figure 31.2). Besides subsistence, the island's cultural and nat-ural heritage provides an opportunity to develop tourism in a manner that is less harmful to key habitats and benefits permanent residents. Islanders could de-velop exciting new tourism experiences and introduce new niches.

We developed seasonal diagrams to be used for programming activities throughout the year (Figure 31.3). For example, the farming of crops that produce yields in the seasons when fishing and clamming are restricted can improve the availability of food and reduce vulnerability to coastal hazards. In addition to sea-sonal food security, this enhances climate resilience in the longer term if rising sea levels and a warming sea reduce coastal biodiversity. In order to identify and allocate the seasonal processes and elements on the island, the diagrams are used with maps.

In the island landscape, existing cultural and natural resources provide the base for a flexible design that accommodates envisioned program(s) and practices in the northern part of Itaparica. The strategy suggests extraction reserves (a Bra-zilian environmental conservation unit), agroforest, and leaving current forests for artisanal extraction and rituals. Design interventions focus on rediscovering and connecting cultural sites and interesting locations in the island landscape, in-cluding connecting these places in time relative to their seasonal significance for instance.

The main road could transform into a connecting 'food mile' with open-air market space and cooperative facilities for commercializing local products rang-ing from seafood and fruit to palm oil and cassava meal. In addition, the proposed marine connections re-establish cultural-historical routes and facilitate commer-cialization of products and commuting to the city. They can adjust to seasonal flows of tourism and produce.

---

1 In the Afro-Brazilian religion Candomblé, natural elements like the sea, rivers, stones, trees, and topography have spiritual significance and affect the location of temples. Plants are central for rituals, medicine, and decoration. Whenever possible, they are extracted from the adjacent forest, but in urban situations, they are often bought or exchanged – thus, in Salvador, there is market potential.

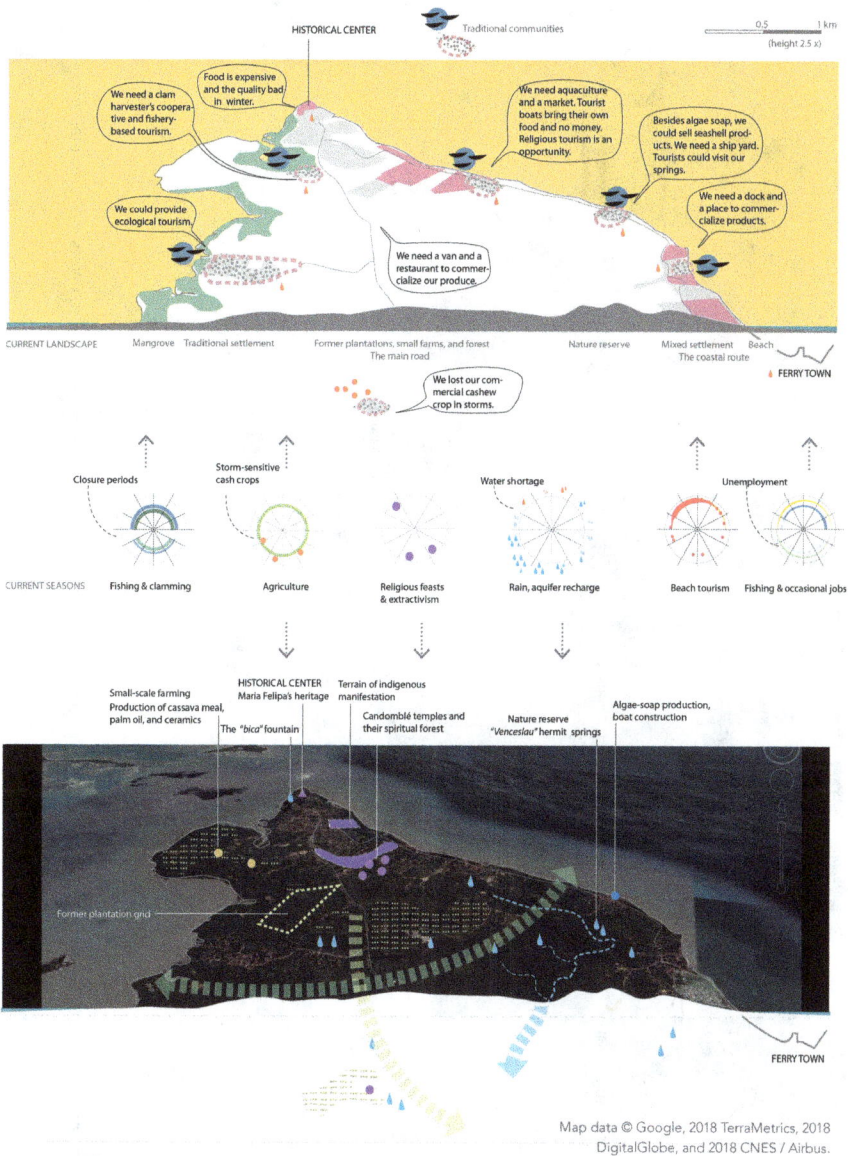

Figure 31.2: Mapping needs and wishes of coastal communities (top) and existing cultural and natural potential in the landscape (bottom),and linking them with seasonal phenomena (middle).

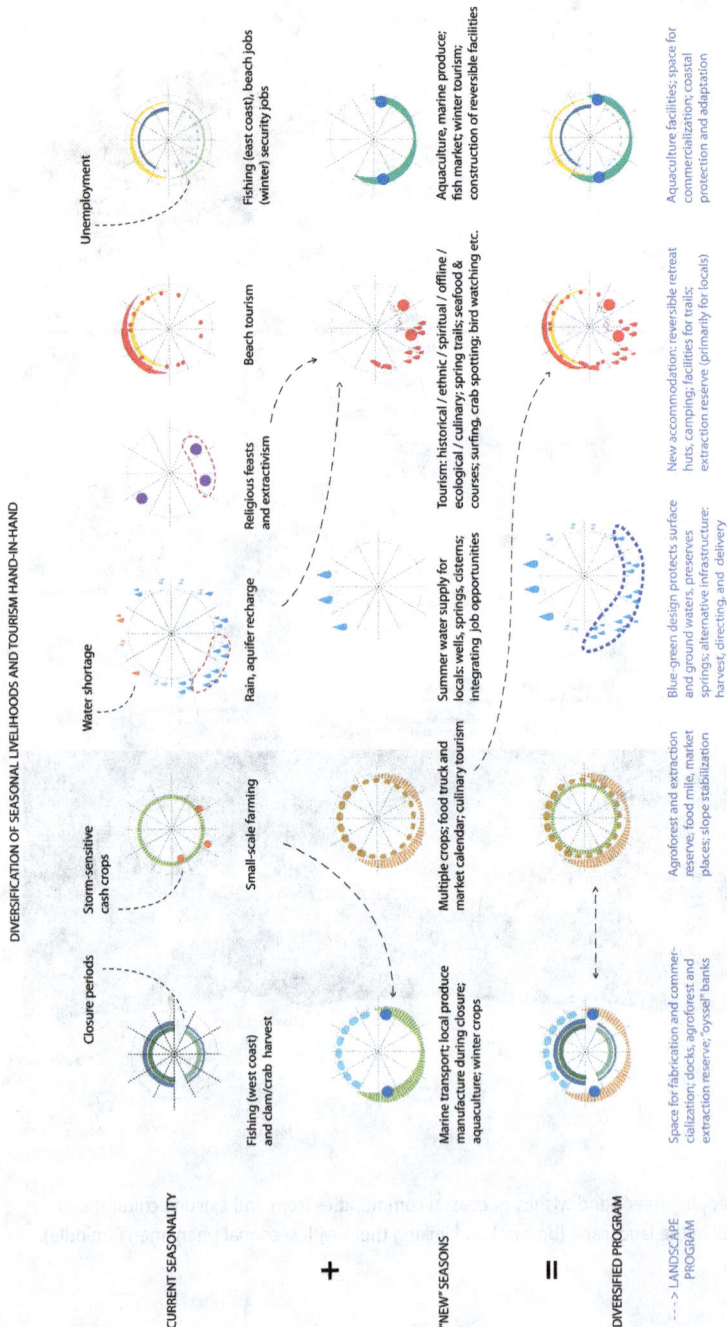

DIVERSIFICATION OF SEASONAL LIVELIHOODS AND TOURISM HAND-IN-HAND

CURRENT SEASONALITY

Closure periods

Fishing (west coast) and clam/crab harvest

Storm-sensitive cash crops

Small-scale farming

Water shortage

Rain, aquifer recharge

Religious feasts and extractivism

Beach tourism

Unemployment

Fishing (east coast), beach jobs (winter) security jobs

+

"NEW" SEASONS

Marine transport; local produce manufacture during closure; aquaculture; winter crops

Multiple crops; food truck and market calendar; culinary tourism

Summer water supply for locals: wells, springs, cisterns; integrating job opportunities

Tourism: historical / ethnic / spiritual / offline / ecological / culinary; spring trails; seafood & courses; surfing, crab spotting, bird watching etc.

Aquaculture, marine produce; fish market; winter tourism; construction of reversible facilities

=

DIVERSIFIED PROGRAM

---> LANDSCAPE PROGRAM

Space for fabrication and commercialization; docks, agroforest and extraction reserve; "oyssel" banks

Agroforest and extraction reserve, food mile, market places; slope stabilization

Blue-green design protects surface and ground waters, preserves springs; alternative infrastructure: harvest, directing, and delivery

New accommodation: reversible retreat huts, camping; facilities for trails; extraction reserve (primarily for locals)

Aquaculture facilities; space for commercialization; coastal protection and adaptation

Figure 31.3: Using diagrams to document current seasonality and finding timing for potential new seasons in order to diversify the annual seasonal program that concerns livelihood security and tourism.

Besides the existing algae soap factory, aquaculture and other new income sources can be introduced. Bioengineering and food production can be combined to 'Oyssel' beds (2) that buffer waves and grow with sea level rise. In the rainy season, agro-ecological practices can prevent erosion on hills. Natural springs are considered as decentralized water sources to cover for the seasonal infrastructural shortages. Their protection is proposed to enhance water quality and retention for the summer season. The springs could also become an attraction in the winter. Moreover, abandoned colonial farm structures and forgotten sites of indigenous and Afro-Brazilian heritage can be integrated in the spatial program. A consultative process in local communities and with the municipality and private sector is needed to develop suitable livelihoods and to elaborate a "seasonal livelihood program" (3), considering culturally sensitive aspects.

The primary goal of the strategy is securing livelihoods of the local habitants. Tourism also plays a key role in the island economy and affects the health of the island ecosystems. This in turn affects the island's and the islanders' capacity to adapt to climate change. It is thus meaningful to address tourism from the seasonal-spatial point of view. The seasonal flux of national tourists depends on the holiday calendar, but looking to international tourism markets for unique and authentic island experiences could help to extend or to create new seasons, for example: spiritual retreats, bird and crab watching, participation in the harvest and production of traditional products, and children's tourism such as treasure hunts or camping experiences. With minimal infrastructure or amenities, these activities could be located in the interior areas of the island in order to relieve the pressure on the coastal zone. Programmed to take place during the off-season they could improve income possibilities throughout the year.

Learning to adapt

'New Seasons' encourages islanders and visitors to manage and use the island space in a sustainable way that is respectful of nature and cultural heritage. The seasonality of livelihoods is embraced as a characteristic of "island time" on Itaparica: seasonal jobs can be a valid solution instead of a conventional idea of permanent employment. The New Seasons strategy creates opportunities to move from single-source income towards improved subsistence, while cherishing heritage and protecting biodiversity. Diversified livelihoods and enhanced food security reduce stress on marine resources and coastal habitats. Looking towards inland opportunities and attracting tourism beyond beaches can do the same, if total numbers stay moderate and appropriate infrastructure and waste management are implemented. Mobile technologies such as a "season app" could make up a key strategy to include local youth and the increasing segment of new-comers. Altogether, such developments can improve the socio-economic situation of the islanders.

The strategy of uncovering and creating new seasons draws attention from coastal activities to the island interior. It raises the question of whether a spatially and temporally concentrated tourism peak season is better than a dispersed, wider, and longer impact around the island and throughout the year. Island tourism can hardly be environmentally sustainable as long as it has an increasing footprint (4). Many of the proposed interventions depend on capacity-building, land ownership, and tourism management. A lack of community initiative and municipal resources has been an obstacle on the island, but a pilot development in Matarandiba community has shown success. More detailed knowledge about the seasonality of resource extraction, crops, cultural manifestations, tourism statistics, and their relations to space could provide a solid basis for building resilience.

Climate change adds uncertainty and irregularity to seasonal cycles on Itaparica island. However, seasons can be a tangible timescale for humans to engage with their environment and adapt to climate change. Longer-term processes are difficult to perceive, and some extreme phenomena may be sudden. The annual cycles of natural habitats, seasonal livelihoods, crops, cultural activities, and tourism provide recurring opportunities for experimentation and reversibility. The interventions and elements can be modified in another season towards multiple "safe-to-fail" (5) solutions. Embracing seasonal rhythms can thus facilitate learning to adapt to climate change.

The author

Vilja Larjosto is a landscape architect and Doctor of Engineering (2019) specialized in climate adaptation. She has studied seasonal phenomena and building eco-social resilience on islands. She currently lives and works in Finland on urban biodiversity and climate adaptation projects in different scales. Larjosto is a professional dreamer, and her job is to envision better futures.

References

1. Larjosto, V. *Dynamic Urban Islands – Seasonal Landscape Strategies for Resilient Transformation.* Leibniz Universität Hannover, 2019.
2. Reise, K., C. Buschbaum, H. Büttger, & M. K. Wegner. "Invading oysters and native mussels: from hostile takeover to compatible bedfellows." *Ecosphere 8* (2017).

3. Baldacchino, G. & I. Kelman. "Critiquing the Pursuit of Island Sustainability: Blue and Green, with hardly a colour in between." *Shima: The International Journal of Research into Island Cultures 8* (2014):1–21.
4. World Food Programme. *A WFP approach to operationalise resilience Part 2: Seasonal livelihood programming.* World Food Programme, 2013.
5. Ahern, J. "From fail-safe to safe-to-fail: Sustainability and resilience in the new urban world." *Landscape and Urban Planning 100* (2011): 341–343.

Floris Boogaard

32 From grey to green infrastructure in a changing climate

Addressing changing patterns of stormwater runoff

Processes of urbanization and climate change are affecting the water balance in our cities, resulting in challenges such as flooding, droughts and heat stress. In many places worldwide the development of watersheds has increased the impervious land cover and led to an increase in stormwater runoff volume, with resultant flooding. Now, with increased high intensity rainstorm events predicted in many places under a changing climate, we often cannot rely on channelling away stormwater in large concrete pipes under the ground. Recognising changing seasonal patterns of runoff, we must make room for water in our public spaces. This has prompted some shifts in how we design for stormwater in our cities. You can see that stormwater management has changed to include techniques that reduce runoff volumes and peak flow rates, while improving runoff water quality. Basically, it comes down to a greening of cities that goes by various names, such as 'Sustainable Urban Drainage System' (SuDS), 'green infrastructure' (GI) and 'nature-based solutions' (NBS). We see a transformation from grey underground infrastructure (stormwater drainage by concrete pipes) to green infrastructure such as bio-swales: a vegetated depression or trench that receives rainwater runoff (from roofs, roads, and parking lots) to store and infiltrate water into the ground and filter out pollutants (Figure 32.1, right).

In this chapter I will show how these green infrastructures, as measures for adapting to a shifting seasonality in runoff, are in themselves introducing new seasonal rhythms to our cities, changing their seasonal appearance, efficiency and use.

This green transformation is progressing slowly due to lack of space in urban dense cities, but you might recognize some green infrastructure "popping up" in your street, neighbourhood or city (Figure 32.2 shows Dutch cities, as an example of this trend in cities worldwide). You can recognize it by talking a walk in the

Acknowledgements: The mentioned research was funded by many Dutch cities and the city of New Orleans (supported with a grant of the National Disaster and Resilience Competition) and by SIA, grant number SVB/RAAK.PUB07.015 project 'Groenblauwe oplossingen, kansen en risico's' (Green Infrastructure: changes and challenges).

Figure 32.1: From grey underground infrastructure (left) to grey-green surface infrastructure (right). (Photos by: Floris Boogaard).

rain and following the route of the rainwater from the roofs and pavement into green canals or raingardens. A raingarden is a lower, planted area that rainwater from roofs and roads (runoff) runs into it and soaks into the ground. With the storage and infiltration of rainwater, it can prevent flooding but also mitigate the impacts of drought by recharging groundwater tables.

Building green infrastructure into our urban areas is not only the job of city engineers. All city dwellers can track and contribute to changing the balance of green space in our cities. Online knowledge-sharing platforms on green infrastructure have enabled people to map and promote more green and blue spaces in urban areas. The implementation of small-scale 'nature-based solutions' such as bio-swales, green roofs, raingardens and green walls requires the involvement and enthusiasm of many different city dwellers and private and public stakeholders in their initiation, design and maintenance. ClimateScan (1) (Figure 32.3) is an example of an online 'citizen science' platform that stimulates stakeholder engagement and promotes nature-based solutions. On this map you can see the pop up of green infrastructure around the world.

ClimateScan has adopted a 'bottom-up' approach in which users have freedom to create and update content. Within just a couple of years, this has resulted in an illustrated map with over 12.000 nature-based solutions projects around the globe, and thousands of visitors every week.

Green shifts in cities' seasonal appearances

The appearance of green infrastructure varies with the seasons, (re)introducing a natural seasonality to the urban environment. Lush green raingardens in spring may turn fetid brown in autumn, changing the colours and smells of a neighbour-

Figure 32.2: Pop up green infrastructure in The Netherlands (source: search keyword 'raingardens' on https://www.climatescan.org/).

hood, and prompting discontent from some residents who are no longer accustomed to plant rhythms in their city. And as we raise our sights to long-term climatic change, we can see this is altering the design and appearance of green infrastructure. We know that with drier summers or periods of more intensive rainfall we will need to adjust what we plant, toward species more resistant to

Figure 32.3: ClimateScan. In 10 years over 10 000 projects related to climate adaptation in cities, including green infrastructure, were mapped by over 1500 people around the world (source: www.climatescan.org).

inundation or dry soil, or even salt resistant in our deltas facing sea level rise. The vegetation of our cities will change.

For citizens, the appearance of green infrastructure is very important, since it shapes their living spaces and can become treated as extensions of their front gardens. Cities are therefore increasingly designing, constructing, and maintaining green infrastructure according to the wishes and experiences of citizens, through public participation. Public participation leads to increased community acceptance and support for green infrastructure and contributes local knowledge and expertise to its design and implementation. This can increase infrastructure's efficiency but also its fit to the aesthetic, social uses, and cohesion of neighbourhoods.

Amsterdam provides a good example. Many city stakeholders have raised doubts that there is place for green infrastructure in high-density urban areas, while others questioned its efficiency in Amsterdam and other cities like New Orleans (2), which are situated below sea level with high groundwater tables and poorly permeable soil. This stresses the importance of public participation in finding space and new routines and habits for living with green infrastructure, including the seasonality of activities associated with maintaining them. But with over 500 examples of green infrastructures in New Orleans and over 5000 in The Netherlands on ClimateScan, we see growing proof that they can be adjusted to urban environments and are finding acceptance. To take one raingarden in Amsterdam for instance, it is located on public land owned by the municipality and has become highly prized by the residents of the surrounding buildings as an extension to their garden. Residents take care of this raingarden in collaboration with the municipality, through weeding it for example. Raingardens look different in different seasons, and this can see their popularity change over the year.[1] There is a greater public appreciation for the summer garden in flower, than the winter garden.

The seasonal efficiency of green infrastructure

The efficiency (3) and functionality of green infrastructure is arguably more subject to seasonal variability than grey infrastructure. In Figure 32.4, for instance, we can see a swale in wet conditions with ponding and green grass, in contrast to the same swale, brown and cracked after 7 weeks of drought. There is a lot of

---

1 For a video comparison of a raingarden in Amsterdam in summer and winter, see: https://www.youtube.com/watch?v=8uAV4nGT5co (case: https://www.climatescan.org/projects/921/detail).

debate among groups managing green infrastructure, such as water authorities and municipalities, about how the seasonality of swales may affect their infiltration rates, or how quickly the water drains into the soil. But it is very complex and varies from site to site. On one hand, the dry brown swale may have a much lower infiltration rate than the green swale, but on the other hand, the cracking of the soil may create deep holes and ruts that allow the preferential flow of runoff so that the water can, in some situations, disappear faster. After just a little rain the swale will go back to its green regular state, which is healthier since the roots and life in the soil will restore their regular infiltration capacity (3).

In this way, the green shift means swapping hard, static piped infrastructure for systems characterized by their own seasonality. Green stormwater systems adjust to annual patterns of rain and runoff, their functionality varying with the rhythms of plants or changes to the soil structure, and the ways this interacts with urban runoff. This is changing how we think about a city's stormwater infrastructure capacity, from a fixed capacity to a capacity that varies seasonally. With a view to climatic change, those designing green infrastructure are mindful of whether the seasonal rhythms of their infrastructure will remain synced to shifting patterns of rainfall.

Figure 32.4: Bio swales in wet conditions and after 7 weeks of drought (https://www.climatescan. org/projects/1114/detail).

Green infrastructure is shaping our use of city spaces

Shifts to green infrastructure are changing our seasonal habits and routines in urban spaces. Our green lawn infrastructure is changing with the knowledge we need nature in our cities. Bio swales and raingardens are transforming lawns into small pockets of biodiversity – of plants and insects – in our cities, put also altering the use of these areas. We see old neighbourhoods such as Betondorp in Amsterdam (Figure 32.5) change from lawn to biodiversity swale, with a loss of open spaces for other activities. This neighbourhood is famous as the birthplace of the legendary soccer player number 14, Johan Cruijff (1947–2016), but it is challenging to play football in a bio swale, even as they are an answer for flooding, drought and biodiversity.

Figure 32.5: Paradigm shift. Left: grass and bushes (2013). Right: low lying bio diversity in swale (2021). (https://www.climatescan.org/projects/2224/detail).

One challenge is to make city dwellers aware of the infrastructure functions of that green low-lying lawn in front of their house. Terms such as bio-swales or permeable pavements are not widely known, and often there is little public information available. Sometimes there is water on people's lawn for some days, which might be annoying for them when they want to walk their dog, or they don't like the muddy clothes of their kids playing in the green depressions filled with water. But this is something I have been working with, through engaging with urban citizens. While monitoring green infrastructure with tank trucks, I have been engaging interested residents in discussing what controlled flooding is all about. People are often very interested, ask many questions and like to tell their neighbours about what they've learned; how their extended garden may be helping to fight climate change and keep their houses dry, with lower temperatures. It might even help stop their houses from subsidence and damage to their wooden foundations. They might spot more bees and butterflies and know that mosquitos are not a problem since the bio-swale drains within two days and a mosquito needs about a week to incubate.

As the ClimateScan platform shows, green infrastructure projects are popping up worldwide, and I have been working in my own way to make people aware of how these projects can help urban communities adapt to shifting patterns of runoff under a scenario of climatic change. The seasonality of this green infrastructure is changing how people think about a city; its appearance, its use and the efficiency of its water systems. You might see that a low lying lawn is actually a swale or a raingarden. You have the knowledge that green infrastructure has important urban functions related to flooding, heat stress and drought and its appearance and functionality will change with the seasons, which you start to see pulsing in your city. My hope is that as you see the seasons and changing seasonality in green infrastructure, this will stimulate your engagement and participation in the process of greening cities and making your own environment more resilient and beautiful. You can be part of the growing global community contributing to urban change and sharing their experiences online, in the promotion of more green and blue spaces in urban areas.

The author

Professor dr.ir. Floris Boogaard has over 25 years' experience in research and consultancy in international climate adaptation. His projects integrate the worlds of spatial planning and water management with a focus on the implementation of nature-based solutions and sustainable urban drainage systems. Floris Boogaard has been a professor at Hanze University of Applied Sciences in Groningen since 2013 working on urban climate adaptation around the world in close relation with international (applied) universities. Floris Boogaard is currently a consultant in water management and subsurface at Deltares and an affiliated researcher at The Global Centre of Adaptation that accelerates climate adaptation by recognizing, building and promoting excellence among stakeholder groups.

References

1. www.climatescan.org
2. Boogaard, F., D. Rooze, & R. Stuurman. "The Long-Term Hydraulic Efficiency of Green Infrastructure under Sea Level: Performance of Raingardens, Swales and Permeable Pavement in New Orleans". *Land* (2023): 171. (https://doi.org/10.3390/land12010171).
3. Boogaard, F. "Spatial and Time Variable Long Term Infiltration Rates of Green Infrastructure under Extreme Climate Conditions, Drought and Highly Intensive Rainfall". *Water 14* (2022): 840. (https://doi.org/10.3390/W14060840).

Mark Thomas Young

33 Artifacts and seasonality: How we guide the built environment through time

Mark Thomas Young is a philosopher whose work explores practices of maintenance and repair of technology. In this contribution, he adopts a narrative approach in the form of a short story about an engineer in order to examine the temporality of the built environment and invite philosophical reflection on the relationships between technology, time and human practice.

"It will have to wait until summer anyway", June said, shrugging her shoulders as she gazed out over the white streets below.

He had expected this response. But while he would have liked to have seen the work done sooner, he had suspected that it may already be too late to schedule it for this year. Here in the Midwest, summer is known as the "repair season" and coincides with a flurry of activity around roads, bridges and buildings.[1] Summer is time for painting and paving, when long sunlight hours provide the conditions necessary to achieve a good finish. Once the cold sets in however, standard surfacing techniques can no longer be used. Instead, potholes and cracks must be given temporary fixes which last only until the weather begins to warm once again and permanent repairs can be undertaken (1).

"Don't worry", she says reassuringly, "I'll talk to Ahmed and explain the situation. This won't be a problem."

He smiles, hiding the fact that he's not convinced it will be so easy. After all, he knows Ahmed's policy on these kinds of questions, and he's seen before what happens when work falls behind schedule. They had planned to repave the roads already last summer, but due to a number of other projects running over time they'd missed the window before the weather changed. Explaining this to the client won't be an easy task. But in any case, he thinks, it's no longer his problem. He now has enough information to submit the report, which means that his work is done for the day.

"Sure, let me know when you hear back OK?"

Back in his office, he clears his belongings from his desk and shuts down his computer before taking the lift to the bottom floor and heading out into the crisp dusk air. Covered in fresh snow, the parking lot glows orange in the light from the large neon sign sprawled across the front of the building: ARCA ENGINEERING. The cars all look identical under a blanket of snow, so he listens carefully for the muffled chirp of his alarm and tries to discern the faint pulse of the indicator

---

1 I'd like to thank Diane Michelfelder for pointing this out to me.

lights. He finds his car near the entrance and zips his jacket all the way up to the neck before beginning to scrape the ice and snow from the windshield. By the time he's finished, his fingers are numb and he hurries to get inside and close the door. Starting the car, he notices that the battery is low, and he tells himself that he must remember to charge it when he gets home.

In the falling snow the cars drive slowly, and he follows them through the flurry of snowflakes illuminated in his headlights. As he turns off the highway and onto the winding road that leads to the small town where he lives, he's taken by how smooth the car feels as it travels down the valley. The potholes and cracks which litter the road beneath have now been covered and filled by the falling snow. What used to be a loud and bouncing passage in the summer months is now eerily smooth and quiet. However, underneath the silken snow he knows that the ice is driving the road itself apart – and that more damage will be revealed when the snow melts in the spring.

When he reaches the bridge, a man in a yellow jacket waves for him to stop. The maintenance team that spent the summer painting the bridge and cutting back the foliage that had grown around the approaches have long departed. Instead, workers are now spreading salt over the bridge deck from large canvas bags. As the wind picks up and salt blows from the bridge towards the freezing river below, he recalls how the bridge itself had given rise to heated debate at the last town hall meeting. Some council members had argued that because of climate change the bridge now occupied an environment vastly different from that which it was originally designed to inhabit. They insisted that the design of the bridge needed to be changed, that the drainage needed to be altered to facilitate the movement of more water as rainfalls become heavier and that the pylons needed to be altered to withstand a predicted increase in major flooding in the river. But these suggestions were met with strong resistance from many in the audience. Some questioned whether a council that struggles each year to secure funding even for routine maintenance of the roads and bridges could afford to make such changes. Others questioned whether the climate was in fact changing. As the conversation inevitably devolved into bitter dispute, the future of the bridge was left uncertain and undecided.

He arrives home, parks the car and hurries inside. The door that previously creaked throughout the summer closes now without a sound. But the house is cold and dark. In the living room he begins stacking logs of wood inside the fireplace. The newspaper starts to burn and he closes the door, listening to the sound of the metal ticking as the heat begins to travel through the frame. In the glow of the fire, he reaches for the guitar that is propped up against the arm of the sofa, only to discover that its badly out of tune.

As he sits there winding the strings, he recalls how a friend of his once told him that the tension in the long cables of the Golden Gate Bridge change according to the rhythm of the seasons, and that the work of tightening them is also described by the workers as "tuning" (2). It strikes him suddenly how the things we make: the buildings and bridges, guitars and cars, breathe with the seasons as much as the natural environment which surrounds us, expanding in the heat as the days grow warmer and contracting in the cold as the days grow shorter . . .

Rather than being an external force against which our artifacts – the things we make – must be protected, seasonal change is in some ways already present in the matter from which artifacts themselves are constructed. Even though many like to think of materials like iron and concrete as permanent and unchanging, they are nonetheless always on the move, and their movements are as rhythmic as the shedding of leaves in the autumn and the falling of snow in the winter. What this means of course, is that building artifacts is often a process that extends far beyond the completion of their construction. For the oscillations between cold and hot, summer and winter, night and day, can never be stabilized once and for all. Left alone they will feed upon themselves, building until the wheels are eventually shaken loose from the frame.

In order to keep things going then, we must continually work to dampen these oscillations, by scraping away the ice and strewing salt in the winter, applying paint in the summer and filling holes, and clearing leaves from the gutters in the fall. This is the other half of building – the forgotten half, which occurs after the cutting of ribbons and the popping of champagne corks. The half which is performed while things are still in use, in lanes closed for traffic or high above the roadway tethered to pylons. The half which is performed in the wind and rain, or the blistering heat of the summer, month by month, year after year. This is the half that often goes unthanked, even unnoticed by the commuters who complain of the delays while drumming their fingers on the wheel. Yet this half is more important than people often think. After all, the built environment is not written in stone, but exists as a fragile balance of processes. Without constant care and attention it would not take long before our subways would fill with water, our pavements would split open and structures such as bridges and buildings would begin to fall in upon themselves (3). This is therefore work that must continue as long as many artifacts remain in use. In order to care for the artifacts that surround us, they must be supported through the passage of time, through the peaks and troughs of seasonal change.

Through the window, the sight of snow suddenly slipping off the garage roof into a heap below, breaks his reflections and draws him back into the present. The outer wall of the garage now stands exposed, its peeling paint and bare wood peering out from the path traced by the sliding snow in the thin dusk light. He remembers now that had planned to paint the garage over the summer. But the cans of paint which he had stacked against the back wall remained unopened as the long summer evenings drifted by. And now yet another autumn had passed in which water from the constant rain had undoubtedly worked its way even further into the wood. The garage must be painted, he tells himself. But that is work that must wait until summer.

The author

Mark Thomas Young is a Marie Curie Postdoctoral Fellow in the Philosophy Department at the University of Vienna. His research covers two fields; the Philosophy of Technology, where he focuses on practices of maintenance and the use of automating technologies, and the History and Philosophy of Science, where he explores instruments, craft practices and tacit knowledge in the early modern period.

References

1. Eaton, R. A, E. A. Wright & W. E. Mongeon. *The Engineer's Pothole Repair Guide*. Cold Regions Technical Digest No.84-1 March 1984.
2. GangaRao, H., M. de Lorenzo, & M. M. de Lahidalga. "How Would Engineers Build the Golden Gate Bridge Today?" *The Conversation*, May 26, 2017. (https://theconversation.com/how-would-engineers-build-the-golden-gate-bridge-today-77846) (accessed 10 July 2022).
3. Weisman, A. *The World Without Us*. New York: Thomas Dunne Books, 2007.

Werner Krauß

34 Weather and infrastructure: The Flax Road

Farmers live in the open, and the landscapes they inhabit and work in are weather worlds. This is even more true on the North German coast, where the land is flat, the wind is strong, and the fields are crossed with ditches to ensure drainage. Climate change is not making things any easier. Weather extremes are becoming more frequent and infrastructures have to adapt to this. Fields need irrigation and drainage; it takes electricity for power and roads for transportation. An example of this is the Flachsweg, which means Flax Road in English, a dirt road in a village in Lower Saxony (see Figure 34.1). The village, Büppel, is located not far from the coast, on the Geest, as the sandy moraines left from the Ice Age are called here. The Flax Road passes by the Eekenhof, where I stayed in 2017/2018 as an anthropologist doing research on how people perceive and deal with climate change. The winter was unusually warm, wet, and dark, followed by a drought that lasted all summer. These weather extremes required the complex system of infrastructure that keeps the farm running to adapt to these changes. How this was done, and the role the Flax Road played in it, is the subject of the following chapter.

Figure 34.1: The Flax Road in Summer (left) and in Winter (right) (Photos by: Werner Krauß).

Land use has changed a lot in this area, the formerly rural village Büppel has increasingly turned into a suburb of the nearby municipality of Varel. But on the edge of the village there is still a farm from the 18th century, the Eekenhof, which takes its name from the oak trees that stand along the Flax Road. Flax was once the most important crop in the area, it was used to produce oil or linen and was a source of income on the barren lands of the Geest. Times have changed, flax is now produced mainly in China and other parts of Europe, but the old dirt road has retained its name to this day.

Klaus, the current owner, inherited the farm from his parents. He studied agriculture at a nearby university and spent several years as a development worker in Papa New Guinea. When he came back, he turned to organic farming and converted the former barn into a farm shop, or more exactly, a wholefood shop. He leased the farmland to Dominik, a horticulturist who produces organic vegetables, and to a part-time farmer who keeps twenty head of cattle. So that was the scene I entered when I lived on the farm during my field research, trying to get a glimpse of the complex and highly mobile network consisting of people, machinery, weather, soil, and infrastructures.

The winter of 2017/2018 was unusually wet, dark and warm. Only when it is cold enough do the skies clear, and it was rarely cold enough. Instead, the rain fell and pushed drainage systems to their limits. The pumping machines on the dikes ran at full speed to pump the water out of the land, but gradually the vast fields and farmlands turned into swamps. Farmers could no longer drive their tractors into the fields, and they could no longer spread the liquid manure from the stables. They were literally in danger of drowning in shit. It was a hard winter, and Klaus and Dominik were lucky that the twenty cattle in the barn were a manageable size in contrast to the farms that live exclusively from cattle and pasture farming, as the subsidies of the EU still suggest to the farmers against all reason.

When I came to visit, I had to steer my VW in slalom and at walking pace around the puddles of water on the dirt road. The lack of light made things even more depressing. For days the sun never came through the thick cloud cover, and everything was clammy and damp no matter how you set it up. No one doubted that climate change was to blame for this misery. Thoughtfully, my conversation partners told me how they used to go ice skating on the frozen ditches, but their children don't know that pastime anymore. Whether there were more storm surges this winter or not, scholars might argue, but the chairman of the dike association viewed the situation with concern. The weather used to be different.

In spring the situation changed, the sun came out and it was starting to get bright and warm. After the dark winter, it was like a miracle how nature blossomed and green burst out of the trees and the soil. The work on the farm was in full swing, finally there was life again. The weather was great, and it stayed great until people frowned and wondered if there wasn't a drought coming. That's what it was, it stayed unusually warm all summer and way too dry well into October. There was a major drought across the country, which was especially hard on the farmers. Newspapers told of dead cows being spotted in the fields, and it is a fact that farmers ran out of fodder because the pastures had withered. The market caused the prices of feed to rise, and some farmers sold their cattle prematurely to the slaughterhouses at a poor price. Some who could afford it – because they were not too heavily indebted to the banks – gave up their farms.

In the meantime, the Flax Road had turned into a dust road, like a road in Australia. The dust swirled up, my car was covered in it, and the farmhouse was repeatedly enveloped in a cloud of dust. Klaus' partner, Elke, a medical doctor with a practice in town, didn't like the permanent dirt in the house and in the garden, and neither did the customers of the organic food store who mostly came by car. This unpleasant situation required an adjustment to the infrastructure. Klaus decided to have the dirt road sealed. He asked the municipality, which only granted a 30% subsidy, so he had to shoulder the rest himself, for which he received praise in the regional newspaper for committed civil courage.

One day the spectacle began (Figure 34.2). Men in orange work clothes came with a steamroller and filled the holes on the path. Then they laid the new pavement with the big tar machine fed with hot tar from the back of a truck. Infrastructures are made, and here in the countryside it is an event in which people are involved. Children stood at the side of the road, and Klaus brought beer and snacks for the construction workers. The construction workers admired the row of old oak trees along the roadside that grow 300 years, live 300 years and die 300 years, or so they say. Klaus told how years ago one of the oaks was felled by a storm and almost fell on the house, only a guardian angel ensured that the disaster was narrowly avoided. The trunk had been completely hollowed out, the tree weak and rotten. I noticed that Klaus told this story in the local dialect, in Lower German, when he addressed the workers. One word gave the other, their talk added a proper soundscape to the work on the local infrastructures.

Figure 34.2: Paving the Flax Road (left) and installing the irrigation system (right) (Photos by: Werner Krauß).

After a few days, the dusty dirt road shone in smoothly polished asphalt black, and bollards were added, which were moved a little into the road at intervals to force motorists to drive at walking speed. I was not the only one to view the matter with mixed feelings. There had been a great land consolidation in Germany in the sixties, when the crooked roads were straightened and the fields merged, the village lime trees felled, and the village streets turned into thoroughfares for the increasing traffic. But Klaus reassured me, the Flax Road is out of the way, it is traffic-calmed, and the measure served customers and suppliers above all. At night, the trucks come bringing the goods for the organic food store, which carries well over 2000 products. Organic food has also built up its own infrastructure over the last few decades, including a data highway that Klaus can use to order goods at his desk at home. The truck drivers who deliver the placed orders are happy about the new road surface, it makes their work easier at night, and Elke and the customers were happy, too.

The weather, however, did not change. And even though the Eekenhof had few livestock, and vegetable production proved to be less sensitive to the drought, the situation was slowly becoming critical here as well. I felt reminded of my research in the south of Portugal, many years ago, when farm workers in the fields covered their necks with red scarves. Due to climate change, more and more South is coming to the North, and Dominik's helpers also worked with neck protection in the field, where the fruit was slowly but surely withering. Klaus decided to make another investment, building an irrigation system (Figure 34.2). He had a hunch where there was water, and the contractor began drilling into the depths beyond the Flax Road, but to no avail. The contractor said he was also a dowser, and he could try behind the house. Klaus agreed and wondered why he hadn't said so right away. When the dowsing rod struck out in the yard, the drilling turned out to be successful, water gushed forth. In an effort that lasted several days, Klaus and Dominik laid the ready pipes to the greenhouses and under the flax road to the fields on the other side. After some adjustments the work proved successful, the drought was defeated.

Climate change, seen from bottom-up, comes as a challenge to infrastructures. Farmers always have to deal with weather conditions that are contrary to the goals they have just set. It takes an interplay of different forces and a great deal of flexibility to defy the vagaries of the weather. This flexibility comes from mobilising as many actors as possible, while ensuring the dependence on individual actors does not become too great. If the bank is breathing down your neck with loans and the business is only surviving on EU subsidies, the situation becomes critical. In Lower Saxony, more than ten thousand rural farms have gone out of business since 2000. After the land consolidation of the sixties, this means that again an entire way of life and economy is finally disappearing. The case of the Eekenhof serves as an example of how the flexibility of mixed farming, in terms of weather and market demands, is one way of responding to climate change. To preserve a sustainable way of living, Klaus explained to me in many conversations, requires the permanent renewal of infrastructures. The Flax Road is no longer a weather-prone dirt road but guided by bollards and asphalted. It stands for a local way of dealing with the vagaries of the weather, and a network of infrastructures that works with the weather and not against it.

The author

Werner Krauß is a senior researcher at the artec Sustainability Research Center of the University of Bremen. As a social anthropologist, his main areas of interest are landscape studies, political ecology and the anthropology of climate change. He has conducted extensive field work in Switzerland, Portugal and Northern Germany, and he has published about issues such as sustainable development, nature conservation, renewable energy, heritage, climate change, and the Anthropocene.

Scott Bremer and Arjan Wardekker

35 Conclusion: Negotiating changing seasonality

Communities worldwide face changing seasonalities, as the chapters in this book have described from a multitude of angles. This may be caused by large scale processes like climate change, technological progress and societal change, or by small scale and even personal developments, such as moving to a new house or trying to collaborate with people from other places, or a combination of these (1). This book then challenges the common perception of seasons as stable patterns or frameworks, even though they may vary from year to year. A given summer might be rainy, but though some might complain that summer had been passed over that year, few would honestly wonder whether there had been one in fact. Seasons are deeply woven into our societies and worldviews, based on millennia of living with them and even depending on them for survival. And our institutions and ways of life are extraordinarily well set up to deal with weather, water, and the other natural and societal rhythms of the past in effective and efficient ways. We often act on seasons in a subconscious and un-questioned way. But many of these taken-for-granted patterns may no longer hold in a rapidly changing world facing an uncertain future, and living according to outdated seasonal ways of life might be counter-productive (2,3). So how do we respond to the realization that seasons are not so stable after all? What do seasonal patterns still mean for contemporary society, and how do we act on those patterns?

How do we respond when taken-for-granted seasonal frameworks come apart?

One realization might be that our *classic* notions of seasons do still mean something today. Societies have not entirely done away with seasonal frameworks, though seasons may make themselves felt in altered ways. As the chapters in 'Part III: Creativity and the Arts' show, seasons still hold a strong sway in our cultural pursuits and our imagination. For example, the passing of spring, summer, autumn and winter in computer and console games based on temperate climates is important for players to relate to the passage of years, as Op de Beke writes (4). Similarly, seasonal rhythms are used in the virtual reality (VR) simulations described by Nordahl (5) to show the passage of longer time scales, but also to allow participants to transfer their imagination from the artificial setting of the museum or office building in which they are physically present, out into the setting of the 'natural world' in the simulation. Seasons also come up in practical situations – they 'do' something – such as in spatial and community planning. Larjosto's chapter (6) (in 'Part VI: Planning & Engineering'), looks at how planning for seasonal rhythms may lead to more sustainable land use practices, better fitted to ecological contexts. Classic seasonality also affects people on an emotional level, for instance in photography and films, as described by Muir (7). Traditional depictions and ideas about seasons are still very much alive in our culture, psychology, and our imagination of the natural world.

Yet, the chapters in this book present many examples where seasonality is changing, with a noticeable impact. First of all, this impact is felt and expressed emotionally. There is no small measure of nostalgia present in many of the chapters in this book – in 'Part I: Evolving History & Heritage', 'Part II: Relations to Nature', and 'Part IV: Rhythms of Daily Life' – a mix of happy memories of days past to sadness at the loss of something that communities held dear. These feelings are accompanied by bemusement (and some amusement) as people struggle to balance seasonalities, such as the tourist season and the swan nesting season discussed by Jensen (8). There is also hope as new seasonalities may also offer new opportunities, as people and nature have shown resilience to past changes and will likely thrive in new ways in the face of these changes, as told for instance in chapters by Flanagan and Black Elk, Gehrke and Pirie, Kendall, and Strauss (9–12).

Beyond this initial emotional reaction, how do people to respond to changing seasonal frameworks in this book's chapters? One option is not to respond at all, to deny or ignore that changes are taking place, but the chapters in this book show little evidence of this approach. Another response is to attempt to reduce our dependence on seasonality, to become less dependent on natural rhythms and to 'de-season' society. This seems to be part of our modern response; to retreat into artificially lit, warmed, and cooled offices, and engineer our environment to keep the seasons out. Chapters such as those of Larjosto, Pijnappels, Boogaard (6, 13, 14) use this as a starting point, yet show that such approaches work only up to a certain point, before leading us down some unsustainable pathways. De-seasoning might also simply introduce new patterns of seasonality, and as Young shows, even hard infrastructure is much more seasonal than most would assume (15).

A third option is to move, whether this is voluntary or forced. Voluntary moving can be seen, for instance, in tourists traveling for winter sports or seeking out summer weather in warmer climates. More forced movement can be seen in seasonal or more permanent migration, when living conditions in a place become unsupportable. As Strauss observes, our species has always moved, following climatic changes and other pressures (12). Plants, animals, and their relations with humans also shift and may open new opportunities, as shown by Flanagan and Black Elk, Gehrke and Pirie, and Bjærke (9, 10, 16). However, movement may not be easy and can have consequences. Carmona and Rupayan (17), and Flanagan and Black Elk (9) discuss the ruptures faced by indigenous communities moving off their ancestral land, where nature, people, place, and identity are thoroughly intertwined. Indeed, Strauss (12) also notes how "our structures of borders and passports and walls" are making it impossible for most people to leave safely or legally.

A fourth option is to attempt to make the most of changing seasonality and manage on the fly. Shifting seasonal patterns might offer benefits to some. The chapters of Hempel and Meisch (18,19) discuss beekeepers in temperate climates who might benefit from more days when the bees can fly, and beekeepers can modify their practices and activities as their bee colonies require. Of course, this will not be an option for all, such as beekeepers in Southern Europe, where the changes and pressures are much more impactful. A fifth and related response is one of incrementally coping, or to take things as they come and adjust to the conditions in front of them. For instance, Sandré shows how the Greenlandic community of Ittoqqortoormiit instinctively track and adjust to changing sea ice conditions, accepting that this is out of their control and that there are uncertainties (20). Writing from Europe's self-proclaimed rain capital, the editors observed similar viewpoints in Bergen, Norway, where local narratives focus strongly on being prepared for all weather and seasons, and 'going with the flow' with regards to changing seasonality and climate adaptation (21).

Finally, a sixth potential response observed in our chapters is to adapt and be agile. Adaptation here is distinct from coping and taking things as they come, because it means going beyond tinkering with existing seasonal ways of life to rethink what seasons mean and do in a community. We see this response clearly in the community planning and island tourism management of Larjosto (6), in Boogaard's examples of green infrastructure (14), in the flexibility and adaptiveness of farmers described by Krauß (22), and in many of the other chapters' arguments on renewing relations with seasonal rhythms and building on the resilience of communities in navigating changing environments.

Clearly, as shown by the authors in this book, communities respond to changing seasonality in many ways. Whether the response is to retreat from seasonality or reconnect with it, whether it is incremental coping or more adaptive, people and communities react differently to the disruption of seasonal patterns, and that is fully legitimate. If there is one thing abundantly clear from the contributions in this book, it is that seasons themselves are very multi-dimensional. Changing seasonality is not just a scientific issue, the realm of climate scientists, ecologists and hydrologists, and not just a professional one, the practical concern of farmers, beekeepers and engineers. It is also normative, political and personal. It relates to our connections with the natural world, our social structures, history, heritage and identity, among many other facets. Changing seasonality impacts people and their values in diverging ways. What should seasons be? What aspects of seasons do we value and why? Coming to grips with changing seasonality will require agility, both in "the world out there" through flexible approaches to adaptation, and in renegotiating what seasonality means to us personally and our communities at large.

How do we renegotiate seasons?

For chapter authors, recognizing seasons as '*polyrhythmic*' – that there are a multitude of yearly rhythms, variously perceived and acted by groups of humans, plants and animals – demands that communities renegotiate seasonality in the places they live. That is *negotiate* in both senses of the word. On one hand, carefully moving through the year, observing the diverse rhythms pulsing through those places. On the other hand, initiating discussions in our communities about what seasons mean for us, how we can better align rhythms and manage 'temporal conflicts', when our timings clash.

Recognising polyrhythmicity starts from noticing 'more-than-human' populations' seasonal rhythms crisscrossing our environments, the phenology of the plants and the behavioural patterns of insects and animals. Though modern societies increasingly detach themselves from these rhythms, they still make themselves felt in our daily lives. For example, through our food production – consider the fruit pollination work of bees in Hempel's chapter (18) – or frightening clashes with animals, like Jensen's encounters with swans (8). For some, this noticing means reconnecting with traditional worldviews of humans coexisting with other species in nature, humans as part of ecosystems (9, 13, 17). As Flanagan and Black Elk (9) note, where human ideas of seasonality fall out of step with plant phenology, "it is the plant that is right", and we should respect the integrity of natural rhythms. At the same time, we need to recognize the growing heterogeneity of modern societies, which are increasingly diverse and specialized. While a pastoral community last century may have lived by a common set of agricultural, religious, and family rhythms (23, 24), many modern communities today are a melting pot of cultures from around the world, busying themselves with an array of activities – from road maintenance to teaching or tax returns – and there is seasonality to many of these activities. How do such multitudinous rhythms come to coordinate?

For Gan and Tsing (25, page 102), seasonal patterns emerge over time, in landscapes like the *satoyama* forest; border zones between foothills and arable flat land. The timings of people, plants and the woodlands come to be coordinated through "evolutionary and historical accommodations to life cycles, seasonal rhythms, and activity patterns". That is, over time plants, animals and humans are incrementally adjusting their rhythms to attune to each other in an environment. There is no conductor, but the different instruments of the orchestra settle into a yearly melody, ever-changing, moving in and out of discord. O'Kane (26) provides a glimpse of this in his deteriorating greenhouse complex, where wild plants invade the abandoned structure, and a new seasonal rhythm takes up for a while in the greenhouse. But dramatic changes to rhythms can see clashes in these patterns or see them collapse altogether. Consider the mismatch between the breeding seasons of the puffins and the herring run in Bastian's chapter (27). Or Jensen's (8) swan attacks, as human activities clash with the swan's nesting cycle. Or how the harvest of *piñones* no longer syncs with the start of the school year, so that the Pehuenche don't have money to send their children to school (17). Or indeed the dystopian computer games described by Op de Beke (4), where players negotiate worlds where seasonality has disintegrated, to be replaced by a string of extreme events. How should we negotiate seasonal patterns that no longer hold? How can we recalibrate seasonal rhythms into alignment?

Well, we could wait and see what new seasonal patterns emerge. We may be in a destabilizing moment, when our seasonal ways of life fall apart, but we can trust that over time a string of "evolutionary and historical accommodations" will see communities settle into new – possibly quite stable – patterns of seasonal life. That through continuous processes of negotiating timings, trial-and-error and 'messing around', our human communities will forge new seasonal links with nature, and coordination between our activities. Indeed, authors describe how plant and animal communities are likewise experimenting with alternative seasonal patterns (10, 27). We will learn to live in this modified environment and draw seasonal cues from new signs; the flowering of an 'alien' plant (16), or the second flowering of species over longer summers (27). The transition will be painful, some species and cultural ways of living will be lost, but we will adopt a new seasonality and the seasons of yesteryear will be seen as belonging to "another time" (17). If this future is upsetting, it is that we have grown attached to a pastoral vision of seasons which – if we're honest – could never have held. As authors like Bastian (27), Gehrke and Pirie (10), and Bjærke (16) write, there is nothing inherently bad about an environment in transition. It is the nature of our environment to evolve, as was made very clear by the indigenous communities discussed in this book. The Ittoqqortoormiit community (20) did not try to reason about or control the sea ice around their village but gave themselves up to local seasonality; 'to flow with an order beyond their control' (17). The Native authors of Minnesota likewise adopted an attitude of celebrating wild harvests that still occur, while rethinking what forage foods to focus on, replacing wild rice with acorns for instance (9).

But if left unchecked, new patterns of seasonal life can inscribe unsustainable habits and deepen inequalities. Some emergent seasonal cultures have damaging impacts on the environment, society, and our health (13). For example, in the introduction we discussed a trend in Norwegian society to fly internationally for finding summer conditions, and Larjosto's (6) chapter similarly describes the impact of seasonal tourism on coastal ecosystems and livelihoods on the Brazilian island of Itaparica. Another concern relates to the seasons we notice, and who we charge with noticing them. Authors are worried that societies' growing detachment from nature means we overlook the multitude of more-than-human rhythms, and focus on what experts can effectively measure and predict; temperature and precipitation. This is leading, Venning shows us (28), to farming decisions being made for East African communities by experts that may be sitting thousands of kilometres away; removed from context and with little stake in the harvest. This also serves as an example of how powerful groups of international experts actively displace and dispossess communities of their own ways of telling time, the traditional farming calendars in East Africa in this case. The politics of time – they who wield the power tell the time – will come to influence any new seasonal patterns societies will settle into, even in ways at odds with the rhythms of our bodies. To return to Ittoqqortoormiit, there is an ongoing debate at the national level about Greenland's time zone and seasonal 'daylight saving time'. Some push for a rapprochement with Europe for better connections and trade. But critics are worried that Greenlanders will not get enough sleep with the time change and associated longer duration of daylight (29). The debates on seasonal timings are hotly contested!

So, for several authors our transition to new seasonal patterns should be accompanied by some conscious negotiation of what seasons mean in our communities, and how we choose to live seasonally. What seasonal traditions we value and retain, and what other traditions we let go. It is a normative discussion, where we question out loud the norms of what we *should* do when. These kinds of cultural re-negotiations are nothing new, they are on-going. Seasonal cultures develop as a messy combination of different ideas stuck together over time, often organically, but sometimes intentionally. Cornish (30) for instance, talks about how the contemporary witch's Wheel of the Year is unlikely a pure reproduction of ancient pagan rituals, and more a modern-day re-interpretation drawing on many traditions. And in a globalised world, witches in places less well described by the Wheel are discussing how best to time their rituals. Cultures which don't shift are dead cultures, Strauss notes (12).

One aspect to this negotiation is around whose seasons we recognise. Pearson (31) shows India exerting cultural and political influence over the region by claiming the heritage value of historical seasonal trade routes, while Axtell and others (32) start their chapter from the historical violence done to Minnesota indigenous communities by colonisers, including dispossessing people of their cultural worldviews. For some then, negotiations should bring up and value traditional cultures and calendars, especially those historically marginalised, to see what they can tell us about living seasonally today (13, 31–33). As Pijnappels (13) shows us, there is a deep but mainly invisible stock of traditional calendars we could draw inspiration from for seasonal living if only we recognised them. Indeed, the Tao seasonal calendar she introduces is itself built on a constant re-reading of seasonal conditions – around flying fish – and a renegotiation of the calendar (and fishing management practices) each year. Kendall (11) and Strauss (12) likewise give us a glimpse of communities drawing on traditional cultures in managing seasonal practices and landscapes, through conservation efforts to plant the coastal zone for example.

Another aspect to this negotiation means recognising how seasons make us feel. As Muir (7) show us, we ascribe a rich palette of emotions and meanings to even just the qualities of the light that we experience at each period of the year. And as Macauley (34) notes, seasonal affective disorder affects the mood of many of us at different junctures. Axtell and others (32) show how feelings of reconnection – both reconnecting to traditional calendars and reconnecting those calendars to local seasonal symbols – was a therapeutic exercise of coming to grips with living in a place that is not one's ancestral home. Altogether, this shows how emotionally-charged such negotiations can be. We are not only discussing the future of seasonal activities like skiing, but we're bringing up cherished childhood memories. As we note above, people's first reaction to seasonal change is often emotional, before they devise a strategy for how to respond.

How can we relearn to take notice and attune to seasonal patterns?

We started this conclusion discussing the array of responses employed by individuals and groups wrestling with seasonal change, and we close with a call – common to many authors in this book – to take notice of, and reconnect to, the rhythms of our communities and environments.

For many this starts with relearning how to read the natural rhythms of our environments. There is a common argument (35, 36) that communities are disconnected or insulated from the natural world sustaining them, and this is leading to unsustainable and vulnerability-inducing ways of life. We do not realise how dependent we are on a healthy environment, and we do not see the damage we are inflicting on that environment and the hazards and risks that come with this damage. Some of the book's authors repeated this message "to pay attention" (9), by setting aside the technologies we look through to understand nature (37), and "spending time outdoors to experience and sense the seasons and calibrate our inner physiology with the outside environment" (13). To see our own human being as "a strand of this web we call life" (17), influencing but also influenced by the rhythms of this web in a way we cannot escape. For authors like O'Kane (26) and Macauley (34), this was about reconciling the seasons without (those 'wild' natural phenomena) with the seasons within (our built living spaces, our cultures and ourselves). O'Kane did this by drawing visitors' attention from the artwork in the gallery to the seasonal state of the tree out the window. Macauley thought about how natural rhythms find their way into his house, as sunlight through the window, or seeds on his socks.

Since embarking on the CALENDARS research project, I (Scott) have been taking notice of seasonal rhythms and noting them down in a seasonal diary and a set of photos from my balcony (Figure 35.1). I was struck by three realisations. One was how, despite living in Bergen for 13 years (having moved here from New Zealand), I remain out of sync with the rhythms of this place. I still find myself surprised by a public holiday that I hadn't noted down, and every winter the skin on my knuckles cracks because I haven't developed the habit of putting on gloves. The second was how oblivious I had been to the year cycling around me. Once I started noting them down, I experienced – saw, smelled, heard, tasted, felt – rhythms everywhere. Some seasonal markers were obvious, like the first spring flowers, or the first day of icy roads. But others surprised me. The way I started to associate summer with the smell of sunscreen lotion. The change in the taste of the strawberries when they came in season. How much more laundry I washed in summer compared to winter. Or the sound of the waterfall. I have a waterfall cascading down the hillside behind my house, and I realised I could tell the season by the intensity of the rushing sound that is background noise in my lounge; from a trickle in spring to a roar with the autumn rains, or silence when the waterfall freezes in winter. The third realisation related to how seasonality affected my body. I became aware of a 10-day period in September when, each year, I feel particularly lethargic; something I've attributed to the shift in light and weather patterns. I'm now more observant of these rhythms, and I like to think I'm more attuned to my environment. At least I don't exert myself too much in September,

I make sure to put the spikey tires on my bike in October, and I remember gloves in November.

What the diary anecdote highlights is that taking notice of seasonal patterns is not limited to connecting to the rhythms of *nature*, such as the waterfall, or my body's energy levels. Coordinating seasonal rhythms in the places we live – aligning the timings of activities with the environment and each other – means we also need to be mindful of the *social* rhythms that mark the year and attune to them; the laundry pulses, or the public holidays. It is not only about harmonising shifting seasonal patterns in the environment, but in society too. This also means recognising that seasons are changing in what they mean to groups today, so that for some people seasons are distinguished more by their social significance than what they can read from the landscape. People now tell the seasons by the timing of sports, music festivals, the release of new computer and console games, or the wear on their infrastructure. These may not be seasonal cultures that are tightly entwined with the natural environment or nurture a deep sense of environmental stewardship, but they are part of the process of society settling into new seasonal ways of life and we will need to attune to (or question) these too.

Another way of learning to notice and attune to seasonality can be through playfully imagining seasons otherwise. Making seasons in virtual worlds – in virtual reality (VR), a computer game, a film or an artwork for example – means first deciding on what seasonal rhythms to capture and how to portray them. We saw this in Muir's (7) analysis of the seasonal qualities of light, and how he manipulates light to create moods in his films; filming in early mornings to emulate autumn light for instance. And in Nordahl's account of the team producing a VR simulation, and the decisions they took on which seasonal rhythms to include in a simplified simulation, as the full complexity of the real world is impossible to reproduce (5). Then, playing with seasonal rhythms in virtual worlds can make them visible and bring insights. Nordahl was surprised at the analemma, or figure-eight shape, that the sun drew in the sky when viewed at the same time of the day each day, over a year in a sped-up simulation. And O'Kane (26), in exploring the dilapidated greenhouses was constantly amazed by the hybrid seasons he found there. Play also extends to imagining seasonal patterns in the future, and how our human communities could adapt and thrive in these (often quite dystopian) futures, as told by Op de Beke (4). There's nothing like playing a character who must shelter from deadly rain showers, or document the "last season", to bring seasonal adaptation to mind. Or the work of Larjosto (6), imagining a different pattern of future tourist seasons on an island.

Figure 35.1: Seasons from a balcony in Bergen, from summer (top left) to spring (bottom right). Though as we noted in the introduction, Bergen's seasons do not neatly fit into a four-season framework. Note cloudy skies as omni-present in a city presented as the wettest in Europe for example. (Photos by: Scott Bremer).

The seasons we notice are the seasons we care for

We introduced this book in chapter one by saying we were less interested in seasons as an eternal law of nature related to the planet's 23.5-degree tilt, and more as a cultural way of noticing and caring for the rhythms and patterns of the year. This is important because seen this way, "It is also up to us – as individuals and communities – to (consciously and unconsciously) choose how we relate to seasons" (1). Seasons are patterns in the world that people choose to see and live by. We all live on a tilted seasonal world, and this gives rise to such an impossible tangle of cycles that we could never hope to bring them all in view. We are forced to focus on those rhythms, those patterns, that are important or meaningful for us, and that stems largely from our ways of life and our activities. The seasons we notice are the seasons we care for, with seasonal patterns slipping in and out of view for groups each day. In Oslo, Bjærke (16) shows us people instituting a new festival – a new seasonal ritual – for imported cherry trees, which they put great care into, adopting and adapting festivities from Japan. But these same people are largely oblivious to the other introduced Japanese plant – the wire weed – that is altering seasonal ecosystems below the surface of the city fjord.

Facing a host of rapid changes, it is up to each of us, as individuals and as part of our communities, to choose which seasons we want to live by. It is the sum of all our individual decisions that will reshape what the different periods of the year mean for us – our seasonal cultures. Is summer a time for Norwegians to board a plane for exotic locations, or to swim in the colder – but still lovely – local beaches and watering holes. What about eating seasonally? What about the festivals we choose to celebrate? What about our attention to the phenology of our native plants? As new habits take hold and spread throughout a population, so will new seasons. And in this way, the seasonal cultures we cultivate have a significant role to play in our communities' transitions toward being more sustainable and resilient.

The authors

Scott Bremer is a senior researcher at the Centre for the Study of the Sciences and the Humanities at the University of Bergen, and research associate at NORCE Climate. His research focuses on governance for environmental challenges – especially climate adaptation – with a focus on the different ways of knowing and acting that guide peoples' decision-making. He is the project leader of the European Research Council 'CALENDARS project', uncovering the often-overlooked influence of seasonal cultures on patterning peoples' thoughts and actions.

Arjan Wardekker is a senior researcher at the Centre for the Study of the Sciences and the Humanities (SVT), University of Bergen. His work focuses on urban & community resilience and climate change adaptation. He is particularly interested in the role of perceptions, narratives and framing, and the interaction between science, policy and society, in building resilient communities.

References

1. Bremer, S. & A. Wardekker. "When seasons no longer hold". In: Bremer, S. & A. Wardekker (eds.) Changing seasonality: How Communities are Revising their Seasons. De Gruyter: Berlin, 2023.
2. Bremer, S., B. Glavovic, S. Meisch, P. Schneider, A. Wardekker (2021). "Beyond rules: How institutional cultures and climate governance interact". *WIREs Climate Change*, 12 (6), e739.
3. Wardekker, A. (2023). "Building climate resilience in deltas amid uncertainty and surprise". *One Earth*, 6 (3), 200–204.
4. Op de Beke, L. "Dark seasonality in computer games". In: Bremer, S. & A. Wardekker (eds.) Changing seasonality: How Communities are Revising their Seasons. De Gruyter: Berlin, 2023.
5. Nordahl, M. Ø. "Simulating seasons in virtual reality". In: Bremer, S. & A. Wardekker (eds.) Changing seasonality: How Communities are Revising their Seasons. De Gruyter: Berlin, 2023.
6. Larjosto, V. "New seasons on a tropical island". In: Bremer, S. & A. Wardekker (eds.) Changing seasonality: How Communities are Revising their Seasons. De Gruyter: Berlin, 2023.
7. Muir, J. "Tilting the frame: How the seasonal characteristics of light informs image". In: Bremer, S. & A. Wardekker (eds.) Changing seasonality: How Communities are Revising their Seasons. De Gruyter: Berlin, 2023.
8. Jensen, M. "Feral swans and frightening encounters". In: Bremer, S. & A. Wardekker (eds.) Changing seasonality: How Communities are Revising their Seasons. De Gruyter: Berlin, 2023.
9. Flanagan, H. & L. Black Elk. "Gifts of the plant world". In: Bremer, S. & A. Wardekker (eds.) Changing seasonality: How Communities are Revising their Seasons. De Gruyter: Berlin, 2023.
10. Gehrke, B. & M. Pirie. "Plants in a world of changing seasons". In: Bremer, S. & A. Wardekker (eds.) Changing seasonality: How Communities are Revising their Seasons. De Gruyter: Berlin, 2023.
11. Kendall, T. "Crimson calamity". In: Bremer, S. & A. Wardekker (eds.) Changing seasonality: How Communities are Revising their Seasons. De Gruyter: Berlin, 2023.
12. Strauss, S. "Time is out of joint: Disruptive seasonalities of the AnthropoScene". In: Bremer, S. & A. Wardekker (eds.) Changing seasonality: How Communities are Revising their Seasons. De Gruyter: Berlin, 2023.
13. Pijnappels, M. "Exploring dynamic eco-calendars for a post-modern world". In: Bremer, S. & A. Wardekker (eds.) Changing seasonality: How Communities are Revising their Seasons. De Gruyter: Berlin, 2023.
14. Boogaard, F. "From grey to green infrastructure in a changing climate". In: Bremer, S. & A. Wardekker (eds.) Changing seasonality: How Communities are Revising their Seasons. De Gruyter: Berlin, 2023.
15. Young, M. T. "Artifacts and seasonality: How we guide the built environment through time". In: Bremer, S. & A. Wardekker (eds.) Changing seasonality: How Communities are Revising their Seasons. De Gruyter: Berlin, 2023.
16. Bjærke, M. R. "Unseen seaweed seasonalities". In: Bremer, S. & A. Wardekker (eds.) Changing seasonality: How Communities are Revising their Seasons. De Gruyter: Berlin, 2023.

17. Carmona R. & J. Rupayan. "Chasing the seasons: Pehuenche experiences of rapid socioecological change in the Southern Andes". In: Bremer, S. & A. Wardekker (eds.) Changing seasonality: How Communities are Revising their Seasons. De Gruyter: Berlin, 2023.

18. Hempel, M. "Losing seasons in the landscape: When the bee season falls out of synchrony". In: Bremer, S. & A. Wardekker (eds.) Changing seasonality: How Communities are Revising their Seasons. De Gruyter: Berlin, 2023.

19. Meisch, S. "I have bee-s/-n up there". In: Bremer, S. & A. Wardekker (eds.) Changing seasonality: How Communities are Revising their Seasons. De Gruyter: Berlin, 2023.

20. Sandré, T., A. Wardekker & J. Gherardi. "While waiting for the sea ice: Stories of changes from Ittoqqortoormiit". In: Bremer, S. & A. Wardekker (eds.) Changing seasonality: How Communities are Revising their Seasons. De Gruyter: Berlin, 2023.

21. Bremer, S., E. Johnson, Fløttum, K.Kverndokk, A. Wardekker, W. Krauss (2020). "Portrait of a climate city: How climate change is emerging as a risk in Bergen, Norway". *Climate Risk Management*, 29, 100236.

22. Krauß, W. "Weather and infrastructure: The Flax Road". In: Bremer, S. & A. Wardekker (eds.) Changing seasonality: How Communities are Revising their Seasons. De Gruyter: Berlin, 2023.

23. Groom, N. *The seasons: A celebration of the English year*. Atlantic Books Ltd, 2013.

24. Lee, L. *Cider with Rosie*. Hogarth Press, 1959.

25. Gan, E. & A. Tsing. "How things hold: A diagram of coordination in a satoyama forest". *Social Analysis 62* (2018): 102–145.

26. O'Kane, E. "The nature of art: Changing seasonality in my artwork". In: Bremer, S. & A. Wardekker (eds.) Changing seasonality: How Communities are Revising their Seasons. De Gruyter: Berlin, 2023.

27. Bastian, M. "Taking a chance in unseasonable environments". In: Bremer, S. & A. Wardekker (eds.) Changing seasonality: How Communities are Revising their Seasons. De Gruyter: Berlin, 2023.

28. Venning, M. "Forecasting seasons: Using climate forecasts to dictate agricultural rhythms in East Africa". In: Bremer, S. & A. Wardekker (eds.) Changing seasonality: How Communities are Revising their Seasons. De Gruyter: Berlin, 2023.

29. Wenger, M. "Greenland's time(zones) changes, but not without problems". *Polar Journal*, Nov 28, 2022. (https://polarjournal.ch/en/2022/11/28/greenlands-timezones-changes-but-not-without-problems/).

30. Cornish, H. "Enchanting cyclical time: Living through the Wheel of the Year". In: Bremer, S. & A. Wardekker (eds.) Changing seasonality: How Communities are Revising their Seasons. De Gruyter: Berlin, 2023.

31. Pearson, N. "*Claiming the winds: Monsoon in the Indian Ocean*". In: Bremer, S. & A. Wardekker (eds.) Changing seasonality: How Communities are Revising their Seasons. De Gruyter: Berlin, 2023.

32. Axtel. S. et al. "*Healing roots and unsettling legacies*". In: Bremer, S. & A. Wardekker (eds.) Changing seasonality: How Communities are Revising their Seasons. De Gruyter: Berlin, 2023.

33. Jensen, E. S. "Thinking with the primstav today". In: Bremer, S. & A. Wardekker (eds.) Changing seasonality: How Communities are Revising their Seasons. De Gruyter: Berlin, 2023.

34. Macauley, D. "Outside-In: Restor(y)ing the seasons". In: Bremer, S. & A. Wardekker (eds.) Changing seasonality: How Communities are Revising their Seasons. De Gruyter: Berlin, 2023.

35. Ingold, T. *Being Alive: essays on movement, knowledge and description*: Oxen: Routledge. 2011.

36. Edensor, T., L. Head, & U. Kothari. "Time, temporality and environmental change." *Geoforum* (2019).

37. Hide-Bayne, D. "Apps and me: How apps are shaping my experience of the New Zealand environment and seasons". In: Bremer, S. & A. Wardekker (eds.) Changing seasonality: How Communities are Revising their Seasons. De Gruyter: Berlin, 2023.

Index